PERMA

WINNER OF THE HILARY WESTON WRITERS' TRUST
PRIZE FOR NONFICTION

NOMINATED FOR THE EVERGREEN AWARD

Named one of the Best Books of the Year by
The Globe and Mail • *Winnipeg Free Press* • CBC

"*Permanent Astonishment* is a mesmerizing story rich in detail about growing up in a Cree-speaking family in Northern Manitoba and later in a residential school. . . . While unstinting about the abuse he and others suffered, Highway makes a bold personal choice to accentuate the wondrousness of his school years resulting in a book that shines with the foundational sparks of adolescence: innocence, fear, and amazement."

—2021 Hilary Weston Writers' Trust Prize for Nonfiction jury

"Tomson Highway is one of Canada's most masterful magicians when it comes to literary prose. . . . [He] conjures and evokes emotions like no other. . . . The land, language and culture weave throughout his storytelling of his formative years. . . . *Permanent Astonishment* is many things, as much of Highway's writing tends to be. But the most impactful is that it is a road map to what matters—a moment of pause for any of us who languish in existential angst."

—*Winnipeg Free Press*

"*Permanent Astonishment* propels itself wholeheartedly toward joy, whether it's the joy of the Cree language, the naughty nicknames for friends and rivals, the white-sand beaches of Reindeer Lake, of dances and school sporting events, of escaping harrowing near tragedies. . . . [Highway] writes with so much beautiful detail about the world that [he] was born into."

—*Xtra*

PERMANENT ASTONISHMENT

a memoir written by

TOMSON HIGHWAY

ANCHOR CANADA

Anchor Canada edition published 2022
Doubleday Canada edition published 2021

Library and Archives Canada Cataloguing in Publication

Title: Permanent astonishment : growing up Cree in the land of snow and sky / Tomson Highway.
Names: Highway, Tomson, 1951- author.
Identifiers: Canadiana 20210187891 | ISBN 9780385696227 (softcover)
Subjects: LCSH: Highway, Tomson, 1951- | LCSH: Highway, Tomson, 1951—Childhood and youth. | LCSH: Indigenous authors—Canada—Biography. | LCSH: Indigenous peoples—Canada—Biography. | LCSH: Indigenous peoples—Canada—Social conditions. | LCGFT: Autobiographies.
Classification: LCC PS8565.I433 Z46 2022 | DDC C813/.54—dc23

Permanent Astonishment is a work of nonfiction. The names and identifying features of some individuals have been changed in order to protect their privacy.

Cover design: Kelly Hill
Cover images: (arctic terns) Arctic-Images/Getty Images; (snow) Rafael Garcin/Unsplash

Printed in the United States of America

Published in Canada by Anchor Canada, a division of Penguin Random House Canada Limited, a Penguin Random House Company

www.penguinrandomhouse.ca

10 9 8 7 6 5 4 3 2

Penguin
Random House
ANCHOR CANADA

For all the families who have undergone an experience
such as is described in this book, my heart goes out to you.

Kaagithow eeta-see-ik n'tootee-mak,
kwayas kimam-toonee-thimi-tinawow . . . kapee . . .

PERMANENT ASTONISHMENT

*Growing Up Cree in the
Land of Snow and Sky*

"Don't mourn me, be joyful."

RENE HIGHWAY

6 November, 1954—19 October, 1990

This is a shape-shifter book, residing in the space between fact and fiction, the fantastical place of memory and dream. It is a book imagined—and written in my head and in my heart—in what surely is one of the most joyful and funniest languages on Earth.

NOTES ON PRONUNCIATION OF THE CREE LANGUAGE:

1) the soft "g," as in "gem," exists not in Cree; all "g's" are hard, as in "get." Names such as "George" are, of course, the exception.

2) then there is the double vowel, "ao," that ends many words but is hard to pronounce for non-Cree speakers. *Iskwao* (woman), *naapao* (man), and *kinoosao* (fish) are three examples. My suggestion is that you turn the "ao" into an "ay-oh." Said quickly, it comes out sounding the way it's supposed to. That is to say, it's not "*iskwaa-oh*" but rather "*iskway-oh.*"

3) there exist two kinds of "a" in Cree, the long and the short. *Sagaak* (thick bush) and *asaamak* (snowshoes) are two examples. English equivalents would be "canal" and "attack," which, rightly speaking, should be spelled "canaal" and "attaack." That, in any case, is how I solve my problem: by using both the single "a" and the double "aa."

4) with two-syllable words—and there are, of course, exceptions
to the rule—the stress is almost always on the second syllable.
Examples are: *wachask* (muskrat) which should rhyme with "the
tusk," and *mitaas* (pants) which should rhyme with "a pass."

5) as northwestern Manitoba and northeastern Saskatchewan, the
regions described here, were missionized by the Roman Catholic
Church starting in the second half of the nineteenth century,
and because that church's missionaries were almost exclusively
French from Quebec, they baptized us not only with French
names but names of saints and biblical figures in their religion.
Hence the virtual epidemic of Josephs, Maries, Pierres, and
Annes, to name but four, among our people. Aside from that,
two biblical names which appear in this book are "Zebedee,"
which is Hebrew for "gift of God," and who was the father of
two of Christ's disciples, namely James and John; and "Nicotine,"
which was our shortening and mispronunciation of "Nicodemus."
Nicodemus was a Pharisee who, among three appearances in the
Bible, helped put Christ's body away after his crucifixion. Thus
bringing us to . . .

6) because we, at the time, spoke neither French nor English—nor
read either language—we learned them phonetically, which is
how and why we generally ended up with the hysterical results
you will read here, keeping in mind two other factors in this
equation: a) Cree and Dene—were unwritten languages up to
very recently; in fact, we, the current crop of Native writers, are
the first generation to commit them to paper, thus giving us the
freedom to invent our own spellings, which is what I do with
great pleasure. Here are two illustrations of names and the sense
of humour that makes them special: Jean-Baptiste and Angelique.
As Jean-Baptiste is pronounced in French as "Zha-Baptiste,"
what comes off the Cree tongue is "Samba Cheese," which is how
I, with my Cree writer's license, choose to spell it, also keeping

in mind that "samba" and "cheese" meant nothing to us, just as *kagitoo michisk* more than likely means nothing to you. As for Angelique, it is pronounced in French as "Ann Jzhe Leek" and so comes out in Cree as "Ass-Lick," keeping in mind that the two words, again, meant nothing to us. But because there were several Ass-Licks in the village and other villages on Reindeer Lake—and several Samba Cheeses, for that matter—we had to distinguish them one from the other with certain descriptive prefixes. So because this one particular Ass-Lick was of a certain size, we called her "Big Angelique," which comes out in Cree as "Mist Ass-Lick," keeping in mind that, as in English with its "big" and "large," Cree has two words for "big." The first is *maagi*, as in *maagi pawm* (big thigh). The second is *mist* or *misti* (or "misty," as I like to spell it), the difference being that if the noun the adjective precedes begins with a consonant, the word is "misty" as in "Misty Bob," which means "Big Bob"; and if the noun it precedes begins with a vowel, then the "y" is omitted, so that the prefix ends up as "mist" as in "Mist Ass-Lick." As for the others, they are just the way the Cree tongue tried to accommodate the English (or French) language; examples are Happy Doll (Rudolf), Stare (Esther), Aroozalee (Rosalie), Chichilia (Cecilia), and Half-Ass (Alphonse).

NOTES ON A FEW ADDITIONAL TERMS:

Maameek—in Cree, there are two words for the idea of "south." One is *saawanook* which means the cardinal direction. The other is *maameek* which also means the cardinal direction but is more sociological in connotation. Slightly disdainful, it means "in the south where the *Moony-ass* live," the insinuation being "so who would want to go there."

Metis/Half-breed—the original meaning of "Metis" was someone who is half Cree and half French. It comes from the French word for "half," as in *moitié* (pronounced "moi-chee-yay"). A Half-breed, on the other hand, is someone who is half Cree and half English or half Scottish or half any-other-kind-of-white-European.

Moony-ass—a generic term, a nickname if you will, that we use to indicate non-Native people. Strictly speaking, it has no meaning. In fact, the closest I can come to defining it is "he/she who is not very good at whatever he/she is doing." But then that's not it either. It just sort of touches ever so slightly on the act of teasing. Ultimately, it is a charming word; far from insulting, rather does it throb with guarded affection.

Neee and koolth-sli—the first Cree, the second Dene, both are the most common words in either language. And both are expressions meaning "good grief" or "as if" or "oh, come on." With the Cree, the more outrageous the story being told, the longer the reaction to it, as in *neeeeeeeeeeeeeee*.

Two-spirit—the Indigenous term, said in English, for "homosexual," "queer," "fag,' "dyke," or whatever, only much less abusive; in a word, more respectful. It means a person has two spirits, one male, one female, and that both are equally valid. Frequently (though there are, of course, always exceptions), they are magic people who bring the colours of the rainbow to the black/white—and boring *and* dangerous—world of heterosexuality. Let's put it this way: without them, Cher would have nothing to wear and have no hairdo.

Weesaa-geechaak—the Cree incarnation of the Trickster, the "god of laughter," the insane clown spirit who "motors" the Cree language. Central to their character is their unfettered concupiscence. For their sexual pleasure has no limit, which is why virtually every second word of the language pulsates with sexual innuendo, hence the over-the-top, wild sense of humour that lives at its core. Indeed, one finds resonance of this aspect of the Trickster's persona in the figures of the Greek gods Priapus and Dionysis. (Cree has no gender.)

Weetigo—the Cree cannibal spirit who eats men's flesh and, more important, their souls, their spirits. He, in fact, is a metaphor for starvation which, in those parts back then, was an ever-present menace. He is also, by association, a metaphor for evil, the nearest idea we have to Satan (*Machaa-is*).

PERMANENT
ASTONISHMENT

1

I was born and raised on the most beautiful location on the face of the Earth, northern Manitoba where it meets Saskatchewan, the Northwest Territories, and what, since 1999, has been called Nunavut. Not only has this region of the world been blessed by nature a thousand times, its remoteness ensures its status as the world's best-kept secret. To this day, no one has seen it, and no one ever will, except for those of us who come from there: the Cree, the Dene (pronounced "Day-nay"), and the Inuit. And even then so few are we in number that we are almost invisible against such vastness. And vast it is.

This from my sister, Louise, who saw it all . . .

As with all Decembers going back to the 1920s, Cree caribou hunter Joe Highway and his wife, Balazee, are crossing this part of the world by dogsled. The only mode of travel up there at that time of year back then, this *ootaa-paanaask* ("sled" in Cree) is made of birch, a wood that guarantees the vehicle's lightness and therefore its fleetness. In essence a toboggan some eight feet long with knee-high sidings made of canvas, its prow curls up like a candy cane. Pulled by eight harnessed huskies walking or running in single file, some of them part wolf for, indeed, they look like wolves, it can hold six passengers if some of them are children of which, today, there are three, and still have room for cargo. A rolled-up tent, bedding, cooking appliances, clothes, food, the vehicle is packed. Moving about these endless snowscapes with their entire home in tow like this, Joe and Balazee Highway are monarchs of the north, sub-Arctic royalty.

They are travelling today—the fifth of December, 1951—under a snowfall with down-sized flakes from their hunting grounds in the area just under the Northwest Territories the one hundred and fifty miles south to Brochet ("Bro-shay"), the village that serves them as home base but home base only for they are almost always out on "the land." In a fully loaded sled, such a journey can take five days depending, of course, on weather. And what brings them to the house they own in that village which stands at the northern extremity of a lake called Reindeer are weddings, funerals, births, and feast days such as Christmas. Which is why, as good Roman Catholics, they are heading for Brochet to celebrate the birth of Jeezoos (Jesus) with extended family and to replenish their supply of flour, baking powder, porridge, bullets, other staples of the sort—and, of course, Dad's great passion, coffee. And, most important for this trip in particular, to be with Pitooria Wachask, the legendary midwife, the reason, in the end, for their early departure this year from the high sub-Arctic.

For as with every second year through twenty-three years of a marriage jam-packed with love, Mom is pregnant. Again. The eleventh of what will be a final tally of one dozen children, I am due to arrive the week before Christmas. Or, at least, so has gone speculation, according to my sister Louise who, that winter, is twelve years old and the eldest of the three Highway children then in that dog-sled. I, however, am impatient. I can't wait. I *won't* wait. Which makes for an unexpected, and rather dramatic, turn of events. Because here we are crossing in a silence so extreme that heartbeats are audible, one silver-lined, ice-and-snow-covered lake after another and one hoarfrost-lined, snowbound forest after another, when a voice cries out from the stern of the vehicle.

"*Poogoo tagi-peechee-aak.*" It is my mother's. Covered to the neck by a goose-down sleeping robe, easily the thickness of two large duvets, she is seated, though uncomfortably at this point, in her usual position: seat splayed flat on the sled's birch bottom, spine perpendicular against its backboard, front facing forward, legs straight out. Kneeling at the prow with her back to her family, her mitt-bound hands clinging for balance to the curve of the "cane" and gorging her eyes on the endless whiteness before her, Louise twists around to look to the rear. The expression in the eyes that look back at her from the foxtail-lined hood of her mother's canvas, goose down–stuffed parka says it all—her time has come. From the middle of the sled where they sit also facing forward, Florence, eight, and Daniel, four, look up at their elder sister, Louise, with eyes wide open. They *know* that something major is about to transpire.

Standing upright behind his wife clutching the backboard for steering and balance and, like her, parka-encumbered, Dad knows in a flash the work at hand, work he has engaged in ten times prior. Her Cree plea—"we have to stop"—slices through air the temperature of which is minus forty, Celsius, according to Louise. And it isn't even night yet, when it will plunge even lower (at such latitudes at that time of year, day starts fading at 3 p.m.).

"*Cha!*" Dad shouts at his lead dog, Kip. Smooth as the curve of a falcon's flight, the sled swerves right, for Kip, a female—lead dogs are always female—knows instinctively that a drama awaits them. And now she is heading for a well-treed island, for the three thin columns of smoke that grace it are proof that humans inhabit its rock-pocked shoreline.

Northerners know the land by heart; they can navigate it in the darkness of night guided by silhouettes—of promontories, rocks, islands, the curve of summits of spruce and pine—and, of course, celestial phenomena such as stars, moon, and *waawaa-steewak*, the northern lights. They also know the general parameters of each other's traplines. The territory each trapper uses for his trapping can vary in size from ten square miles to fifteen or twenty. Based on family tradition, legal formalities such as property rights, deeds, line demarcations, and such are, for these people in this culture, non-existent and thus unnecessary when it comes to these traplines. Thus does Joe Highway know that this mid-sized island of the thirty or so on this lake called Mariah constitutes the fiefdom, or a part thereof, of a Dene hunter named Henry Beksaka (for this territory is so far north it is actually not Cree but Dene country). This Henry Beksaka's language is as different from Cree as English is from Korean; Dad has learned it through the course of the years he has lived here, which has opened the door to lifelong friendships with this Henry Beksaka and his cousins, Beejee-aazay and Adoo-naazay, among other Dene. The man won't mind, goes Dad's quick thinking, if he, Joe Highway, pitches camp on his island; will he not, after all, be engaging in the act at its far other end where he won't stand the risk of crowding Henry Beksaka's family? Having no time to deal with such questions, Dad stops his sled and there, in a meadow, throws up a tent. The canvas structure's pegs, poles, and frame are far from "pre-fab," as they are for modern-day campers of the *Moony-ass* persuasion—he has to carve them himself from trees using axe, strength, and skill won by years of practice. A chop-chop up here, a tug-tug there, a general billowing of sail-white canvas greyed by smoke and, poof, the tent is up.

Once it is ready with its carpet of green boughs snapped from spruce and its small black woodstove is roaring with flame—the appliance carved from the hulk of a five-gallon barrel of motor gasoline without which nomads travelling in sub-Arctic regions risk death by freezing—the next question is: Where to find a midwife when Pitooria Wachask, as Joe Highway knows, is still some one hundred and fifty miles south of his current location? The answer is obvious: Henry Beksaka's wife. *She* has experience.

If that night, I am set to take my place as the eleventh child Joe Highway has sired and Balazee Highway is carrying, then they have lost five already to what was considered, even back then, to be an infant mortality of a rate unheard of. With such a lifestyle? Babies born in snowbanks regular as clockwork with nothing but a layer of canvas—the walls of the tent—shielding their nakedness from minus forty weather? Or, in the case of lean-tos, which some are born in, nothing at all? Or, not much further north of us, babies born in houses made of ice? Or on ice floes? With the nearest hospital a thousand miles away? A child catches a chill, that chill turns into pneumonia, he dies, it is that simple. So according to Louise—and, of course, Mom and Dad—the count in our family goes like this . . .

The first child was Viola. Born in a snowbank on Windy Lake in 1929, we call her Vi; she lived to adulthood. The second was Swanson. Born in a snowbank on Egenolf Lake in 1931, he lived to adulthood. Next came Marie-Adele. Born in a snowbank on Whiskey Jack Lake in 1933, she died of pneumonia at age nine years. Fourth was Sylvia. Born in a snowbank on Nueltin Lake on the Manitoba–Northwest Territories border in 1936, she died of pneumonia at age seven years. Next came Louise. Born in a snowbank on Clifton Lake in 1939, she lived to adulthood. Sixth was Jeanette. Born in a snowbank on the Cochrane River in 1941, she died at three. The cause? Pneumonia. Next came Florence. Born in a snowbank on Casimir Lake in 1943, she lived to adulthood. Then came child number eight, whose name was Weezoo (Cree for Louison). Named after Mom's father, who drowned at sixty (when Mom was forty), he was born in a snowbank on Ministik Lake in 1945 but died as an infant. Of pneumonia. Next came Daniel. Born in our house which sits on a hill in Brochet village in December of 1947, he lived to adulthood. Then came Hermeline. As child number ten, she was born in a snowbank on Beaver Island on Reindeer Lake in 1949 but died as an infant. Of pneumonia.

And now here we are in the final month of the year 1951 and child number eleven—me—is ready for his entrance on, again, a snowbank, the question being: If Joe and Balazee Highway have lost five children already to death by pneumonia; if there was, in fact, one extended period of four years of heart-wrenching sadness where they lost four children in a row, Marie-Adele in 1942, Sylvia in 1943, Jeanette in 1944, and Weezoo in 1945; if the death of Sylvia at age seven years in 1943, in particular, had hit Dad so hard that he had wept for a year—she was "special," Louise says sadly—then how long would he weep for me, the sixth one to die, here in this snowbank on Henry Beksaka's island?

Besides Mom and Dad, the family dogsled, that day, carries what remains, at least at home, of their then ten children. Now twenty-two and twenty respectively, Vi and Swanson are on their own, Vi, in fact, with the first four children of the fourteen she will have in the next two decades. And, of course, the remaining five are gone up to heaven. Dad's presence necessary to his wife's survival—if that stove goes out, she dies as does his baby—this leaves Louise as the only person available for errands. Such as fetching a midwife. Accordingly, Dad dispatches her to the island's other side. The life of "your little brother depends on you," he tells her, says Louise to me some ten years later, as he holds open the tent flap for her exit. How he can take it for granted that I will be a boy is beyond Louise's comprehension for she misses terribly her late little sister Hermeline, who died as an infant just two years before. Off she goes with trepidation. Why trepidation? For three reasons: a) she doesn't know the island, b) it is night, and, c) there are wolves.

Two miles separate the Beksaka camp from ours. The snow still falling, Louise will sink to her knees in its powder-fine softness, thus making her crossing of such a distance slow and difficult—she might not make it in time for the birth. With snowshoes, she just might. Not having her own, Dad lends her his. Two sizes too big for a girl of twelve, they will do, Dad reassures her, though she will have to go straight through the island as opposed to circumventing it by walking on lake ice—"there is no time."

Without aid of a flashlight, a trail, or even a map, her progress will be stunted, doubtful in course. Fortunately, just then, the cloud cover lifts. The snowfall arrested, a half moon emerges, plunging the landscape into a riot of tinsel-edged white and twinkling lights. Her journey no longer hindered by absence of light, she takes heart. Standing as they are less than two hundred miles south of the treeline where start what we call "the barrens"—that is, the treeless tundra—the trees do their part to aid her: a) the excessive latitude prevents them from growing beyond a height of nine or ten feet and, b) they grow sparsely. Meaning to say that she won't have to fight her way through *sagaak* (thick bush).

Behind the tent, up a slope, and into the forest she trudges intrepidly. In her Mom-made, flower-patterned cotton granny smock, thick wool, flesh-coloured stockings, beaded lace-up moccasins, and down-filled parka of bright red canvas with its pointed hood trimmed by fur of red fox, she feels like Weesaa-geechaak (the Cree Trickster figure) in flight through time. All black spruce enrobed in snow, the trees start giving the impression that they are swaying, breathing, moaning. In fact, most could pass for people wearing shrouds, they stand that low. She stops, pants, catches her breath, turns.

There, a half-mile down the knoll, her family's tent. Lit from the inside by a kerosene lamp, it looks like a lantern suspended in mid-air with a silver balloon, that great half moon, all but touching it, the stars on guard high over its chimney with its curl of smoke. Oh, how lovely her hearth and home, the sigh breathes through her. When she turns around to resume her trajectory, she sees them: a girl of nine smiling. At her. Her eyes twinkling, a vision wearing some diaphanous material, she floats like a mist a half-foot above ground some five feet before the youthful traveller. Then a girl of seven materializes in kind to the right of the first apparition, followed, to her left, by a girl of three followed in a trice by two infants hanging in their beaded cradleboards (a laced-up bag made of bead-decorated caribou hide for carrying babies on one's back) from the branches of spruce. It is, she knows, her five late siblings, in order of age: Marie-Adele, Sylvia, Jeanette, and the babies Weezoo and Hermeline. The tail of red fox that serves her as muffler shudders from a breeze that has ambushed her. Which is what breaks her trance. And she is on the point of taking her first step to resume her journey when a sixth small figure appears. This new one unborn, it hangs there naked in fetal position, unattached to solidity, and transparent. A girl? A fifth dead sister? A sixth ghost sibling? The one to be born, or stillborn maybe, within one hour? Dumbstruck, spooked, Louise stands transfixed. Until a snowy owl hoots from the summit of a spruce tree, sending a shiver up its five-foot spine. Locating the bird's perch from a trickle of snow it has set falling with a wing it has just adjusted, she looks up at it. What is he saying? That the baby won't live? That Mom will die? She starts crying. Somewhere behind her—ten feet? Twenty? A mile?—a lone wolf howls. Then a second then a third. She screams. And runs for her life.

Fortunately, this is an island and, on islands, one can't get lost, children most especially. Which is why Native families always choose islands to camp or live on. Still, this knowledge doesn't stop Louise from careening from one tree to the next as if they can save her from the starving pack of wolves. Their pink tongues drooling, their white teeth glistening, they will eat her in a flash, she can smell it, she can taste it. The cold no matter, sweat breaks out across her forehead. Until suddenly, she hears barking—Henry Beksaka's dogs have smelled her. At which point she perceives three orange lights glinting through a copse of willows aglow with hoarfrost embroidered by moonlight.

In those days, we called the Dene "Chipewyans." Not Chippewa but Chipewyan. Chippewa is the name for that part of the Ojibway nation that spills over from Ontario's Great Lakes region into the northern extremity of American states such as Minnesota and Michigan but whose language, interestingly enough, is Cree's first cousin. Both Algonquian languages in the same sense that French and Spanish are Latin languages, they sound similar and share words liberally. Chipewyan, by contrast, is an Athapaskan language. As with Loucheux in the Yukon and Slavey around the Northwest Territories' Great Bear Lake—a European equivalent would be Russian and Polish as Slavic languages—it is as different from Cree as English is from Arabic. That is to say, not one syllable do Cree and Chipewyan have in common. It is only some three decades after my birth that we Cree will start calling the Chipewyans "Dene," which is the catchall term for Athapaskan-speaking peoples whether Loucheux, Slavey, Chipewyan or, for that matter, Navajo in the American Southwest. The arrival of electricity in old Brochet in the summer of 1973 was the catalyst, for it ushered in two forces that would change our lives forever: television and, with it, the English language in amounts unheard in the north. The shift, of course, was gradual; but, until that time, the term "Dene" simply did not exist in the Cree language, as it still doesn't. For reasons of civility, however—and even though we called them *Oochee-pawnoo-wak* ("Chipewyan" pluralized) all my life, as we still do when we speak Cree—I will call them Dene in this narrative.

They also look different. Strictly speaking, the Dene are a sub-Arctic people. Inhabiting as they do the Yukon and the southern half of the Northwest Territories (though not as far east as what is now called Nunavut), they serve as a sort of buffer between the Cree and the Inuit, the latter of whom are the true Arctic people, the people who are born in houses made of ice. The Cree, by comparison, are more southerly, coming as they do from the northern three-quarters of the three prairie provinces as well as Quebec and Ontario. "Spill-over," however, transpires between the Cree and the Dene which, of course, is usually the case between nations that share a border. In fact, so far north is Brochet that it actually lies in Dene territory— which is why the village, back then, is half Dene and half Cree and intermarriage is engaged in with increasing regularity. Where the Cree have paler complexions and look more European, due to white blood that seeped into the more southerly areas of Native territory earlier in history—in fact, many Brochet Cree are actually half white—the Dene, being more distant from the *Moony-ass* in terms geographic, are of purer extraction. Thus are they not only swarthier of complexion, they look Asiatic. For example, the Chief of Brochet at the time of my birth, Louie Dankaazay, is Dene. Grace of French missionaries who arrived in the north in 1860, however, we call him Chi-Louie. A diminutive of "Petit Louie" which, in its native French, is pronounced "Pechi Louie" with the "Pe" clipped off and almost inaudible, it comes out as "Chi-Louie" and means "Little Louie." Besides being "little"—that is, short—Chief Chi-Louie looks like Mao Zedong. And a Dene woman named Stare Loon, wife of Modest Loon, looks like Mrs. Chiang Kai-shek, whose picture, together with that of Mao Zedong, has been seen in the pages of a magazine that Mist Ass-Lick Beksaka once ripped from its staples in Father Cadeau's visitors' parlour to show them to her friend, Stare Loon.

Their appearance aside, the Dene are known for their vulnerability to phenomena unnatural. They take fright easily. If you step on a spider, they turn ghost-pale. If you point to the sky at full-moon time, they cross themselves (for they are so Catholic they make us Cree look like heathens). If they hear a sound that is unusual, say a squawk or a gurgle from a source unknown—an unfed stomach, say—their eyes dilate, their hair stands straight. So when this Cree girl of twelve, my sister Louise, announces herself from her position, which is ten feet behind the trio of tents that stand there facing that part of the lake, aglow from their kerosene-lamp-illuminated canvas interiors, that's what happens—their eyes dilate, their hair stands straight. Don't malignant spirits that steal men's souls communicate with humans in the dulcet voices of pubescent girls? asks Henry Beksaka of Dad, at Christmas that year, with embarrassment.

"Is anyone home?" Louise has to shout, in Dene, to make her bell-like soprano audible above the cacophony of sled dogs barking. Happily for her, being half wolf they are tied to tree trunks behind the encampment so thus can't bite her. And happily for her, a man leaps out from each of the tents. The light shed by these flimsy shelters on the sub-Arctic darkness limits Louise's vision to silhouettes. In fact, all she recognizes is Henry Beksaka, from his gangly frame and his lynx-like manner of prowling for quarry.

"*T'lagaa?*" asks Henry Beksaka. (Dene for "yes?" or "what is it?") With a few exceptions, Henry Beksaka among them, most people in Brochet of our parents' generation at the time in question speak both Cree and Dene to a greater or lesser degree of fluency. The next generation is not so blessed. Louise, for example, speaks Dene, but only in a manner that is considered elementary. When it comes, for example, to subjects as advanced as pregnancy, childbirth, and midwives, she is a write-off. Tonight, all she can muster is a timorous "My mother is ill." If the three men's eyes were dilated when their owners first emerged into Louise's field of vision, they dilate even more at this information. And their hair now looks like bristles on a scrub brush.

"Ill?!" The dim light forcing them to squint tight wrinkles, it takes them a second to recognize the girl as Joe Highway's daughter.

"Yes, ill." Unfortunately, because of their vulnerability to phenomena unnatural, the Dene men jump to conclusions. Misinterpreting the girl's terse message as "mentally ill"—as in "my mother has lost her mind"—all they see is the *Weetigo* of Cree myth, the cannibal spirit who has, it is clear, come to possess the mind and soul of Balazee Highway, wife of Cree caribou hunter Joe Highway. And the next thing Louise knows, she is running through the forest behind three men each armed with a weapon: a rope, an axe, and a rifle. The barking of dogs fading behind them, they run so fast, in their snow-shoes, that they leave behind them an *oopas-choosoos* of consider-able virility. They run so fast that the little girl of twelve has to pant like a husky to keep up with them. (An *oopas-choosoos* is the wake a motorboat leaves behind it; the greater its speed, the farther behind its *oopas-choosoos*. The same thing can happen with snow if one is going fast, as on skidoos in later years.)

When they get to the tent where lies my mother moaning out one ardent Hail Mary after another and clutching her rosaries to the point where her knuckles creak all but audibly, they call Dad out to "come and face the music." When he won't jump out on the instant, they smear him with insults. They call him a coward, they call him a bastard. Imprecations colourful echo like gunshots from one end of the island to the other. And when he does emerge but two minutes later, a merry tussle follows. Snow flies this way, snow flies that way, fists do this, legs do that. Henry Beksaka shoots Dad. Dad ducks. The murderous bullet zooms over his shoulder and into the tent. Ripping through the canvas, it misses the belly—me!—of Balazee Highway by an eighth of an inch, according to Louise, before it goes whizzing through the wall on the tent's other side and into the forest. According to the Dene, the woman's inflated state is "evi-dence aplenty" that the evil spirit who eats men's flesh has come to bedevil their sacred island.

Whatever they think, Dad sees red. He wrests the rifle—a Winchester .30-30, powerful enough to kill two moose with a single shot—from Henry Beksaka and bangs him on the head with its steel-toed butt. Apparently, as he says to Dad that Christmas, Henry Beksaka sees the constellation Queen *Kaaski-pichi-gan* ("Cassiopeia" in Cree) waving her wand.

Here the story gets murky, for it is now past midnight and Louise is tired. In fact, she falls asleep in a corner of that carpet of spruce boughs so fragrant it makes her woozy, so probably dreams this next small section. To the end of her days at age seventy-two, she is not sure how it happens but, as it turns out, Henry Beksaka's wife, too, has just given birth that morning. To a boy named Zah whom, at residential school, we will call Caayoots (a Cree corruption of "Coyotes," a word we hear in a country song at said institution). So even if she is the most skilled midwife in all *keeweet'nook* (the north), Marianne Beksaka, that night, is unavailable for just such a service. So much for "Plan A." Fortunately, a "Plan B" appears. There just happens to be a second midwife of repute at the Beksaka encampment. Who else, after all, would have eased into this world the newborn child to be called Caayoots?

Wife of Ma Gloire Looraah, an old Dene man from Wollaston Lake in Saskatchewan, some two hundred miles northwest of Brochet, Titty Ray Looraah is of age "indeterminate" and dwarfish of size. Which doesn't stop her from being admired across Dene country for her midwifing know-how. In fact, legend has it that she has midwifed a thousand babies, five hundred more than Brochet's Pitooria Wachask; Caayoots Beksaka is only her most recent product. And wouldn't you know it but Caayoots is born just in time to free the old Dene woman for the "maternal demands" of Balazee Highway. In fact, so closely do the two births transpire that it is suspected by some people that I might be Caayoots Beksaka, switched at birth by the dwarfish but crafty Titty Ray Looraah. But how a woman of an age so advanced—they say she is ninety—has transported herself from one side to the other of an island that is two miles in radius in a space of minutes is anyone's guess; she must have flown like a *cheepay* (ghost), is Louise's speculation. By whatever means she arrives, there Titty Ray Looraah squats crouched over my mother in the middle of the night, exhorting her through her writhing contractions, her brook-like gurglings, her general delirium. In her half-sleep, and over the humps of Florence and Daniel's little sleeping forms in the goose-down duvet she shares with them, Louise remembers seeing the midwife's shadow projected on this white flannel bedsheet that Dad has hung from the centre beam of the tent to give Mom some privacy, an *ersatz* maternity ward that will mask my entrance.

And there, with nothing separating my mother from that snow-bank but a thick wool blanket and a carpet of spruce boughs—with our huskies tied to trees behind our tent, howling with their cous-ins, the wolves, on the mainland two miles away, a plangent chorus that makes one weep—I am born not male, not female, but both, in the early-morning hours of the sixth of December, 1951, the Feast of St. Nicholas. Which is why and how it gives me so much pleasure to explain to the world my favourite activity, which is laughing—I share a birthday with the King of Laughter: *Saanchi Giloss* in Cree, Santa Claus in English.

2

The norm is that families who have gone through a test such as this will stop their travel for a day, two, or three to allow child and mother to recover. Southerners are astonished, indeed have difficulty believing, that such births transpired like regular clockwork, but the truth is that, back then up there, Native women gave birth to not just one, two, or three but twelve, fourteen, even eighteen children in such circumstances. For us far northerners of a certain epoch, it is par for the course, tradition, a part of the culture.

Accordingly, the plan is for us to stay put for two days at least, says Louise. Just one day is out of the question, as the last thing Dad wants is to put the life of his eleventh child at risk. After losing five? Unthinkable, he says to Louise. Then we will continue to Reindeer Lake and our humble home at its northern tip beside Father Egg Nog's two-storey, grey-walled, green-roofed rectory. Except that something happens that brings to an end Dad's forty-three years of life on Earth. Or almost does.

The morning after my birth, he is chopping wood, something he has done three, four, five times daily since age ten. In fact, he is known for his prowess with an axe and wood. It's true, however, that skillful swimmers have been known to drown in bathtubs, experienced drivers to be killed on streets. Even trapeze artists known for their daring have been known to hit a brick wall or two, at least metaphorically. Which is the kind of freak accident that visits itself upon Dad that morning—he chops his foot. With the forty-pound head of a wood-cutting axe and an impact powerful enough to cut through bone. Distracted by a bark—for, tied to trees behind our tent, the sled dogs are never out of hearing range; a ptarmigan fluttering from tree branch to snowbank; or a cry from a newborn, no one knows, no one remembers. He just cuts his foot. Steel-toed boots unknown back then, at least to us northerners—everyone wears moccasins of caribou or moose hide—the weapon cuts right through the beadwork, the hide, the three pairs of socks of double-layer wool, the veins, the flesh, and into the bone. All Dad sees as he hobbles to the tent ten feet behind him, he will tell me at his deathbed some four decades later, is blood pulsating inside his skull; all he hears is a piercing wail, an unchained legato.

Mom, of course, is still too weak to help him. As for Louise, she does her best to dress the foot but proves herself inadequate—she is too young, she is no nurse. As for the Dene on the island's other side, they have had, for some reason, to decamp unexpectedly and rush to the north, Wollaston Lake, is one speculation, where they have relatives (it is wrong; we will see them at Christmas in Brochet). Fleeing from the *Weetigo* Balazee Highway has just given birth to is the second speculation, for Henry Beksaka must be embarrassed "as hell" about his overreaction to my mom's situation. Whatever the reason, kudos go to his wife and child, who prove their mettle by travelling onward one mere day after the birth of Henry and Marianne Beksaka's infant. Which doesn't nullify Dad's need for medical assistance. *Professional* medical assistance.

The problem is that the nearest hospital is situated some two hundred miles to the south, in the mining town of Lynn Lake, so this is impossible; we have no planes, no trains, no cars. Our two other problems? By day's end, we will be out of firewood and thus will freeze to death. Worse, there is no food.

In the throes of fever, his face like wax, Dad lies prostrate beside his wife on their makeshift bed of fresh green spruce boughs and goose-down duvet. With no painkillers, the pain must be beyond endurance. Still, not one second is to be wasted—he *has* to go hunting, get a caribou, a beaver, a muskrat, anything. His brood must eat, his dogs must eat, or they go nowhere. Fast.

Still bedridden with a day-old baby stuck to her breast, Mom directs Louise as best she can. Rustle up some scraps of caribou hide that can be found among our provisions is the girl's first task. What she comes up with would make three pairs of adult-size moccasins if times were normal. Except, of course, that times are not. In the present case, they will have to do for one large moccasin, for Dad's foot is swelling with a speed most frightening to watch, says Louise. Then Mom gets the girl to bring her her sewing kit. From the homemade bag of black velvet with its red embroidery she extracts a needle, thimble, thread, and pair of scissors. By the time she starts sewing, Dad's left foot is the size of a roast.

In, out, in, out, goes Mom's *saapoo-nigan* (needle), its silver streak flashing in the light of a sub-Arctic morning (at such latitudes in early December, sunrise comes at 10 a.m.). Going beyond her weakened state, she works as fast as time will let her. All as she breastfeeds her newborn and Louise works like a demon on her Dad's left foot: staunch its bleeding, wash it, apply iodine, and wrap it in a length of flannel torn from a bedsheet. Then she helps him ease it into three clean pairs of wool socks, tugs and shimmies the new moccasin on, and does up the lacing. Still in his parka from his labours chopping wood, Dad just manages to pull himself to a standing position. Then he takes his rifle and, with physical agony etched as with charcoal into his face, drags his foot out into the cold. Unable in his state to harness his dogs, he ties a rope to the prow of the sled which now sits empty, lays across its bottom a canvas tarp and a bag containing a spare sleeping robe, a kettle, and a knapsack with basics such as bannock, tea, matches, twine, an axe, and a scrap of *paastee-weeyaas* (dried meat). (Bannock is a Native bread. Round like a pie, of the same circumference, and one inch thick, it can be baked, fried, or grilled over an open fire). And off he limps dragging this sled. Down the slope to the lake, across it, and off to the islands, for the one we are on is just one of thirty.

The life of the family now in Louise's hands—her mother, an eight-year-old sister, a four-year-old brother, and a newborn baby aged eight hours—she is daunted if not scared outright although she later claims she masked it. Not only does she have to feed four people with what crumbs she can find in the grub box, she has to make Mom fresh tea on the hour, keep changing my diapers—of which we have few, so that she has to keep washing and then drying them in front of the stove. Most important, though, is that, with a naked baby present, she has to keep that fire going inside that stove. Which means she has to keep throwing on her parka and going outside to chop more wood from logs Dad has left, if inadvertently. And when she runs out of logs, she herself has to wade through the snow into the forest behind the tent with her axe—we always have two, for emergencies such as this—to cut down more trees, lop off their branches, drag them back to the tent, and chop them down to six-inch lengths, that is, small enough to fit into the stove, which is tiny.

Still, the hardest part of the experience, she says years later, is that she isn't allowed to fall asleep. If she does, Mom warns her, the fire will die as will the family, the baby especially. All day does Mom have to rack her brain for ways to keep her little girl awake until her husband's return, which she knows from experience will not be soon, perhaps by noon next day, at best. Fortunately, Peechoochee, Dad's wicked sister whom he hasn't talked to in over two decades she is that wicked, once informed Mom that smoking cigarettes keeps one awake. Having no choice, she decides to try that novel technique on Louise that night.

Cigarettes as we know them today exist not up north, not back then. People make their own from cigarette papers and loose-leaf tobacco that comes in these tin containers the size of a muskrat and with drawings that are colourful, all available at the Companeek store in Brochet ("Companeek" is our word for the Hudson's Bay Company, the English-based fur-trading enterprise). A smoker all his life, Dad enjoys these "roll-your-owns," as does Chief Chi-Louie, as does Mrs. Chiang Kai-shek's Dene lookalike, Stare Loon. In fact, the second-last thing Mom does every night before she retires is roll twenty-five, enough for a package that will keep Dad happy all day next day, then put them in a pocket-sized cigarette case made of plastic with a cover that slides in and out to ensure water-tightness, fits to a T a man's shirt-pocket, and so is ideal for fishermen. Or hunters. After a lifetime of rolling these cigarettes, not only does Mom's speed impress—we all grow up watching her fingers whir like propellors in the kerosene light and her pink tongue darting to lick the gummed edge of the papers—so do the cigarettes. So perfect are they that they could pass for those smoked by *Moony-ass*.

Propped on a pillow in her sickbed that evening, Mom makes another twenty of these "roll-your-owns"—only, this time, for her daughter. So there at the stove sits this Cree girl of twelve smoking one cigarette after another after another the whole night through. Every time she nods off, Mom hisses her awake and tells her to light up another. As my sister will say about that night years later, she smokes herself blue in the face. She smokes so much that, after that night of near-death crisis, she never wants to see, ever again, another cigarette.

Meanwhile, Dad drags his foot, now inflated to proportions unprecedented, across one mile after another of snow-covered ice. Every step is excruciating beyond human limits. Finally, when his entire being is screaming from the pain and he can barely crook a finger let alone a knee, he stops for the night on an island some five miles away from our camp. Here on the shore of this island, against all odds, he constructs a lean-to. A shelter for travellers that is made out of logs chopped down for the purpose, some fifteen of them are tied with twine in such a way that they end up making what looks like a raft. Except that this "raft" is propped on a frame so that it "leans" at a forty-five degree angle over the ground. There under the half roof formed by this structure, the traveller will prepare his bed. Then, insofar as one can heat a space that is open on one side to the elements, the traveller builds a fire two feet in front of it. Fed with wood at intervals through the course of a night that will be long, this and the sleeping robe he lays out under the lean-to are what will keep him alive till morning. That is to say, Dad sleeps outside. In the snow. In temperatures that plunge to minus fifty. And does it, moreover, with a foot that screams. And screams and screams. If gangrene sets in—his thoughts, too, scream—it is gone, fallen victim to an operation he has only heard of called "amputation." And *then* what will happen to his family?

His sleep is fitful, the infection worsening, the germs thereof wriggling like a vatful of maggots devouring his flesh, he can feel them, he can see them. The pounding throb from his mangled extremity aside, he keeps seeing—in dream? In reality? He can't tell which—the five of his children who have died already, five winged creatures like dragonflies fluttering in a circle two yards above their father's prostrate figure. Its fur snow-white, an Arctic fox comes skulking by to sniff out the knapsack that lies enticingly, but empty, a foot from the stricken hunter's head. But this the hunter doesn't see, at least not then. Until he perceives a sixth child—a third baby; the three others are no longer babies—joining the circle of five dead children flying their orbit and humming a melody like bees in a meadow. Snapping to a sitting position and total awakeness, Joe Highway screams out his anguish.

"*Mawch!*" ("No!") The fox jumps back and, empty-jawed, zooms back into the forest. Which is when Dad sees her or, at least, the spectacular bush that is her tail swishing off like the flame from a torch coaxed thus by a breeze. Then he weeps. He weeps to the point of hyperventilation.

"Please God," he sobs, "don't take my son. Take me instead." And then he sits shaking. And shaking and shaking. Until stark agony combined with exhaustion plunges him into pitch-black darkness. He faints.

The next morning—though it is almost noon by the time day breaks—Florence and Daniel are playing in the snow on the shore down the slope from where stands our tent while Louise is kneeling inside it nursing our mother and her new baby brother (whom she pretends to herself is a girl). All of a sudden, she hears Florence and Daniel yelling. She pokes her head out the tent flap to see what has caused such exuberance. It is Dad. Even from this distance, they recognize his limp. And the sled he is dragging. Still walking as if his left leg were a stump, he advances stubbornly. Except that his sled is no longer empty; you can tell by the way its tarp now bulges and the way he drags it, with much more effort than at his departure. Obviously, it is weighted down. But with what?

Running to him would be useless. The snow is too deep, certainly for children. So Florence and Daniel wait on the shore in the only way that children know—they jump up and down, they run quick circles, they play tag, they pick up handfuls of snow and throw them aloft so that they come down as snowflakes sparkling in the light of an exposed sun, they laugh, they shout.

When Joe Highway gets there, he throws off the tarp. Now streaked with blood, he has placed it there to conceal its treasure. For there in the sled, glistening with flesh that is freezing by increments, lies a fresh young caribou, all butchered by him, all set for the feeding, for a week, of a family of six and a dog team of eight. In his weakened condition. With the force of a will as strong as Samson's, he has saved his family, me not least, just one of the many times he will do so through the course of a life jam-packed with daring, with unstoppability.

That afternoon, Mom has Louise take one of her sewing needles, boil it, and lance Dad's foot. Then she has her drain the infection. Two more days do we stay on that island, long enough for the swelling of the foot to subside to a point where Dad can walk, if with a pain that is just bearable, hitch up the dogs, pack our belongings, take down the tent, load up the sled. And go.

3

The part of travel by dogsled that is most striking is its silence. The vastness of the land demands it—immense, a sigh that yawns, the swelling of a lung divine in nature. It helps, of course, that the sled is engine-less. The cacophony of cars thus non-existent, the hum of powerlines, the blare of radios, television, or gramophones, the babble of voices human or otherwise, none of this is there to distract it. And if the cawing of a crow, the squeaking of the sled on crisp new snow, or Dad's mellifluous baritone exhorting his dogs left, right, or forward do break that silence, if rarely, then the blanket of snow that coats that landscape muffles such events, renders them sibilant, irrelevant. So that what that silence ends up doing after an hour of non-stop gliding through virgin snow is paralyzing its listeners with a music beyond experience. And the visuals that go with that "music" confirm that trance.

There is no trail; we make our own. And we make it on snow just freshly fallen, snow of a whiteness that is seen nowhere else in God's good kingdom, snow so white it hurts one's eyes. And we weave our way through mile after mile of stands of spruce trees thus finely cloaked, lake after lake—large, small, and medium—each likewise enhanced, river after river each likewise white. White, a general, a universal white. A hopping rabbit here, an Arctic fox there, a ptarmigan, a weasel, all four species in their seasonal white, a chickadee here, a junco there, a lynx, a squirrel, the forest is alive, the forest is an act of soundless magic. Then there is the air. Direct from the North

Pole, not once on its entire more than twelve-thousand-mile-long journey down to our homeland has it passed through any conceivable source of pollution so that, by the time it gets here, it makes lungs gasp, it makes lungs sing. And newborn babies sleep like angels.

For vast as it is, this region of the world still forms but a portion, and a small portion only, of Canada's Arctic. To take one point of comparison, the distance from the Manitoba–Nunavut border at latitude sixty to the country's northern extremity at latitude ninety—that is, the North Pole—is the same as that from Vancouver to Halifax. Another point of comparison: the territory of Nunavut, with its population, in the year 2021, of 39,000, is the same size as all of western Europe, with its population of a near half-billion. And that's just one territory of Canada's thirteen provinces and territories. So that from the perspective of an eagle surfing the breeze a half-mile overhead, the Highway family must look, "down there" that sunlit morning, like a line of ants traversing a bedsheet. I don't, of course, remember the journey, but I will see that landscape innumerable times throughout my life. I will live it, dream it. And between Mom, Dad, and Louise, who will tell me the story a thousand times as I grow up, I have it on excellent authority that this, indeed, is the trip we make that tenth day of December, 1951.

Finally, after four excruciatingly slow days of progress in order to accommodate Dad's injured foot—that part of the journey normally entails three days, if that—we burst from the forest and onto the surface of a river called the Cochrane. Lined in summer by swaths of wild grasses that come to the chest of a full-grown man and sway like dancers when coaxed by breezes and with willows that lean over the riverbank like tearful widows, the Cochrane River winds its way from just under the Northwest Territories' border to the northern extremity of Reindeer Lake, a distance of one hundred and fifty miles all told. In so doing, it follows the warp and weave of endless eskers (glacier-carved, sky-high, miles-long land formations that look like molehills), connects one lake to another and another, and is marked by rapids large and small at intervals irregular. In winter, naturally, these chutes don't freeze. The churning movement of water won't allow it. The result? Ice sculptures chimerical in shape that rise from the depths to heights of yards and mists that churn, billow, hover, ghostly in shape, a phantom presence. Our passage across such stretches thus blocked completely, we are forced to climb the river-bank and pass through a short stretch of yet more forest before we slide back down to the river post-rapids, thus allowing us to resume our homeward trajectory. And the largest of these rapids appears just before the river opens out to Reindeer Lake. A passage that is legendary for its great schools of pickerel, it fires the dreams of rod-wielding fishermen from Texas to Europe.

An ice-cream cone in shape, this titan among lakes straddles the border between the provinces of Manitoba and Saskatchewan. Tab-ulated as the twenty-third-largest lake in the world, its northeastern tenth lies in Manitoba, its southern nine-tenths in Saskatchewan. As for its length, its northern extremity lies one hundred and fifty miles south of the Northwest Territories' (now Nunavut) border, its south-ern, 1,500 north of the US border. One hundred and fifty miles of water from north end to south and forty from east side to west, that's Reindeer Lake. Picture Lake Ontario with five thousand islands, many of them ringed by gold sand beaches. That's Reindeer Lake. Picture Lake Erie with water so clear you can see to its bottom and so clean you can drink it with your hand, untreated. That's Reindeer Lake. Picture your family with thirty-five islands all to itself. That's Reindeer Lake. With some eight hundred people at its northern tip (Brochet, just inside Manitoba), twelve hundred at its southern (Southend, just inside Saskatchewan), and two dozen in the middle (Kinoosao, right on that provincial border)—two thousand people all told on a lake half as large as the Netherlands with its population of 17 million—the three communities are separated by so much dis-tance that, no matter which island you camp on, you get the impres-sion that you are alone, that you have the entire lake to yourself. That's Reindeer Lake. And the village of Brochet sits perched like the cherry on that ice-cream cone.

Having just skirted the last and largest set of rapids on the Cochrane River, we enter the expanse of Reindeer Lake, a breathtaking sight no matter how many times you make that passage. Passing four islands large and small to our left and the mainland to our right, we burst from the strait that separates Gunpowder Island from Moomoos Island. And there, glittering in the sun like shards of glass strewn willy-nilly, sits Brochet. One more half-mile and we are home.

From that distance, Brochet looks like a village made of assorted candy (it no longer does; time has changed it like it has everything and everyone). Log cabins with tarpaper roofs in red, green, and blue dot the plateau that it sits on. With no electricity, none have central heating, so each is crowned with a blackened tin chimney. All emitting smoke like trains in transit, the two square windows that front each house with the porch between them make them look like faces in a children's storybook—they wink at you, they smile. And with no roads, not to the world, not inside it, it is free of motorized traffic. Only walking trails for humans and dogsleds wind their way here, there, and everywhere.

The settlement comes in three distinct sections: central, western, and eastern. The central section is dominated by Companeek—the Hudson's Bay Company—with its store, two warehouses, and factor's residence (a "factor" is a manager in Companeek parlance). All white clapboard and with roofs of tile in *weesageemin* (cranberry) red, the complex ends down the hill at the water with the dock where bush planes moor at least thrice weekly. Behind them and inland stands a fenced-in compound which houses a weather station. Manned by a *Moony-ass* who lives there with his wife and two young children, its purpose, apparently, is to monitor the climate of sub-Arctic regions for Transport Canada. Thus the billboard that marks it: D O T, which is what we call it, for "Department of Transport." Just to the east of its five white buildings with their red-tile roofs which match Companeek's lies the Dene quarter. Contrasting vividly with its neighbours, this is an encampment of white canvas tents stained grey by smoke, smokehouses (tepee-like structures for smoking wild meat and fish), and mangy sled dogs tethered to posts, eight per tent. This entire section, comprised of Companeek, weather station, and Dene encampment, faces Brochet Bay.

Also facing Brochet Bay, the second section stands to the west of the central. Here stands the old church. Built in 1860, its walls of tin flash mirror-like in the sun as if to remind us that, even though it has long been supplanted by a new house of worship, it holds its place if only as storehouse and sometime cinema. To the right of the old church as one stands facing the lake, and slightly up this slope, stands the old priest's residence. Green-roofed, grey-walled, two-storeyed, it is followed in its turn by the new church, which was built in 1950. Which is why the new cemetery, for people who died post-1950, lies a quarter of a mile behind where starts in earnest the virgin forest.

At this point, the slope descends by increments to accommodate the schoolhouse for non-status children—that is, Native children whose ancestors did not sign treaties with the Crown. One-roomed, blue-roofed, white-walled, it marks the beginning of the non-status quarter, which flares out fan-like into the forest behind it. A neighbourhood of clay-caked log cabins with colourful roofs well-spaced one from the other, a few cling stubbornly to the shoreline west of the school and right to a headland that is marked by a crucifix of spruce painted white. The last house, in fact, is the domicile of Filament Mosquito and her husband, Archie. A Metis couple of long standing, they are known for their complexions which are white as parchment, thus proving incontestably that many non-status Cree in Brochet are actually half *Moony-ass*. Last, the aforementioned cross that juts from the headland behind the Mosquitos' cabin marks the old cemetery, the one where lie people who died pre-1950 when the new church was built.

As to the settlement's third and final section, it stands east of the Dene tent village and across the river. Here live the status Cree—that is, Native people whose ancestors did sign treaties with the Crown. And even though that river is actually an inlet crossed by a causeway, we still call it *seepeesis* (little river). Being status Cree, the midwife, Pitooria Wachask, lives in this neighbourhood with her husband, Alfred. It is she, in fact, who gave it its name, Seepees-seek (Where the Little River Is), or so it is said. In English, a reasonable equivalent would be "Riverdale." Whatever the origin of this cute little moniker, the neighbourhood of log cabins with colourful roofs is eventually swallowed by the forest on that side of the settlement. Here live hidden by stands of pine the Companeek clerk, Maagisit McMillan, his wife, Fire, and ten children, eight female, two male. This is Brochet's layout with, as always, exceptions to the rule—one of which is the elderly and crusted Moomoos Perkins and his extended family, who live on two islands across from Companeek, the smaller one of which we call Moomoos Island, which is non-status. (His eldest daughter having married Cheechup Kamaa-magoos, she lives therefore on the larger island, which is status but has no name.) The other exception is us. Though status to the roots of our jet-black hair, our house stands firmly on non-status land just east of the priest's house and west of the D O T.

By now, it will be clear to the reader that four fractious elements nullify all Brochet's chances of unity: geography, politics (status and non-status), ethnicity (Cree, Dene, and English, with, grace of missionaries, some French thrown in), and language (ditto—and no one speaks all four; a good half, in fact, speak one language only, the *Moony-ass* especially). Within the sphere of politics alone, for example, all Dene are status, where only half the Cree are. Meaning to say that one side of the village is governed by a town council with mayor (the non-status side), the other by a band council with Chief (the status side); and even then, the latter is divided by race (Cree and Dene) and language (ditto). For a village of eight hundred people?

"That's too muchie," says Chief Chi-Louie to "His Worship," Zebedee Zipper (my mom's youngest uncle), one August day, if only to apprise him of the fact that, besides his Dene and *apisees* (little bit) of Cree, he knows some English. By comparison, Mayor Zebedee knows ten words of English, fifteen in Dene, and "thousands" in Cree. All of which reduces communication between the two leaders to grunts, grimaces, and wild gyrations. In fact, the only thing that unites the disparate communities of Dene, status Cree, and non-status Cree is religion, which is Roman Catholic. *Ergo* Father Egg Nog's privileged position as King of the Indians, his sidekick this rotund little Brother with a head so bald it looks like a *waawaa* (egg).

K's'chees-naanis, we call him (our "Big Little Brother"). A sort of semi-priest who serves Father Egg Nog hand, foot, and soul, he, among other duties, also plays the harmonium (an air-based organ, like an accordion, that is pumped with the feet) in church for services and rings the bell in the steeple that summons the faithful to Mass on Sundays. Which brings us to the part in this narrative that describes my induction into the ranks of this star-crossed religion.

4

My father, Joe Highway—Joseph was his father, he just Joe—comes from Pelican Narrows, a Cree First Nation in northeastern Saskatchewan. With a population, in his youth, of some eight hundred people, it is situated seventy-five miles northwest of the border mining town of Flin Flon, Manitoba, which, in turn, stands halfway between the American and Nunavut borders (though, back then, the latter territory was, of course, still just part of the Northwest Territories). "Pelican" thus stands on the network of freshwater passages that drain Canada's western sub-Arctic into vast, salt-watered Hudson's Bay some eight hundred miles downstream via a network of lakes and rivers. Prime territory for a British enterprise called the Hudson's Bay Company to launch its dream, it would prove a fertile breeding ground for many a young Cree adventurer. Like Joe Lapstan Highway. ("Lapstan," his nickname, is just two syllables slapped together for no greater reason than to make people chuckle; as with "Peechoochee" and "Chaggy-wat," whom you'll soon meet, they mean nothing.)

Companeek was founded in London, England in 1670 with the objective of trading for furs with the Indians of Canada. Our great Northwest being an area known for its richness in beaver, the company's mode of shipping thus had to answer to extensive and arduous lake and river travel to access it. When you consider that that region as a whole boasts lakes that number some fifteen thousand, and countless rivers, the portages alone would make men tremble. (Portages are places where a set of rapids make a river impassable so that the traveller must carry his boat and cargo to connect with the next lake or river.) *Ergo* the York boat. Named after York Factory, a trading post built on the flat and swampy shore of Hudson's Bay 120 miles southeast of Churchill in 1684—as opposed to the spectacular, esker-riven, lake-pocked landscape that marks our side of northern Manitoba—the hardy York boat carried trade goods upstream on the Nelson River and onward, and furs downstream from there to be shipped off to England. Preferred by the Company for their greater capacity to the Native canoe, the boats were built by "Orkney men" (of whom more shortly). The young Cree men hired to row them thus had to have the strength of steel. Impossible for one team to row the entire length of the Hudson's Bay drainage system, which stretches all the way to the Rocky Mountains, they worked in relays *and* in teams of six or eight per boat. One such man was named Joe Highway. Born on the twelfth of March, 1908, to Joseph and the fiercely handsome Josephine Ballantyne, he was rowing and portaging with the best of them by age eighteen. From Pelican Narrows up the Churchill River up the Reindeer River across the south-north length of Reindeer Lake thus entering Manitoba from whence Brochet, the Cochrane River, and what was then the Northwest Territories, this was his route. A distance of some six hundred miles of roadless land, the feat would have laid low men of lesser mettle. But not Joe Highway. The second eldest of thirteen children, nine of whom survived to adulthood, he passed Brochet on a basis semi-regular going north with trade goods—tea, flour, baking powder, guns, bullets, and canned goods such as beans—and south with furs. Which is how he met this dark-eyed young woman who, like him, was the second eldest of thirteen children, nine of whom survived to adulthood. A match made in heaven, said Joe Highway to this woman whom he married in a trice. He, aged twenty, she, seventeen, the God-blessed union fell on the sixth of November, 1928.

Born in Brochet on the eleventh of January, 1911, thus giving her the number, 11/1/11, that made her life an act of magic, my mother, for her part, came from a family of criminals, according anyway to the Government of Canada. The story goes that when Louis Riel's efforts to establish an independent French-speaking country in Canada's west were crushed in 1870, a bounty was set on the heads of those Metis and Half-breeds who had participated in the rebellion but survived the fate met by Riel and many others: hanging for treason. And even though the bounty might have been mere hearsay, it was real enough to make them flee. Cree-speakers all, these mixed-race die-hards sought refuge in places so remote that the law would never find them. Thus Reindeer Lake and thus Brochet. (If both are impossible to reach even today, imagine them in the nineteenth century.)

A summer encampment for Dene hunters who came by canoe from northern Saskatchewan and the Northwest Territories where roamed their cousins, the equally nomadic Dogrib and Slavey, Brochet made room for these homeless vagabonds, refugees from sectarian violence. The result? Within three generations of peaceful co-existence by these two nations, the village was largely bilingual in Cree and Dene. And being as she was a member in good standing of the third generation of Half-breed refugees, Balazee Highway's adopted Dene rivalled her native Cree in fluency. In fact, as the second eldest child of Weezoo Zipper and Adelaide Gunpowder, her speed in either language was such that she could make lip-readers go blind with one Hail Mary, is how legend has it. The first proof-positive that her magic number worked? She gave Joe Highway their first-born child on the sixth of November, 1929, one year *to the day* after their wedding.

And speaking of Hail Marys, ever since Europeans first set foot in what to them was the "New World," the various denominations of the Christian religion have engaged in a race for the souls of the hemisphere's Indigenous peoples. In some regions, the Anglicans won, in others, the Methodists, in others, the Baptists, in still others, the United Church. In large swaths of southern Canada, the Evangelicals have made great strides in the second half of the twentieth century. In southwest Alberta, it is the Mormons. Even the Jehovah's Witnesses have managed to get their foot in the door in certain corners of the Native community. In Canada's north, the Roman Catholics won hands down with the result that, all across that vast territory, when you see an Indian on his knees with his lips contorting and his eyes turned skyward, you can bet your bottom dollar that he is praying to the Virgin and rattling his rosaries. So it is with northern Saskatchewan, so it is with Pelican Narrows, so it is with northern Manitoba, so it is with Reindeer Lake, and so it is with old Brochet.

So it was that Roman Catholic missionaries first started arriving by paddled canoe on Reindeer Lake in the 1850s. Oblates of Mary Immaculate, an order of priests founded in Aix-en-Provence, France, in 1816, their mandate was missionary work the whole world over. In Canada, its recruits for the most part came from Quebec—which is how the letter "L," previously unknown in our language, found its way in with words like *la messe*, *lachook* ("*la tuque*," the winter hat made of wool), *lapwachin* ("*la pudding*"), and *pawpilly-cum* ("bubble gum"). It came, that is, from the articles *le*, *la*, and *les* that anchor French, and the names of the children these priests baptized betrayed in kind such Gallic influence as in Jean-Baptiste which, pronounced in Cree, comes out as "Samba Cheese," Pelagie ("Balazee"), Charlotte ("Salad"), Philomene ("Filament"), etc.

By 1860, these missionaries had erected a church in Brochet proper. Named after the mission, which they called St. Pierre, it stood on the hill just up from the lake halfway between Companeek and Minee-waati-meek (the Point) where live Archie Mosquito and his wife, Filament. In use for some eighty-odd years until it started creaking and sagging—and "smelling like shit," as claimed Masky Jimmy Perkins, the self-appointed village interpreter of signs and symbols (and grandson of Moomoos Perkins)—it was replaced in 1950 by a brand-new structure some forty yards west of the old, with the rectory, that is, the priest's house/residence, between them. Which is the church to which I am taken on the morning of the fifteenth of December, 1951, for my baptism.

Normally, a newborn baby about to be inducted into "the faith" in this manner so arresting is provided with two godparents, one of each sex, both picked by his parents. My younger brother, Rene, had Nora Gunpowder, my wicked Aunt Peechoochee's third of five stunning daughters, and Ben Wah Naatawee-oos, the grandson Zaa-Marie and Rosie Gunpowder had raised as theirs because his mother, their daughter, had died in childbirth. Daniel had both, one of whom was Chief Chi-Louie. Florence had both. But all I was given was a woman, one reason for the pronounced femininity of my persona, I have always thought. Her name was Tarees (Cree for Thérèse) Naasi-peeti-meek. The wife of Samba Cheese Weetigo (his last name, too, a nickname only), she lived downhill from our house, right by the lake which is why her nickname: "Tarees Down-by-the-Lake" (for her real last name was Gunpowder, as was her husband's). Straight-backed at the time (which she is no longer), round-shouldered, and swarthy of complexion, Tarees was Dene; Samba Cheese was Cree. One of the first instances of cross-tribal marriage on Reindeer Lake, they were applauded by the priest at the time, Father Egg Nog, who had warned from his pulpit that inbreeding had been known to result in two-headed children, which terrified the Dene into submission. Which was his purpose.

Now, Father Egg Nog was interesting on two counts. One was that, like all priests of the era, he wore his foot-long, gilt-edged, black wooden crucifix wedged into the sash that girded his cassock at belly-button level, the waist thereof rather skeletal for he reputedly ate pemmican almost exclusively (pemmican is moose or caribou meat first smoked to a state that is crusty, then pounded into a powder which is then "glued" together by animal fat and wild cranberries; with no electricity and thus no refrigeration, this was how we pre-served our meat). The way he wore that symbol of torture, however, and the way he walked, which was with strides so aggressive they scared small children, the cross looked like a weapon; it looked quite capable of stabbing and killing. Another was that, unlike all the other missionaries who were French to the last—that is, Québécois—he was a *Chaariman*. In fact, his real name was Egenolf, but as no one in Brochet could pronounce it, the best they could do was "Egg Nog" (which, to us, was not a drink but garble).

"Much easier on the tongue," mused Masky Jimmy Perkins, whose limp was so violent it made you dizzy to watch him walk, which is why his nickname: "Lame Jimmy." Father Egg Nog, that is to say, came not from Quebec but from, of all places, Germany which, of course, is what made him a *Chaariman*. The cantankerous old codger had been in Brochet since 1890 so, by the time I was born, he was ninety.

"Old as the eskers," said Masky Jimmy Perkins. Authoritarian to the roots of his snow-white hair, he ruled Brochet with a fist made of iron *and* a face to match that gnarly extremity: fur-like eyebrows, glowering eyes, a falcon nose. He forbade, for example, the art of dancing which, as bad luck would have it, was Samba Cheese Weetigo's favourite activity. If anyone was caught dancing, Father Egg Nog thundered from his pulpit on Sunday mornings, "*kwayus tawee-sagee-gasoo machee-skooteek*" ("he will burn to a crisp in the flames of hell") for, God knows, like all missionaries of the time and place, the crafty old *Chaariman* had learned to speak Cree like a chickadee speaks chickadee. His descriptions of hell, according to Louise, were so detailed, twisted, and terrifying that no one in Brochet ever contemplated one step of a jig much less a *skweetaas* (our pronunciation of "square dance"). But back to my baptism . . .

According to Louise, there we are in St. Pierre Church ●at butt-freezing morning in mid-December, clustered around the baptismal font that stands at ground level to the side of the altar which, in turn, stands three steps up a pinewood platform. My parents, my sister Louise, my godmother, Tarees Naasi-peeti-meek, and Father Egg Nog. The priest enrobed in a green silk stole, a matching maniple (a sort of sleeve-cum-napkin worn hanging from the right forearm), and a starched white surplice that flows like a curtain over the upper three-quarters of his thick black cassock, he looks like a statue, according to Louise. So cold is the water in that font—a bowl made of white stone cupped by a hollow at the top of a pinewood column four feet high—that filaments of *maskwami* (ice) cling to its surface, again according to Louise. As there always are in such circumstances, curious onlookers kneel scattered across the cavernous chamber to witness the ritual. Of these, the only one she remembers with clarity is Jean-Pierre Yazzie, the grizzled, potato-nosed Dene *k'seet'noo* (old man in Cree) who is notorious for clearing, very loudly, the snuff-manufactured, greenish-brownish phlegm from the base of his esophagus in the middle of church services and other such unlikely places

and times, making the shoulders of all who hear him cringe with re-
vulsion. And so they should, because the sound he makes when he
does this amounts to a growl, with great gobs of snot at the base of
his throat followed on their heels by a sharp spitting sound and then
by a *splat* at the bottom of his ambulant spittoon, the empty Libby's
brown beans tin can he carries with him wherever he goes, to
Companeek, for instance, to buy his snuff. I know the sound because
I, too, hear it with disgusting regularity in the years that follow.

Knowing this will happen sooner or later and dreading it, Tarees
Naasi-peeti-meek holds me in her arms as if I am the world's last
baby. Ardent praying and soulful chanting in a liberal melange of
Cree, Dene, and Latin open the proceedings. And they do this, that,
and the other, according to Louise. Father Egg Nog waves his arms
this way, that, and the other. Until they come to the crux. When the
priest asks me—and by way of me, Tarees Naasi-peeti-meek—if I am
ready to renounce *Machaa-is* (Satan) from my body and my heart
together with all his empty promises and wild whorish ways, Jean-
Pierre Yazzie, from ten rows behind us, horks out his phlegm with his
usual gurgling, hair-raising gusto and spits into his can with a *splat*,
thus neatly camouflaging my godmother's answer—and by way of
her, *my* answer—to that testy little question, is how my sister Louise
recounts the old yarn. Which is why I have always had a thorny relationship with this whorish *Machaa-is*, is the general consensus in
family lore. I don't, of course, remember the holy water hitting my
forehead but I imagine it is cold for, apparently, I wail out in a manner
that makes it impossible, apparently, for Jean-Pierre Yazzie to drown
it out this time, if his phlegm-clogged old gizzard is so inclined.

And then they give me the name for which I will pay dearly all my
life. "Tomson Highway?" people will inquire and burst out laughing,
"Sounds like an address." "Tomson Expressway," "Tomson Freeway,"
I hear them both, and more, year in, year out. On top of which, as
bad luck would have it, a year or two after my birth, *Moony-ass*
prospectors discover nickel in the rocks some three hundred miles
southeast of Brochet. For the north of the time, which is roadless,
three hundred miles is a daunting distance. In fact, my eldest brother,

Swanson, leaves Brochet at age twenty, at the very time of my birth, apparently to help clear land for the mine site and the town that will spring from the granite to serve it. But he might as well have left this planet for all we see of him throughout that period. When he finally does appear, I am four years old and don't even know him. The name given the town that he helps clear land for, in any case, is "Thompson," the road constructed in the years that follow to connect it to Winnipeg the "Thompson Highway," which causes confusion and rancorous debate wherever I go, even on the beaches of Rio de Janeiro.

Yes, my name is "Tomson Highway." Not "Thompson," not "Thomson," not even "Thomas," but "Tomson." "No 'h,' no 'p,'" I have to explain—to bank tellers, airline ticket agents, policemen, one-night stands—my entire life.

As for the spelling, it is highly suspected that Father Egg Nog's weakest subject in school was spelling. When it comes to inscribing names into his baptismal registry, for example, he misspells everything. Still, he must be forgiven because life in official northern Manitoba at the time functioned, as it still does, not in Cree, not in Dene, not in German, not in French but in English. He registered my eldest sister Viola's name, for instance, as "Voila." He misspells Hansen as "Handsome," to cite another case, which ends up a boon for Handsome Hell for he isn't handsome at all, not as a boy, not as a man. So when it comes time for the withered old *Chaariman* to inscribe my name into the baptismal registry as "Thompson Highway," which is my father's desire for a reason I'll get to shortly, he either inadvertently leaves out the "h" and the "p" or he has no idea they exist. Whereby hangs a tale that will titillate all who read this story . . .

History states that, in the 1930s, as Hitler's shadow was oozing its way across increasingly large chunks of northern Europe, citizens of nations within the German orbit of influence were plunged into a fear unknown till then, as can only be imagined when one looks at the final tally. And as conscription was the rule in these countries, young men of conscience left their countries as an act of protest. Much like American draft dodgers would do in reaction to the

Vietnam War some four decades later, they fled their countries to preserve their principles. And their lives. Disgusted with human behaviour, they sought out as refuge the most isolated parts of the planet that they could think of, where they would never have to set eyes on another accursed human being. Hence sub-Arctic Canada. The Scandinavian countries, in particular, fell victim to this exodus, a trickle as it was. Which is how the area that borders northern Manitoba and Saskatchewan on the one hand and what was then just the Northwest Territories on the other—that is to say, my home-land—ended up harbouring these Scandinavian-hermit trappers—for that's what they became, hermits. The region unimaginable in its vastness, it just swallowed them. And being Norwegian, Swedish, and Danish, with names like Larson and Olson and Patterson and Peterson and Anderson and Johnson. The Highway family traversing perennially the territory these hermits had chosen as refuge, Dad was practically the only human contact they had. And this not often. And being the prince he was, they liked him, trusted him, he was the sole friend they had on Earth.

Still, a hermit's existence did not suit them all. Some of them, in fact, married Cree, Dene, and Inuit women and begat children. With the result that, some seventy years later, northern Manitoba and Saskatchewan are chock-a-block with Cree Indians whose last name is Olson, Anderson, and Peterson. My parents begetting five boys and seven girls as they eventually did, Dad started naming his sons after these "friends." Thus my eldest brother is called Swanson. And I am called Tomson, thanks to a combination of my father's Norwegian friend, Something Thompson, my illiterate (in English) father him-self, *and* Father Egg Nog's dyslexic spelling.

As for the "Highway" part, there is only speculation. It was the winter of 1972–73 and I was living in London, England, studying, of all things, with a concert pianist. The game of soccer as much a pas-sion there as hockey is in Canada, it was omnipresent, in the print media, on the radio, on TV. And among the teams from the various English cities, the one from Liverpool had a particularly rabid fan base. And the star of that team at the time was an Irishman from

Dublin named Stephen Derek Heighway, a soccer hero in his day as big as David Beckham was in his. That's the only other place where I have ever come across this family name. Which makes it doubly striking that, today, in northern Saskatchewan for the most part and northern Manitoba to a lesser extent, there are hundreds of us Highways, perhaps even thousands. My father's youngest brother, my Uncle Adam, alone, had twenty-two children! Meaning to say that, up in those parts, the name is normal, a part of the landscape.

Now jump back some three hundred years. As mentioned earlier, the Hudson's Bay Company was founded in London, England in 1670. To get to northwest Canada, which it had identified as the richest place in the world in fur-bearing animals, the ships that it sent there sailed from London, out the Thames River, and into the North Sea. France and England forever at war, turning southward and going via the shorter route of English Channel and westward was considered too vulnerable to piracy, a practice encouraged by both French and English. *Ergo* the route that went north instead, up the east coasts of England and Scotland, around the northern tip of the latter country, across the Atlantic Ocean, and into northern Manitoba via Hudson's Bay. The last stop they made before their great crossing was a cluster of wind-blasted, rock-bound islands off Scotland's northern tip. Called the Orkney Islands, this is where they got their last supply of drinking water *and* recruited the labour they would need for the trading posts they planned to establish across Canada's sub-Arctic. Grace of their Viking past—for seafaring peoples, the distance of five hundred miles of sea that separate Norway from Scotland is nothing—not only were these island's residents more Scandinavian than Gaelic in look as in character, they also had an education system, at the time, that was superior to Scotland's. The young men hired here by the HBC, some of them a mere eighteen, thus were literate, not least in mathematics which, of course, was a skill essential for the practice of commerce. Hence the clerks and factors who came to man the Companeek trading posts scattered across our great Northwest. That many of these men also had the skill to design and construct their forebears' Viking longships is the reason that the aforementioned York boat looked so similar. And these "Orkney men" came with names like Flett, Loutit, and Linklater, names since passed down to the Cree of our area. In times of war when young men ran short, the ships would have stopped at the north end of Ireland, which is where they would have picked up at least one Heighway—but that's speculation.

As for those Scotsmen who worked, as well, for the HBC in numbers respectable, they came with names like McCallum, Ballantyne, Spence, and McKay. And even if they didn't marry Native women, as did Anderson and Olson, then here's what happened: when it came to the signing of treaties with our people, Cree and Dene names were frequently impossible for the *Moony-ass* to spell. Beejee-aazay, Old Dice Chagaazay, Apaag-waachees Mooraah—all would have stumped them. So they "borrowed" names from "the boys" who happened to be sitting at the counter drinking coffee and smoking cigarettes, names they could spell, and slapped them onto those documents. Thus am I one-quarter Highway (my father's father's last name) and one-quarter Ballantyne (my father's mother's maiden name), one-quarter Zipper (my mother's maiden name), and one-quarter Gunpowder (her mother's maiden name), the last two names of which, respectively, come from England. As for the Cree part of my bloodline, it goes back eons, to a time before the arrival, on our shores, of the first lost *Moony-ass*. It comes from the soil, it comes from the veins of the Earth itself.

But far too often have I wished that I was blessed with a name like Bill Johnson, Bob White, Ron Cooper, or Mstislav Michiskovich. Or even, for that matter, Paul Gagnon, Michel Tremblay, or Row Bare Go Bare (Robert Gaubert, pronounced in French but spelled in Cree). But no, I am just bizarre, unusual, ridiculous, multilingual, optimist unstoppable, laughter-loving, piano-playing—and utterly unique—Tomson Highway.

5

Six feet tall, straight-backed, square-shouldered—a bull moose with antlers surveying his kingdom from a hilltop—his face is chiselled even if it shows evidence of youthful acne. Full, meat-like lips, a firm square jaw, an aquiline nose with slender nostrils, wavy black hair, thick black eyebrows that, at the same time, are just this side of bushy, eyes that dance forever on the cusp of exuberance, of unbuttoned levity, that is Dad. Like all Brochet men of the time, he wears when outdoors a *napa-gastoo-tin* (flat hat), a pie-shaped hat of worsted wool with a button at the top and a visor at the front, his feet with moccasins a-splash with colour, beadwork crafted by Balazee Highway. Weightless footwear, they give his feet the wings of birds. When not engaged in tricksterish endeavour, his eyes speak patience. And of kindness, humility, respect for God, respect for Man. Never does he have an unkind word to say of anyone; if something or someone peeves him, a dark cloud floats across his face and then is gone. Never a preacher, his tacit lesson is: If you have something unpleasant to say of someone, say it to his face. Or say nothing.

Mom, on the other hand, is short and elfin. Which doesn't nullify the fact that she is as strong and as supple as a length of rubber. Wire-like muscles and steel-like bones render her capable, even at age seventy, of bearing a half-size canoe turned upside down up a hill on her shoulders, her hands gripping its gunwales, her head concealed in its hull. We have the pictures to prove it. Oval-faced, full-lipped, the forehead not quite as high as one would want it but attractive still, a loon-like neck (though not, of course, quite as long), eyes as mischievous as Dad's prank for prank, her *pièce de résistance* is her legs which are streamlined, fine-boned, the legs of a runner. When she stands on one leg with the other bent lazily at the knee, she gives the impression of verging on sliding into a waltz. Rain or shine, she wears a floral-patterned cotton granny smock of tasteful colours. Emerald, magenta, sapphire blue, these are favourites. The dress she herself has made, as with all Brochet women of the time, using her manual sewing machine and from material she has bought at the Companeek store. When finished, it comes to just below her knees, flows like a curtain, and is as finely crafted as anything one finds in the Eaton's catalogue.

As with the men, lace-up moccasins with fancy beadwork are the footwear if not quite of choice then of necessity—the landscape decides; on her back a sober-coloured windbreaker or pastel-tinted wool-knit sweater with buttons down the front. (In winter, of course, these are replaced or covered by a parka stuffed with goose down.) A multi-coloured, faux-silk kerchief covering her head with ends tied loosely under her chin complete what, in essence, is a uniform worn by all Cree women of her time and place. Raised by kind people, she is kind. And, like Dad, nurtures her penchant for the ridiculous.

"You wants some the coffee?" she will ask her husband of a given sunny morning to show off her English, which is non-existent.

"You makes the good coffee," Dad will answer. And will lance into the air a robust, full-chested laugh. And if they are good-looking, then so are their siblings and their progeny and all that progeny's progeny with, of course, exceptions. I have male cousins who look like Elvis at the height of his beauty, same olive complexion, same jet-black hair, same thick lips. I have female cousins who look like Katharine Ross, the American actress who co-starred with Dustin Hoffman in the film *The Graduate*. In fact, it has been said, on more than one occasion by more than one person, that the concentration of physical beauty in Brochet is extraordinary, the result of the mixing, over the course of untold generations, of Cree and *Moony-ass* blood. Among other "strains,"—English, Scottish, Irish, and French, among them—Viking blood from the Orkney Islands, I am convinced, has contributed. In fact, wags claim that the letters "HBC" stand not for the "Hudson's Bay Company" but for the "Horny Boys' Club"; boys will be boys . . . Still, the most beautiful of them all—the most beautiful man ever to walk the face of this planet, it will be said by all who see him—is about to be born to this Cree couple who are now in their mid-forties. His name? Rene Highway.

If Titty Ray Looraah midwives babies out on the land, as she did me, then Pitooria Wachask, Mom's best friend, midwives babies in Brochet. Her real name is Victoria—Victoria Wachask-née-Fitzgerald, elder sister of Alec Fitzgerald who himself will have eighteen children—but everyone calls her "Pitooria" which is Cree for "Victoria." So far as is known, Pitooria Wachask has midwifed every birth that has transpired in Brochet between 1930 and 1960, which means that she has brought into the world a good half of the village. And she would have continued with her nocturnal ministrations to age one hundred if the federal government didn't introduce, in 1960, a programme whereby Native women in the final stages of their pregnancies are flown by bush plane the three hundred miles south to The Pas (The Paw), there to wait out their term at a hospice. When this time comes, they are driven to the only hospital in town, St. Anthony's, some ten blocks away, there to give birth. Which is why those of my nephews and nieces born in 1960 and after were not, like me and nine of my eleven siblings, born in snowbanks. The government's objective, of course, is to lower the infant mortality rate which, prior to 1960, is brutal, as witness my family. Fortunately for me, I am born eight years before 1960 and so am spared an urban birth, that is, birth by doctor in a *Moony-ass* hospital. As is my younger brother. Born in 1954, he will be the last of our family of twelve.

Being status Cree, Pitooria Wachask lives in Seepees-seek with her husband, Alfred. In fact, they live at the far end of the causeway where starts the neighbourhood so that they "guard" its entrance, if inadvertently, as the three-headed dog of ancient Greek myth whose name I can't pronounce guards the gateway to hell, has explained Father Egg Nog who despises Alfred Wachask because he harbours proclivities shamanistic—that is, proclivities pagan—or so rumour has it. Pitooria and Alfred have four children which, for a Cree couple, is considered sterile, though the number is supplemented by an orphan girl Pitooria Wachask was given by an itinerant Swedish trapper whose Cree wife had died in childbirth—as well as two other "progeny" who remain a secret, conceived from "flings" somewhere "down there" (our way of saying "where live the *Moony-ass*") before she married this Alfred Wachask. It is said that one such fling transpired in the arms of a *Moony-ass* bush pilot who flew cartographers to the Arctic on a basis semi-regular to map it. The insinuation that this white bush pilot who has five sons—all, like their father, to become legendary bush pilots—might have sired a love-child with our Pitooria Wachask remains just that, an insinuation, for the midwife's lips themselves are sealed as with *pawpilly-cum*.

Still, most eerie for us children is her left eye, which is clouded over with what looks like smoke, its pupil, its iris, and its retina thus half-hidden by a nimbus that swirls, as if it harbours an oracle. Mom says that people so afflicted are blessed with a vision. And it's true, when Pitooria Wachask looks at you, you feel exposed, as if she is reaching into your soul's inner passages and rifling around inside its folds. They say she can fly. They say she can speak the caribou language.

When his wife is sufficiently advanced in her pregnancy to make birth risky, a man sometimes goes north to hunt and trap by himself, allowing her the safety of birth in a house as opposed to a snowbank, a tent, or a lean-to. In my case, my parents planned to reach Brochet in time for my birth which was expected the week before Christmas. Except, of course, that I arrived two weeks early. In my little brother's case, it is evident from the start, apparently, that he will be born in early November. Which is why my father leaves my mother at our little log house on Brochet Hill that October and drives his dogsled north by himself. All by way of saying that I end up out-lucking Rene in the sense that I am born in a snowbank, he in a house. Then again, he will out-luck me in many other ways. Now fifteen, and this being early November, Louise is away at boarding school and thus not in Brochet to witness his birth. Which is why the narration at this point in this story is taken over by Pitooria Wachask, Brochet's great mid-wife and Mom's best friend. So this from Pitooria . . .

For some reason, most people in Brochet are born in winter. So on certain nights when the stars are visible and the snow is knee-high, Pitooria Wachask is seen at intervals irregular, always in silhouette, crossing the village (she will tell Rene and me these stories as we are growing up like they are ghost stories). Her back hunched over, a canvas packsack upon it, a walking stick aiding her progress, all who see her know that a miracle is imminent, that the crone of sixty is about to perform yet another one of her acts of magic. The late evening of November the fifth, 1954, is no different. Parka-clad, she crosses the causeway from Seepees-seek, crosses the Dene encampment with its chimneys smoking, weaves her way between the Companeek store and the D O T, trudges past the house where lives in solitude Poosees Gunpowder, the Gunpowder matriarch, thus arriving at our home.

Now eleven, Florence, too, is away at boarding school which leaves Daniel, now aged seven, and me, now aged one-month-short-of three, sleeping together on a mattress splayed out on the floor of what would be the living room if this were a house that belonged to a *Moony-ass*. So no, no tales from Louise, Florence or Daniel about the arrival of our new baby brother. No Henry Beksaka brandishing a rifle and yelling obscenities to the starlit sky, no Titty Ray Looraah sprouting the wings of a nighthawk and zooming through the night to be with Mom, and no fresh snow as bed for an infant.

Pitooria Wachask tells us that Rene's birth in the early morning hours of the sixth of November, 1954, goes off "swimmingly," that no mishaps happen, that all is on schedule though one would think that, by child number twelve, an infant's passage through his mother's birth canal would be smooth sailing, no pain for the mother, no pain for the child.

"Twenty-five years, *to the day*, after our wedding," crows Dad when he gets home from the north some six weeks later.

"And twenty-four years, *to the day*, after our first-born," Mom echoes, thanking in her heart—she tells me years later—her magic number, 11/1/11. And it's true: this new child's birth, the youngest of our twelve; the birth of the eldest of those twelve, Viola; *and* our parent's marriage take place on the sixth day of the eleventh month of the years 1954, 1929, and 1928, the last two digits of which three years add up to 111. That he is healthy, strong, and cute as a *waaskee-choos* (pine cone) is a given. That his beauty will bloom to jaw-dropping heights is also a given as we already have members of the extended family who look like gods. He is named Rene at his subsequent baptism by his godparents, Nora Gunpowder, elder sister of Rene Gunpowder (Aunt Peechoochee's third son of six)—from whence comes the name "Rene"—and Ben Wah Naatawee-oos.

The midwife crouches on the floor of our "living room" in our little log house that looks, from the outside, like a cake with its mantle of snow, its kerosene lamp, and its chimney smoking (this last description from Rene Gunpowder, then fifteen, who has run over to help stoke the woodstove with wood he is chopping. And chopping and chopping). The stars out together with the northern lights in all their splendour, the air rings out with the usual call-and-response chorus of sled dogs tethered to posts throughout Brochet, and their cousins, the wolves in the distance. In the north, we all grew up falling asleep to this haunting sound; it was our lullaby. As indeed it is to this infant just born.

Fast-forward one winter. I am now four, Rene one year. Mid-morning already, the interior of our house is a-splash with sunlight. Open in concept, the kitchen, dining, and living areas are all one piece, the division between them nonexistent if it were not for the dog's paw, wrought-iron woodstove in the middle and a little to the right as one enters. Daniel, now eight, is away at boarding school with Louise and Florence. But Swanson, now twenty-four and as handsome as his cousin, Samba Cheese Gunpowder, my wicked Aunt Peechoochee's first-born, is home from clearing land for the building of a railway that is snaking its way north from The Pas to the new mine in Lynn Lake, a town rising from the bush seventy-six miles as the crow flies southeast of Brochet. And he is standing there just inside the front (and only) door drinking coffee from a mug, his wavy black hair slicked back with Brylcreem. Rene, meanwhile, is sitting on the floor in his little red plaid flannel shirt, faded blue denim coveralls, and lace-up, beaded, caribou-hide moccasins the size of dolls' shoes. The conversation murmurs like a babbling brook. "*Tamithoogee-sigow paa-am anooch kaagee-sigaak*," says Dad. "*How*," says Swanson, "*apwee-tigwee n'ga-maachaan. Kagee-ayawa-in naa kiteemak?*" ("I think it's going to be nice today." "Yes, maybe I'll go hunting. Can you lend me your dogs?")

Nobody has noticed that Rene is now standing, albeit with help from a kitchen chair to whose aluminum leg he clings with hands the size of a puppy's paws. By dint of child effort, he has hoisted himself to an upright position. No one knows how long he has been standing there. Me? I hear silence. The mouths of my parents and my eldest brother move mutely. Time hangs likewise. Then I see Rene's left foot lift off the pine-plank floor and take its first step, independently, free of chair, free of Mom's hand. It is one of the clearest memories I have from that part of my life.

"*Ana n'si!*" ("Look at him!") exclaims Swanson. Rene's second step I don't remember. Nor his third or his fourth. But he is walking now, though "staggering like a drunk" would do more justice to the act. And he is thrilled—a newfound freedom, his first step of *skweetaas* (square dance), a dance he will love with all his heart. And the remainder of that day fades first to grey then to black.

6

Rene and I grow up like twins. In Cree, the word is *neesoo-cheewak*, which means "two maggots," from *neesoo* (two) and *oocheewak* (flies or maggots; "*oochao* is a fly; the "*wak*" pluralizes and the "*oo*'s" of the two words are simply collapsed into each other—don't ask why. That's just the character of our Trickster language). As twins, therefore, we are inseparable. Regretfully, this is not the case with me and Daniel, the next in line in the family going up—that is, from youngest to eldest. Because of the loss of our sister Hermeline, who came between us and died as an infant, four years separate us, too wide a gap to bridge with common interests. As for our other siblings, to us, they are fossils. All of which leaves Rene and me in a state of fraternity uncommonly close, uncommonly personal. *We* have common interests, *we* have a bond that is unbreakable.

If Daniel's interest is sports, especially ice hockey, ours is the arts. What I remember next are the games we play, Rene and I, as we are growing up on the islands of Reindeer Lake, of Mariah Lake, of Robinson Lake, of lakes a hundred, two hundred, three hundred miles north of Brochet, right into the then Northwest Territories. And it is always islands we live on, never the mainland, and that for reasons of a theory held by all northern parents.

Islands, in effect, are enclosures. There, children can play at liberty without fear of getting lost. *K'stagaa-mak* (the mainland), on the other hand, is dangerous. In a land so vast, one wrong turn and you are lost forever. Then there are the animals, bears for example, or wolves or lynx. Worse, there is *ma-chimes-chigoosoo*, the "bad *Moony-ass*," who is this crazed, filth-encrusted white hermit with eyes, they say, as wild as those of Keesk-weeya-i Salamoo (Crazy Solomon), a mentally disabled Cree man who wanders Brochet with bare feet in winter (legend has it that he lost his mind when his wife died young). A bogeyman of sorts, *ma-chimes-chigoosoo* roams the forests of the mainland looking for children to eat, says Mom. Her way of deterring us from wandering too far and never crossing to the mainland, for we sometimes have an extra canoe *or* can build rafts, this *ma-chimes-chigoosoo* exists only in the realm of a child's worst nightmares. Still, that doesn't stop us from looking for him whenever we happen to be travelling by or through *k'stagaa-mak*. Right into our teens do Rene and I peer into the forest hoping for a glimpse of that filthy coat, that dirt-caked face, that tangled knot of greasy hair, and that diabolic stare. Even today, whenever I'm up there, which is almost every year, I still catch myself looking for him in the deep dark forest if a chill comes upon me.

Fictive or not, this man is a reminder that Rene and I are privileged enough to have entire islands to ourselves as playgrounds. Or entire beaches. Or entire series of islands *and* beaches. The rocks on those islands, for example—shards of granite as old as time—are sometimes as large as one-storey houses and square as boxes, so we climb them and, from their flat summits, wail out songs of our own making. Or create dances complete with music that we make by banging sticks together while we babble nonsensical syllables. And because our nearest neighbour is a hundred miles away south, east, or west—to the north, try ten thousand—we have no playmates besides each other.

According to Dad, Reindeer Lake has five hundred bays, some on islands, some on the mainland. The best known is called Paskwaa-chee Waasaak (Stump Bay). Just inside Manitoba from its border with Saskatchewan, it is feared for its size; when you drive past it, it looks like a mouth that is yawning, the forest beyond it made blue-grey by distance. And then there is Perch Bay, much smaller but also on the

Manitoba side, some fifteen miles behind Brochet. One has first to circumnavigate the stunning two-mile-long sandbar called Thigh Daddy to get to the abandoned cabin Dad knew had been there for years and, with his skills as a carpenter, reconstituted. Which is where we are living when I turn five and Rene two. Our other siblings either all away at boarding school or flown the nest to start their own lives, it is just us and our parents on Perch Bay that winter. (The name of the sandbar is actually Thighdarry, with the "r's" rolled thickly—it means "Sandy Point" in Dene—but to us Cree, it sounds like "Thigh Daddy," so that's what we call it.)

Dad is out hunting, so the dogs are all gone. Nothing unusual there; he does it all the time. To keep boredom at bay, for herself as for her sons, Mom packs a picnic of bannock, pemmican, and *namee-steek* (smoked whitefish or sucker), a lunch she says we will supplement with black tea boiled on a fire fed by spruce on an island somewhere out there.

We get there, we eat, we play, we leave. And now we are on our way home.

The sun is low. The sky is clear, though its blue is fading which means one thing—dusk will soon be upon us. The strait we are crossing looks like glass, for very little snow conceals its surface, this, after all, being early November and the winter blizzards yet to arrive. Mom is pulling a child-size toboggan. Inside the box made of plywood that Dad has nailed there sits Rene wrapped like a stuffed toy, me running along beside him. Also running along is Itchy, Rene's little salt-and-pepper house dog whom he loves to a fault. Her pink tongue hanging, her breath puffs of vapour, Itchy Highway, as Rene calls her, returns that love heartbeat for heartbeat.

Besides the sled dogs who are always eight in number, Mom always has a house dog. The only ones domesticated enough to be let into the house, or tent, and sleep there, eat there, these dogs are not so much pets as family members. They come in useful, says Mom. For instance, they warn her of foxes who have this habit of sneaking up at night and stealing *paastee-weeyaas* (dried meat). They chase squirrels, they chase chipmunks, they make you laugh. Always black, female, and small, crossbreed mutt/terrier types are her favourite. A dramatic contrast to her husband's robust, muscled huskies who look like wolves, Itchy not only looks like a wind-up toy, she barks like one.

I still remember all those little black dogs over the years, still have some of their pictures in my photo album. There was Chummy followed by Itchy then Topsy then Doggy then Tigger and there were others before Chummy that go back years. Chummy Dad received as a gift from his brother, William. But Itchy is special. Her, Mom gives to her baby as a gift, something she never does, or will ever do again, with her other dogs.

With Itchy loping happily along beside her master, we are rounding our third small island—our cabin will come into view within minutes—when, without warning, her eyes glinting with Trickster mischief, Mom starts running. And running and laughing and running and laughing. Forty-five years old that winter, she runs faster than a man half her age across that ice. And only gradually does it dawn on me why she is running—she is not alone in the act. Wolves have appeared to our right by a quarter of a mile and they, too, are running a half-dozen strong across that ice. The race is on.

Encouraging Mom, Rene and I are squealing with glee until Mom, too, to our child's eyes, is a wolf, sleek, muscled, with fur that shimmers in grey and silver. *And* in a light that tells us it's over, this day filled with wonder. Snow starts falling. Flake after flake as large as duck feathers and as weightless, it floats from heaven as gifts from God. Now singing in his chime-like soprano, his arms akimbo, crystals of snow turning to liquid on his angelic face, Rene flies along in a vehicle that is, at times, airborne, that's how fast Mom is running. In fact, she outruns her lupine competitors. Fading to nothing, they are swallowed one by one by the sub-Arctic darkness. And with Itchy yapping excitedly beside me, I run after Mom.

7

The year comes to an end. A new year starts. Three months after our adventure on the Perch Bay ice, we are out ice fishing on Reindeer Lake, some five small islands past the spruce-treed entrance to Perch Bay itself. It is Sunday, Dad's day off, so, for him, this is pleasure, not work, a day he gets to spend with his family. On a cloudless day uncommonly benevolent for the month of February, we have just finished eating on the shore of yet another island yet another picnic with *namee-steek* grilled on an open fire. One endless picnic, that's Highway life in *keeweet'nook*.

With freshwater fishing, the fisherman uses nets made of emerald-coloured nylon fifty yards long and two yards wide—or what, in fishing lingo, is two yards deep. That's for fishing in shallow water for fish like pickerel. For deep-water fishing, for trout, for example, the nets are two yards deeper. In either case, the upper border of the net is lined with floaters the size and shape of hot-dog buns while the lower is lined with lead weights the size and shape of adult index fingers. When the net is not in use, it sits coiled in a crate made of birch. So that when the fisherman lifts the net, yard by yard, from its crate and eases it into the lake, the counterweight of floaters to weights ensures that the strand unfurls as it enters the water with the result that, once in that water, it hangs like a curtain which, to fish, is invisible.

The other technique employed in the north is to string two or three of these nets end to end thus creating a "super net" one hundred or two hundred yards long. That way, the fisherman catches more fish

in one location. Once in the water, each end of the net hangs anchored to the bottom by means of twine tied to a rock the size of a
volleyball; pinned by such rocks at both ends, the net stays put; it
does not float to the surface. Then, by means of a second length of
twine that rises from the anchoring rock to the end of the net to the
surface of the lake, this also at both ends of the net, *this* length of
twine completes its climb at a buoy visible to the fisherman from his
boat as he approaches from a distance. Two buoys topped by a bright
red pennant—to, of course, ensure its visibility—floating separated
by a hundred yards of water thus indicate two ends of a net floating
like a curtain for a hundred yards *under* that water.

In winter, this technique is adjusted to accommodate the factor
of ice. At this latitude in the dead of the season, sub-Arctic ice can
float some two feet thick, so the first thing a fisherman has to do is to
chop a hole one foot in circumference in that ice with a needle nose,
an elongated crowbar that looks like a spear with one end sharpened
to a point like an arrow. Then there is the jigger. A yard-long plank of
spruce the width of an oar but with a kind of Geiger-counter-cum-
compass installed at its centre and a steel hook at one end, its purpose is to drag one end of the net, by means of this hook, under the
ice to a second hole of similar size the fisherman has chopped in the
ice a hundred or two hundred yards away from the first. The length of
the net decides this distance. Once the fisherman has tied, with another length of twine, one end of the net to the hook at the rear end
of the jigger, he puts this jigger facing forward into the first hole in
the ice, aims it at the second, sets its Geiger counter–like mechanism,
and off goes the jigger. For this, one must keep in mind that there
always remain at least three inches of space between the surface of
the water and the ice's underbelly. And this is the space that the jigger
navigates like a miniature torpedo, the second hole in the ice its
vaunted target.

Once all is going, the fisherman lifts his net, yard by yard, from
its crate behind him and eases it into the first hole. As it enters the
water, the net unfurls, becoming a filigree, a thing of beauty. By the
end of the process, the crate is empty and the entire length of the net

is strung from one hole to the other. Then the fisherman ties the back end of the net to yet another length of twine which, in turn, he ties to a rock the size of a volleyball placed on the ice a good three yards from the first hole. This will stop the net from being dragged by its jigger past the second hole. Once his net is unfurled in its entirety, the fisherman runs to the second hole, there to meet the jigger. If he doesn't get there in time, he stands to end up with a mess. The jigger being stopped by an unexpected force without a human hand to receive it, it would careen all over the place under the ice, leading it to who knows where and making it impossible to find from *over* the ice. If this happens, the fisherman risks not only losing his net but his jigger. And jiggers in the north mean life or death; the nearest store, twenty miles away in Brochet, would take one entire day to reach. You lose your jigger and you fish no more, not that winter; your dogs starve, you can't travel, your family starves.

While Dad is doing all of this some six feet offshore from the island we've just eaten lunch on, I am running on the ice around him playing "fetch the stick" with Itchy. As for Mom, she is sitting in the sled nearby with her back to the backboard and two-year-old Rene on her knees. Basking in the sun, both are dozing. The sled dogs, meanwhile, are lying haphazardly in front of the sled, they, too, relishing the warmth. We all are, and life is good.

Suddenly, the dogs start barking. They jump to their feet. We look. And there, a half-mile off, sits a red fox. Ensconced on her haunches, she is waiting for us to leave so she can eat our leftovers. The sled dogs take off—come hell or high water, they will get that fox. The problem is that they are still harnessed to a sled in which sit mother and child. If the sled goes flying, which it does, then so do they.

"Whoooooooooooa!" shrieks Mom. Besides her parka, her sweater, her cotton granny smock, a slip, and her *poppily-cum*—that is, her bloomers—she is wearing her usual wool flesh-coloured stockings and beaded, lace-up moccasins of caribou hide, neither of which last two items stops her from throwing her legs up, out, and over the sled's canvas sidings, jamming them into the snow, and digging in as deep as she can; no matter what happens, that sled must stop; she can't lose her baby. She *won't*. Unhappily, her legs are no match for a team of eight huskies out for blood. Flanked by two gigantic sprays of powdery white snow caused by Mom's splayed extremities, the sled looks like a snowplow barrelling along at forty miles an hour. And Mom is wailing. Yapping in her own inimitable fashion, Itchy goes bounding after them—lose her master she will not.

My first instinct is to run after the sled. Before I do, however, I turn to Dad to see what he thinks. His forehead furrowing, he is looking at the sled. I look at Mom, whose size is receding. I look at Dad. His forehead now sweating, he is still easing his net into the water, for one thing is certain: grace of the jigger, the net won't stop. At which point I decide—I am staying with him. He might need me.

Dad's dilemma? If he lets go of his net, he stands to lose it *and* his jigger. But if he stays with it, he stands to lose his wife and baby. Which is more important, his net or his wife, his jigger or his child? Can his wife stop the sled on her own? Eventually? Can he run and catch up with them in time for him to run back and meet the jigger at the second hole and thus save it *and* his net? From the receding distance, his wife's voice echoes—"whoooooaaaaaa!"—decreasing in volume with each passing second. The voice's decrescendo puts the fear of God in him. Finally, he curses, "*salapree!*" (from the French *saloperie*, which comes from *la salope*, which means "slut," a curse he learned from, of all people, Father Cadeau), drops the net, and runs off madly. Behind him, the net continues sliding its way into the first hole in the ice, the crate it comes from now nearing empty. At five years of age, I am too small, not strong enough to help Dad, and we both know it so I run. And run and run and run.

The sled dogs, meanwhile, are prevented from running at their usual speed by my mom's legs which, insubstantial as they are when compared to their strength, still act as brakes, if brakes working at half-power only. And the fox is long gone anyway; having had enough of licking her chops in anticipation of a meal that will not be, she has run off, back to the mainland from whence she came. The dogs stop. And Dad catches up. With my much shorter legs, I, of course, lag but, by the time I get there, Itchy is jumping up and down at the side of the sled yapping and yapping and Dad is standing there laughing through his panting. What else can he do? He pants and laughs and pants and laughs. My mother, at first, is reticent; this whole incident has cost her too much effort for her to engage in levity. But then she rallies. Looking up at her husband's beaming face, she gives in. She laughs. And laughs and laughs. Rene joins in. Unable to resist, I, too, start laughing. The laughter is raucous, without limit, universal, the north resonating with its vaulting music.

When we turn the sled and dogs around to retrace our steps, we see that the sled has left one long furrow. As have Mom's legs and feet on either side. *Mom the bulldozer*—the thought flits through me and I smile. She is my hero. Dad is my hero. Both are my heroes. And I can't remember this part of the episode but, as is his way, Dad somehow succeeds in retrieving his net *and* his jigger. And all ends happily.

8

And now it's May. To prepare for spring which, of course, comes late in the north, we are dogsledding it back to Brochet from Perch Bay, there to put our sled in storage and replace it with our motor and canoe to get set for summer. Meaning to say that this will be the last trip by dogsled that we will be making this winter.

Travelling by dogsled as opposed to canoe, circumnavigation of the sandbar we call Thigh Daddy is not necessary. We simply cut through the snowbound forest and a string of lakelets to head directly for our destination at the north end of Reindeer Lake. That is to say, we approach Brochet from the back. Thus is the duration of the trip cut in half. Following trails other hunters have left behind them, we come to a clearing on a spit of land between two lakelets. Dad knows the trails; he's been through here hundreds of times before. He knows the clearing. Lunch stop, he says, and ties the sled to a tree so the dogs won't give chase if a rabbit happens by. Or a lynx. Or a fox. Then he makes a fire with his usual alacrity. Reindeer moss, birch bark, spruce wood, all rise from the flames as aromas to entice our appetites. As Mom sets to work.

Digging into our travelling "grub box," a crate made of pieces of plywood cut in squares with handles on the sides made of straps of moose hide, the staples are flour, baking powder, lard, salt, pepper, onions, potatoes, tea, coffee, and milk, either in a can or in powdered form. Dad's favourite treat, strawberry jam, has long been a memory— to be replenished in a flash at the Companeek store when we reach

Brochet. The main course Dad usually catches with a net from a hole he chisels into the ice down the slope from Mom's makeshift open-air kitchen. And if he doesn't, then there is always the standby of pemmican. And then there are those days blessed by luck when we happen to have "extras" in the sled, items such as rabbit, ptarmigan, a caribou hindquarter, even beaver, even porcupine. And sometimes *wachask*—muskrat. Spring is a good time to catch *wachask* as, indeed, has Dad that week. Since kept frozen, three sit in the sled in a canvas bag waiting to be eaten by a family of five: a man, a woman, two boys, and a dog.

Wachask is a rodent with chestnut-brown fur, like a beaver's but darker, though not quite as lustrous. In fact, it could be taken for a beaver by those not familiar with the animal for it, like the beaver, is amphibious—it lives on land and yet moves in water with equal facility. Which is where it looks closest to beaver—that is, when it is swimming. Still, it is smaller, bonier, not as round like the football-shaped *amisk* ("beaver," rhymes with "the disk"). The size of a rabbit, say, only flatter, it lies closer to the ground, though with ears nowhere near the length of a rabbit's; in fact, they look like buttons, they are that small. Like *amisk*, *wachask* lives in swamps where it feeds on roots and reeds and therefore is musky in odour as in flavour. If cooked with skill, its meat is delicious. It can be roasted, broiled, boiled, smoked, fried—you can do as many things with it as you can with pork, beef, or chicken—but it is best grilled on a spruce-fed campfire. Butchered like rabbit, or chicken, you splay its open carcass, mount it on a stake whose base is planted in the ground one foot from the fire which, by the time you are ready, should be coals red-hot and glowing but with minimal flame. Then with the carcass suspended flat on its front over the fire, you watch its juices sizzle and smell its fragrance ascending. And every few minutes, you lean over to flip it. But the best part for me—and for Rene and Itchy—is the tail.

Amisk, of course, is famous for its tail that resembles a snow-shoe. The tail of the muskrat, by comparison, is nowhere near as striking. Like the beaver's it is scaly, yes, but that's where ends any and all resemblance. Unlike the beaver's, it is cylindrical in shape, tapering from an inch in diameter at its base to a point at its end. In fact, it looks like a whip, if a small one, hanging at about six inches on an adult *wachask*. Having no stores out where we are means one thing to children—we have no candy, cookies, or pop. Only in Brochet can we get them, at Companeek, where, for pennies, Maagisit McMillan sells these chewy little toffees wrapped in coloured wax paper. Most of the time, however, we are not there, so what do we do? We suck muskrat tails.

To backtrack slightly, when Dad skinned the animals in preparation for Mom's culinary sleight-of-hand, he cut off the tails and gave one each to me, Rene, and Itchy. Then, as a game and thrilled pink silly, we boys throw the tails, still raw, on the fire, Itchy's included, and roast them. The aroma alone sends us to heaven. And using willow stakes that Dad has carved for us with his hunting knife, we turn them this way and that in the flames until all sides are cooked. The scorched, blackened skin now sizzling and bubbling with a succulence unknown to the *Moony-ass* nation, we blow on them to cool them, then slurp the thick end into our mouths like one would spaghetti, leaving the thin, pointy ends sticking out by about four inches. To us, they are the equivalent of the licorice Twizzlers eaten by kids in the city. Except that, because the tails are actually vertebral cartilage, a) we can't swallow them, and, b) they jerk and wiggle and bounce and dance as we leap and run about, through the trees, in the snow, on the ice, around our parents, playing tag with Itchy all along, the three of us chewing and sucking and chewing and sucking with complete relish.

Those muskrat tails are better than lollipops, better than licorice. And better, when you think of it, than cod liver oil.

9

Idyllic as they are, canoe and dogsled are modes of travel very limited in their reach. As slow as travel by horse or donkey, as says Father Egg Nog who rode them in Germany as a young man of twenty, they connect local villages but not much more. So to go further afield, Brochet inhabitants have to resort to the bush planes and, even then, few can afford their fares. The arrival of three per week is the average. And they almost always come from Lynn Lake, seventy-six miles to the south, bringing merchandise for the Companeek store. Or government bureaucrats to monitor band council business. Or D O T people. Or medical personnel. Bush planes also take the occasional Cree or Dene passenger to, say, the hospital in Lynn Lake, The Pas, or further south depending on the illness. And bring them back, *if* they haven't died. Indeed, there are times when "occasional" is replaced by "frequent."

And a colourful array these bush planes are, in make as in character. The Norseman, the Otter, the Beaver, the Cessna, even the thick-thighed Bellanca that went obsolete in the late 1950s, all have their sizes, their uses, their stories, their legends, their appearances, their personalities, their sound. The most common is the Norseman, which seats eight people and is the loudest; its scream at takeoff has been known to deafen people who happen to live near the Companeek dock, like Moomoos Perkins on his nearby island. The Otter, on the other hand, drones like a bee; its sound as comforting as a grandmother's coo, it is my favourite. And it seats twelve. The baby of the family, the Cessna, can seat three passengers, one beside the pilot at the front—a position called, for some reason, "riding gunshot"—and two at the back. Not much bigger than a glider, if seen from afar, it looks like a mosquito. And sounds like one. So well do we know these sounds that even children can tell which plane is coming just by its "voice."

It is mid-August, the best month of the year to be up here, no bugs, no wind so the lake is as still as still can be, the temperature exquisite. We are in Brochet because we have been summoned away from our island home on Reindeer Lake by Father Cadeau. Having replaced Father Egg Nog who, overcome by gout and too much pemmican, died at ninety, the new priest has cited medical as opposed to spiritual reasons for his call by "moccasin telegraph" (a term we Natives use for "hearsay") which is why we are here sitting at the table in our house on the hill some forty yards north of this Father Cadeau's residence eating whitefish *arababoo* (a Cree spin on the French *bouillabaisse*, that succulent stew of fish and seafood). A simple recipe, yes, but Mom has a way of doing it that makes it special, especially with her fresh-baked bannock to soak up the juices which is what we're doing when, suddenly, we hear an Otter.

We jump from our chairs, scurry to the door, and look to the sky—that is, me, Daniel, and Florence (I'm aged four; Rene is still too young to leave Mom's side). People in Brochet always do that, then run down to the dock to see who's arriving and what they're bringing. What else, after all, is there to do in a village where nothing ever happens? By the time we get to the crest of the plateau on which sits our house, the plane is flying over Gunpowder Island then Moomoos Island then banking for a landing on the choppy waters of Brochet Bay. And next thing you know, it is putt-putting up to Father Cadeau's dock with the priest standing there in his midnight-black cassock and sword-like crucifix waiting for the rope to be thrown at him by the pilot. My favourite part is the way the plane's propellers—single, of course, as on all Otters—whir like spirits and go *bobby-dee, bobby-dee, bob* as they slow to a stop. It floats to the dock, its front door opens, and out pops the pilot, a fit young *Moony-ass* in green work coveralls and construction boots. A coiled rope in hand, he jumps down to the pontoon and tosses the ligature at the priest who, forty-eight and handsome—for a priest, very good-looking—ties it to posts that jut from the dock. The plane thus secured, the pilot then flings open the passenger door. And into the sunshine floods a gaggle of pale-skinned people who, we are told, are medical personnel. Doctors? Dentists? Nurses? Brain surgeons? We don't know yet. All we know is that they have way too much luggage—*Who will carry it?* we wonder. As if he's heard our unspoken question, Father Cadeau attacks it by deciding on the spot—the Indians, of course. This he says to the pilot, or seems to, for he says it in English and we can't read lips, not, at least, in the *Moony-ass* language. Whatever his words, before you can say "*kimoosoom chimasoo*," the Indians are huffing and puffing their way up the hill with crates, suitcases, and equipment that, to us, look suspect. As there are no roads to, from, or in Brochet and thus no motorized vehicles, and as the *Moony-ass* themselves won't carry it, or can't, we have no choice. Even I carry a small black satchel that contains *maskee-geeya* (pills), or so says Masky Jimmy Perkins.

Whatever this equipment, the Indians bring it into the single classroom at the one school in town which is meant for non-status children and, of course, is vacant for the summer. Once it is ready, we all crowd in to watch the *Moony-ass* put things together. When assembled, they look, to our eyes, like scaffolds, electric chairs—even a guillotine ("*misti-moogoomaan*," a great big knife), as Fire McMillan, the Companeek clerk Maagisit McMillan's firey wife, is reported to be hissing into the midwife Pitooria Wachask's ear about one such erection. It doesn't help, of course, that the entire *maskeegee-it'noo* (medical) crew is now dressed in white, like corpses in shrouds. At which point Father Cadeau brings in this shy, thick-lipped, pock-marked sixteen-year-old Dene youth named Lawrence Loon, second-eldest son of Stare and Modest Loon, to press him into service as interpreter. His last name is actually Dadzin-anaaray, but as the Companeek manager, who is *Moony-ass*, can never pronounce it, he resorted long ago to its English meaning, which is "loon," and it has stuck to our tongues like *pawpilly-cum*. Wasn't this Lawrence

Loon, after all, the first person in all Brochet to reach grade nine? The highest grade anyone in northern Manitoba has achieved thus far? Far surpassing the Companeek clerk Maagisit McMillan's pathetic grade four? And is he thus not one of very few Indians in all God's kingdom who can speak English beyond Maagisit McMillan's already impressive, to us, "your father, he want some the gazzy [gas]?" and "I saw you stoling!"? Indeed. Lawrence Loon has become fluent in Dene which, of course, is his mother tongue, and English, and Cree, this last by way of a fling he apparently is having with Watermelon Perkins, a buxom Cree maiden from Moomoos Island. Which is the ticket for it is precisely such a talent—that is, linguistic, not sexual—that makes him indispensable when it comes to the matter of Brochet people who, of course, speak Cree and Dene but no English, mixing and mingling with the *Moony-ass* who, almost always, speak English only.

His job, however, isn't easy. This day, for example, the people of Brochet have squished into the classroom in numbers unprecedented out of sheer curiosity, only to expose themselves as terrified of scaffolds, electric chairs, gas chambers, and instruments of death in general. To my child's unfettered imagination, in fact—and thanks to Fire McMillan's incendiary abstractions—a guillotine stands in the middle of the classroom, open-jawed and starving.

So here Lawrence Loon is caught between the devil and the deep blue sea. Behind him stands an increasingly impatient gaggle of *Moony-ass* with their arms waving wildly and their hot lips quivering, mouthing unprintable obscenities, for all he knows; before him a seething mass of bug-eyed, teeth-chattering Indians on the verge of fleeing to the bushes and the wilderness in general. And the Indians are about to wrest certain victory from the *Moony-ass* when, suddenly, Father Cadeau comes barrelling in with his black cassock billowing. The gilt-edged crucifix that hangs wedged into the sash around his waist flashing with menace, he threatens excommunication to those who don't heed "the call of modern medicine," and the *Moony-ass* win. Once the volume of this incipient riot has decrescendoed to the level of a civilized *pianissimo*, the X-ray technician—for that's what she is, as it turns out—offers directives that are interpreted with sugar-sweet persuasiveness by this clever, if rattled, Lawrence Loon. Thus it is that Brochet's entire population lines up one by one like beads on a rosary and takes turns climbing what looks like a pedestal, putting their arms around what looks like a window except that its glass is black, breathes in deeply, stops, and thus stands waiting for the blade of the guillotine to drop, at least so hisses Fire McMillan to the midwife, Pitooria Wachask. I know. I hear her. I am standing there, not one foot behind that woman who is known for flying great distances though not on Norsemen (that is to say, it is whispered that she is a witch).

But no, much to the disappointment of the Companeek clerk's bloodthirsty wife, they are not beheaded. They simply have their picture taken. Or at least their chests do, for that's how they are told, through Lawrence Loon, to stand, with their clavicles, scapulas, breasts, and rib cages crushed, as by a magnet, up against that high glass panel, which we children have to stand on a fish box for our little chests to reach. Bad Robber Yazzie, Meat Toss Yazzie, Happy Doll Gaazayoo, Salad Kipawm and her husband Misti-goso; Zebedee Zipper, his wife Ice-keemee Minette, Moomoos Perkins and his wife Jemima, Ptarmigan Gunpowder, Samba Cheese Weetigo, Samba Cheese Gunpowder, Flora Kamaa-magoos and her youngest daughter, four-year-old Melinda Kamaa-magoos, the prettiest girl in all Brochet; Check Wheat He Chissaazay, Verna Hell, Archie Mosquito and his wife Filament, Henry Beksaka, Beejee-aazay, Adoo-naazay, and Lady Beksaka; Old Dice Chagaazay, Modest Loon, Stare Loon, Half Ass Sam Well, Mist Ass-Lick Beksaka, even Keesk-wee-eye-i Salamoo, even ninety-eight-year-old, big-bummed, white-haired Keeyaask-oomay-is (Seagull's Little Poop), all take turns being *eesaap-waap-meechik* (to be "seen through" as through saran wrap; our word for "X-rayed").

After each one is done, the white-uniformed *Moony-ass-kwao* (white woman) stands by the guillotine to ululate cheerily, "thank you"—Lawrence Loon translates the words into Cree or Dene—and the person just "beheaded" (in my child's eyes) steps down from the pedestal and shuffles out the room headless but feeling his or her chest area with renewed conviction. "Next!"—Lawrence Loon tries to replicate the white woman's next ululation with small success for, his balls having dropped two whole years previous, his is a voice that rivals in pitch a moose's lowest groan. And so the pattern repeats itself the live-long day until all Brochet has submitted itself to such invasive perusal.

Being so young at the time, I can't remember the next sequence of events. All I know is that some people end up being flown to a hospital in a Norseman as a result of these "pictures," while most are not. TB *manchoosak* (bugs or germs) are what these *maskeegee-it'noo-wak* (medicine people) are looking for inside our lungs, I learn later. The malignant *bacillus*, apparently, has a way of insinuating itself into the artful construction that is that particular human organ and sucking the air from the tiny little sacs that comprise its bulk. The outcome? Deflation—that is, of those sacs—and death by asphyxiation, at least so explains Father Cadeau.

Then that winter, the Norseman comes for my mother—*she* has TB and might well die like so many others before her, carried off by that Norseman and brought back in coffins. People all over the north are dropping like flies from this sickness. The mere prospect must frighten Dad—to lose five children and now his wife? When his two youngest—Rene and I—are still just babies? Always the stoics, however, neither he nor Mom shows their anxiety, so I don't either. I vaguely remember Mom and Flora Kamaa-magoos-née-Perkins, eldest daughter of Moomoos Perkins and his wife Jemima, climbing into a Norseman perched on the ice downhill from Companeek. Then her face sort of visible behind a fogged-up window, tearless, smiling at me. Balazee Highway never did have time for self-pity. Your mother dies? You cry for a month. Then you pick yourself up and just go on. Then the plane revs up, taxis off, turns, screams like a power saw, and zooms to the sky, leaving in its wake the biggest *oopas-choosoos* seen on Reindeer Lake in recent memory. Then it cuts an upward trajectory over Moomoos Island then Gunpowder Island and flies on southward, leaving the grizzled old Moomoos Perkins stone-deaf for an hour. Again.

Both women thus spirited away are forty-five years old at the time I speak of and, being first cousins—Mom's father and Flora Kamaa-magoos's mother are siblings—look very similar. "The belles of Brochet," Bob Hughes calls them. Bob Hughes? The D O T manager for whom Verna Hell, my sister Louise's best friend at the time, works as a cleaning lady. Which is who overheard plain gangly and bedsheet-white Bob Hughes in his artful meanderings.

As it turns out, the two ailing women are gone for a year to a sanatorium for TB patients in far Ninette ("Nine Ett"), west of Winnipeg halfway to the Saskatchewan border, according, anyway, to the stern but handsome Father Cadeau. In fact, one doesn't make it, the question being which, we all ask ourselves when the news comes through that "a woman has died." Remember: Brochet has no electricity so has no way of confirming such *aachi-moowin* (news). All it can depend on is unbuttoned rumour. And, God knows, in Brochet both then and now, it is unbuttoned.

10

In Mom's absence, Louise has to quit school to care for me and Rene. With Dad gone north by himself to hunt and trap and the others all at boarding school or adults moved on to their own futures, who else is there? Now eighteen and with a grade seven education which, for Brochet at least back then, is stratospheric, she is ready. And thank God she is because tuberculosis, apparently, can take years to recover from, *if* one ever does. So communicable is the illness, says Father Cadeau, that quarantine is necessary—for months or years, no one ever knows in advance. Fortunately, her stubbornness aside, Louise has talents as a cook, housekeeper, and beadworker. With this last, she is so good that she arouses jealousy for her gloves and moccasins, even from—*especially* from—our wicked Aunt Peechoochee. Her recent achievements at school, moreover, mean that she can speak English, if in a sense, and can add, subtract, multiply, divide, and write and read, if not quite Shakespeare then the labels on packages of crackers, cans of soup, and sacks of flour. People in the village consult her on matters of correspondence and the Eaton's catalogue. Even Chief Chi-Louie asks her for advice on a basis semi-regular, on a contract, say, with Manitoba Hydro. They have plans, so Louise reads, for building a dam on the Reindeer River, thus flooding Reindeer Lake to provide electricity for the citizens of Winnipeg. No, she says to Chief Chi-Louie. So no, says Chief Chi-Louie to Manitoba Hydro. Which is how my sister Louise saves Brochet from being submerged in sub-Arctic waters.

If Manitoba is known for winters that can freeze one's extremities, then *northern* Manitoba is feared for winters that torture, maim, and send to the grave. But that winter with Louise, for some reason, is particularly frigid. Central heating as yet four decades into the future, the house, of logs and plaster, is heated by a four-legged cast-iron woodstove. But the fire dies at night so that, by morning, everything is frozen, the water in the pails, washbasins, and saucepans, the fish, the potatoes, the pemmican, even the holy water in Mom's little plastic Virgin Mary vial (giving us license to call it "holy ice"). So hard is our bannock that, if you smash a man's head with it, he will die, right there on the spot.

The three of us sleep crushed like pickles in a jar under a foot-thick goose-down sleeping robe. Her skeleton rattling, her lips *kaski-tee-i* blue (black-blue), Louise climbs out of bed in the pitch-black darkness of 6 a.m., tiptoes in her thick wool socks to the woodstove that has been stuffed with kindling and wood the night just prior, sparks up a match and, poof, the flames take form. And even then does it take one hour before anything is thawed to the point where it is drinkable or edible. Still practically a baby, Rene bawls out his misery. Fortunately, one hour later, grace of our resourceful elder, and beautiful, sister, we are eating hot steaming porridge and bannock smeared with lard and raspberry jam, Rene chirping merrily and kicking his *ooskaat-sa* (little legs) under the table.

Apart from the *Moony-ass*, no one in Brochet has indoor plumbing. So not only do we have to use the outhouse at the back for our "lower necessities," as Father Cadeau calls them, we have to get our cooking, washing, and drinking water from the lake, which takes huge effort. For two Cree boys aged six and three in the dead of winter on laundry day, it is slave labour. But off we trundle down the hill to the lake, Rene and I, uncomplaining, mourning our lot for not one second. Our little lard pails swinging from our be-mitted hands ping and rattle. One pail for Rene, two for me, all three are empty except for the dipper that Louise has included in one of mine. We get to the lake. Ten yards off, Samba Cheese Weetigo, our lakeshore neighbour, has chiselled a hole in the ice for his family but he lets us use it, God bless Mom's cousin, this Samba Cheese Weetigo. We get to the hole, I kneel, I dip my dipper into the water over and over until our pails are spilling out over their edges. And now we are trudging up the hill with the little shards of ice that float to the surface tinkling and rattling inside our pails which are of tin. And the sound has a rhythm. And I like music. So I start singing.

"*Tha kaat kimbaak, tha kaat kimbaak*, sidlee, sidlee, sidlee." I coax Rene into joining me and he does, at least for the part that he can get his tongue around which is "sidlee, sidlee." The part that goes "*Tha kaat kimbaak*" is beyond him. But why "*Tha Kaat Kimbaak*"? Because I have heard it on Apwee-tigwee Gunpowder's old black gramophone a hundred times.

Delphine Gunpowder the woman's legal name, she lives towards Minee-waati-meek (the Point) with her husband, Obert, and nine rambunctious sons of the eleven they will have within good time (they will also have three girls at the end). Nothing new there; most couples in Brochet have fourteen children. What is new is that she owns Brochet's only *kitoo-chigan* (gramophone). To me, this fact is a miracle.

A rectangular box with a handle at one end, it looks, in effect, like a small black suitcase, at least when closed. But when opened, it is something else entirely. What looks like a hammer wrought out of steel stares out at you, the needle at its tip a point of magic. Its black turntable is the next thing I see. This will hold the record that spins, the label at its centre lulling you into a state of hypnosis. Unfortunately, Apwee-tigwee Gunpowder has one record only; the rest, her nine thugs have broken. That record? "*Tha Kaat Kimbaak*."

In those days, records come in 78 rpm format, one song on each side of a disk the size of a dinner plate made from thick, chunky, brittle black vinyl. So brittle is this vinyl that all you have to do is drop a record once on the floor and it shatters in a flash to a hundred pieces. Useless, irreparable. Good-bye Kitty, good-bye Hank, two white gods of country music who are worshipped in the north because we hear them on transistor radios of which there are five in all Brochet. So this "*Tha Kaat Kimbaak*," to me, is a national treasure, the world's last record.

Which makes it that much more urgent that I run to Apwee-tigwee Gunpowder's house at the non-status end of the village every chance I get to play "it." Even in minus fifty weather, I run, non-stop, the half-mile to her house clean across the summit of the plateau on which sits Brochet, on my left, towards the lake, the long old church with its cheap tin roof then, on my right, Father Cadeau's house then the new church then the teacherage (where lives the only teacher in all Brochet, a young male *Moony-ass*) then the non-status school where he teaches then three more houses before I get there. I am obsessed. I am lovesick. Once arrived, I don't even ask for permission. I drop to the floor where sits the appliance—Brochet households of the time have little furniture—and start winding the stainless-steel crank that sticks out of the hole on its right side. Its turntable motionless, the arm that holds its needle glistens with promise, on that turntable the record with the title that makes me ache. When it starts spinning, I put the needle on the record, the music begins, and I lie on my tummy with my elbows propped, my hands to my *tap'skan* (chin), my small Cree feet in their tiny little moccasins kicking in the air with joy inexpressible.

"Daadi-didi-daa, *tha kaat kimback* . . ." sings the man on the record.

"Sidlee, sidlee, sidlee, sidlee," I sing along, for the lyrics are beyond me and I can only approximate; besides, the fifth in line in Obert and Apwee-tigwee Gunpowder's nine-thug household is called Sidlee, which is Cree for "Sydney." And I play that record and play that record until I drive the non-status if handsome Obert Gunpowder crazy and he sends me home.

So up and down the hill we go, Rene and I, all day long hauling water for our sister on laundry day singing to the tinkle of shards of ice that are floating in our pails: "*tha kaat kimbaak, tha kaat kimbaak*, sidlee, sidlee, sidlee, sidlee . . ." And into the house we go with these pails, receptacles Louise then empties into larger pails that sit on the stove, the water thereof to be boiled to a foam and, once boiled, transferred to the washtub in which sits half-submerged a washboard of wood and of glass that is thick, opaque, and corrugated. Done pouring the water into the tub, she stuffs in the clothes and, half bent-over, scrubs and scrubs until her fingers are the texture of raw *moosoo-weeyaas* (moose meat). All day she does this, all day we get water, though one must qualify that, that far north at that time of year, the span of time called "all day" is not very long.

And we are poor. Dad has left a line of credit with Maagisit McMillan at the Companeek store so we can eat. And this we do though there are days when we go hungry, days our sister manages to solve with her usual inventiveness—fish and caribou meat given us by kind-hearted relatives are saviours. But clothing is another matter. So poor are we in this regard that Louise has to keep re-mending Rene's and my clothes until they are threadbare. More than six decades later, I still have Rene's little parka hanging in my closet. A faded, tired old rag of worn grey felt with red flannel lining from which still poke tufts of white cotton stuffing, this winter coat for a three-year-old boy takes pride of place in a transparent garment bag next to my concertizing beaded tuxedo. The parka's hood still barely hanging, metal clasps serve it as zipper, and so many patches cling to its surface that it looks like a quilt on its last legs. The right-hand pocket fell off so often that it was finally replaced with a square of white flannel clipped from a diaper. There is, that winter, simply no money to buy new parkas.

11

Mom is dying. We all know that. All that winter of 1957–1958, we keep getting reminded. How? Dead babies keep passing our window. A river of innocence, they float right past and we watch, mystified. Such an epidemic of infant mortality happens more than likely every winter in Brochet but because we're never here, we never see it. But now we are and now we do.

But why all this death? Grace of the Oblates of Mary Immaculate and their *modus operandi*—spiritual extortion, I will think years later—the Catholic Church is all-powerful in sub-Arctic Canada, so that when men like Father Cadeau thunder from the pulpit that using contraceptives of any kind whatsoever assures you of a place at the right hand of Satan in *machee-skooteek* ("the bad fire," our word for "hell"), you listen. You quake in your moccasins but you listen. The result? Couples having twelve, fourteen, eighteen children is par for the course. That many of these newborns live but days is also a given—with the nearest hospital beyond their reach, what chance is there?—and we have front-row seats for the spectacle, Rene and I, at least that winter.

We are, after all, Father Cadeau's neighbours. Only a footpath separates us from the white picket fence that encloses his property. A piece of land the size of a schoolyard with his house in the middle, beyond it stands his church, the fulcrum on which turns the spiritual life of the village. One branch of this footpath leads to life—the lake, downhill, on whose water we depend. A second, ironically, leads to death—the new cemetery at the rear of the village a quarter of a mile behind our house. The two branches merge at our doorstep, meaning to say that all funeral processions pass our window. And as the table at that window is our favourite perch, the place where we draw our pictures, build our houses with pieces of kindling, and play with Dad's trophy, a silver bowl with ornate edging, proof positive that he, indeed, is the world-championship dogsled racer they say he is, for he won it at the biggest race of its kind in the world, in The Pas, before we were born . . . so here we are ripping wings off houseflies then watching them walk in single file towards this bowl, eight grey huskies on the verge of collapse from exhaustion though Dad won't let them as he is on the verge of winning this silver trophy together with a kiss from a woman called the Fur Queen . . . through this "sieve," we see them all, these funeral processions.

As funeral homes in Brochet are unheard of, people construct their own—that is, their loved ones'—coffins. Generally of plywood, they are pretty basic; they have, for instance, no inner lining or cushioning, not of satin or of velvet of the kind I saw in Father Egg Nog's coffin when I was four, so I ask my sister about dead people (in Cree, it goes without saying).

"Do their backs not hurt?"

"They're dead," she answers. "They don't feel anything."

"Oh," I say, "well, I want Mom's to at least have a pillow." She stops. I stop. We think. And then move on, lumps in our throats, sobs incipient but unrealized. While the men do the carpentry in the construction of these coffins, the women do the sewing—for sewing, indeed, is part of the process, though neither of linings nor of cushions.

I hear the hammers in the distance banging away. Today, it is Happy Doll Gaazayoo and Nicotine Yazzie who are making the box in the Dene encampment, Louise informs us, for it seems that tall-as-a-tower Kinaws-koo Sophie Yazzie and her husband, Meat Toss, Nicotine's cousin, have just lost a baby. ("Kinaws-koo Sophie" means "Tall Sophie," though in Cree and not her native Dene for it was us Cree who gave her the name.)

For the infant coffins, people go the extra distance beyond just plywood. Once the little box has been constructed, the corpse inside it, the cover nailed shut, the men wrap the exterior with lengths of white linen, material they attach by means of nails the size of tacks. The final effect? A neat white box rectangular in shape but not much bigger than Apwee-tigwee Gunpowder's old black gramophone. Which is when the women take over. I see aunts do it, my mother's younger sister, Laughing Aunt Margaret Kipawm, for instance. I see cousins do it, my wicked Aunt Peechoochee's beautiful eldest daughter, Arlene Gunpowder, for instance. Apwee-tigwee Gunpowder, Louise Cheepay, there, four Cree women clucking and cooing as their scissors and needles glint in the light of a lamp fuelled by kerosene.

Taking leftover pieces of this white linen, they cut them into strips one foot long and two inches wide. Then with artful scissor work, they cut patterns of snowflakes, wild roses, or small crucifixes into these strips. The final effect is of lengths of lace a bit rough at the edges though still recognizable as such. These they then tack onto the box's upper edges in such a way that they hang down by an inch or two, like water from a waterfall, on all four sides. When it is finished, the little plywood coffin looks like a cake with the white "lace" its icing. And our favourite, Rene and I? That that icing, so to speak, flutters and dances and glimmers and shimmers in the February breeze, the February sun, as the coffin trundles past our frost-streaked window.

Father Cadeau, of course, leads the procession. His thick beige parka concealing in part his surplice and cassock, a jaunty black biretta (a priest's hat of the time, black, of mortarboard, three-pronged, and tufted at the top) crowns his head. Clutched to his heart with one black-leather-gloved hand sits a missal with its pink-edged white pages. Their words to be read once arrived at the grave, the infant's soul will need their magic when he enters God's presence, says Louise. Next comes the coffin which, because it is weightless, is carried on the shoulder of a parka-clad youth, generally a relative of the deceased. Today, it is Half Ass Sam Well, the baby's uncle, apparently. Next come two altar boys in their tuques, thick mitts, parkas, and cassocks, one holding aloft a crucifix the height of a man. Next comes the family with expressionless faces and drooping shoulders, the parents with eyes like glass that's just been shattered. And last come the usual straggle of nosey onlookers including, inevitably, the notorious throat-clearing, phlegm-spewing, Libby's-brown-beans-tin-can-as-spittoon-carrying Jean-Pierre Yazzie who loves funerals, weddings, and baptisms and has nothing better to do with his time than attend them.

There have been five infant deaths so far this winter, maybe more, but through the filter of memory I see a non-stop procession of these pint-sized coffins carried on the shoulders of handsome youths with names like Isaac Fitzgerald, Samba Cheese Gunpowder, and Polio (Cree for "Napoleon") Gunpowder, the icing on the cake on their shoulders, so to speak, dancing and fluttering and glimmering and shimmering in the February breeze, the February sun.

Death, to us, is not a tragedy but a show, an extended entertainment. Until, that is, my mom's first cousin, Flora Kamaa-magoos, dies not of TB, as it turns out, but of thyroid cancer later that winter, leaving behind her eleven heartbroken orphans aged twenty-four to two. And Mom comes home in a Norseman. Alive.

12

It all comes about as a result of Reindeer Lake's expanding reputation for its richness in trout. So splendid is the beauty of this mythical *aya-weeya* (creature), so succulent is its flesh, so gigantic is it at its largest that the most rabid of fishermen will travel to the ends of the Earth to catch it. And though this reputation is not universal—it doesn't resonate, for example, in Saudi Arabia—it is nonetheless substantial enough to trigger in the minds of enterprising *Moony-ass* from *maameek* the possibility of profit. Thus are hatched extensive plans for attracting big money from Americans by stoking their obsession for this fish in the crystal-watered lakes of sub-Arctic Canada. To these *Keechi-moogoo-maanak* ("Special Knives" or "Long Knives"), as we Cree call them, size not only *matters* when it comes to *nameegoos* (trout), it is God incarnate—so, at least, says Masky Jimmy Perkins. Meaning to explain that if such plans are to be given their go-ahead, our home and native lake will be seething with fishermen from *Keechi-moogoomaan-askeek* ("Long Knife Land," our name for America) faster than a man can say *"kimoosoom chimasoo."*

Still, we, too, stand to profit, says Dad, for he has gotten "confirmation positive" of rumours along these lines through news from Southend, Saskatchewan, where one of his brothers is married to a woman named Rosie Ooteethani. Southend, Saskatchewan? Another Cree First Nation, this one standing at the southern extremity of Reindeer Lake so thus halfway between Brochet and Pelican Narrows, Dad's home "town." Jobs are to be had, confirms Uncle Eelee ("Elie"

in Cree), through a letter he has written in Cree syllabics (a Cree or-
thographic system) to his elder brother Joe, and has had delivered to
Brochet by their nephew, Samba Cheese Gunpowder, eldest son of
their wicked sister, Peechoochee Gunpowder. Just back from Pelican
where he had gone for a visit with his young family in tow, this Samba
Cheese Gunpowder had, of course, and like all travellers traversing
that route, to pass through Southend going in either direction, which
is where and how he got roped into service as a one-man postal
system. The news in that letter? A tourist fishing lodge for wealthy
Americans is opening this summer on a certain island on Reindeer
Lake at the halfway point between Brochet and Southend.

For Dad, the prospect of a job "down south" is attractive. It will
give him a break of at least one summer from the back-breaking
labour that is his fishing enterprise up north. Second, spending a
summer with his beloved younger brother will do "my heart good,"
he says, for he *knows* his Eelee; being a man of his word, he will
be there. Third, it means adventure, and nothing excites Dad more
than "rampant adventure." Seventy-five miles we will have to travel
to get to this island, but after five years of York boat rowing, even
if that was some thirty years ago, it is, for him, *machig-wanaas*
("dirt," i.e. a cinch).

There is nothing quite as messy as springtime in the north. The further north you go, the messier it gets. I mean, think of snow sometimes as much as six feet high and lake ice two feet thick, both of
which have to disappear in order to concede Earth back to the soil,
the plants, and the water, to let them win back the light of day, to let
them breathe. After eight long months of keeping them in chains, as
hostages of sorts? We speak here of a season that can take a month to
complete the transition. Imagine. Four whole weeks where the surface of the Earth in its seeming totality has been turned to a bog, as
treacherous as the quicksand we see in Tarzan movies at Brochet's
old church and sometime cinema. People have to wade in knee-high
rubber boots to get to the store or the church or Seepees-seek. Or
paddle a canoe down the streets of the village negotiating chunks

of floating ice, some small as bars of soap, some large as beds, but chunks, nonetheless, that scrape across the vessel like a nail scratching slate. To cross to Moomoos Island? Forget it, at least on certain days in the middle of the season or at the height of days when the sun is at its warmest and thus turns ice to the consistency of clay. Clearly, one must time one's errands with intelligence. As for bush planes, landing on the lake at that time of year is a bust, on skis *or* on pontoons. The village, in that sense, is therefore marooned. The seasons are at war, spring versus winter, winter versus spring, the question being: Which will win? There are days when half the population of the village will throw its hands up and wail to the heavens, believing to the core that *pipoon* (winter) will beat the living shit out of *seegwan* (spring). Eventually, of course, *seegwan* wins. And by mid-June, people have started crossing the water by using an arresting combination of canoe and dogsled. Travelling in summer *and* in winter simultaneously is what it amounts to. And which is what we find ourselves doing that soggy *seegwan* of 1958. With Mom back with us.

First, because of the season, and like all men in Brochet, Dad employs a different kind of sled. Invented by the Inuit, who call it a *komatik*, this sled boasts skis with a trestle that elevates cargo and passengers six whole inches above ground. So that here we are crossing Reindeer Lake squished like pickles into a canoe that itself sits perched on a dogsled which itself sits perched on a trestle whose base is, in essence, a pair of skis, sled and boat secured by rope to keep slippage and spillage to a minimum. As usual, all our belongings sit inside that boat together with Dad, Mom, Louise, Rene, and me (still in school, Daniel and Florence will join us at the end of June). When you sit inside that boat as it plies that ice, its height is vertiginous—in fact, so vertiginous that you, as a child, believe you are flying.

As for that ice, it is still capable of bearing weight that is substantial. The difference is that it now sits underwater by an inch or two. Or, rather, the water has risen above it by an inch or two. Whichever way the argument goes, the skis now function as mini-submarines. The weight of our boat, sled, cargo, and passengers sinks the section of ice we are crossing even deeper (though, once we have passed, it springs right back to its normal level). Meaning to say that if those skis are travelling underwater and their trestle hanging mere inches *above* it, then the dogs who are pulling both conveyances at one and the same time are up to their ankles *in* water. And are thus wearing moccasins. The whole point being: if the ice were to break then the sled would sink through and, being of wood, it would, like its skis, now be a submarine. All while the canoe slips into service as what it was made to be in the first place: a boat. So into the water slides its belly and, suddenly, we are afloat, so smooth the transition we hardly feel it.

And the dogs are now swimming. Fortunately, dogs make good swimmers and are blessed, moreover, with internal heating systems that stave off hypothermia. So Dad directs them to the nearest piece of land, there to unharness and load them, and their harnesses, into the canoe with us so that we can keep travelling. And *then* that boat is crowded. Still, this rarely happens. Today, for instance, it doesn't.

But dogs wearing moccasins? In spring up north, sled dogs run all day through miles of slush, that is, snow in the process of melting. That custardy texture gets wedged between their toes and, as the day heats up along with their bodies, the slush starts to melt. But then comes night and the temperature plummets and, as the dogs sleep outdoors, this slush refreezes. Between their toes. And it hurts, so much so that, by morning, they have trouble walking. Not good for sled dogs. So to keep that slush from insinuating itself into the spaces between their toes, Mom makes them moccasins of caribou hide. No more than pouches the size of teacups, she strings, at the end of the process, spaghetti-thin lengths of hide around their upper edges. Shoelaces, in effect, they are to be tied in a knot to prevent the footwear they go with from slipping off no matter how violent the animal's foot movements. One whole morning does it take Mom to make them, four per dog times eight dogs per team making for a total of thirty-two miniature, pint-sized moccasins. Whereupon Dad slips them onto the feet of each squirming animal with a dexterity born of long habit.

And now we are crossing a part of Reindeer Lake that I have never seen, for the reason that I have never been this far south. It just goes on, this body of water, southward and southward, a virtual sea with island after island of spruce-treed forest. The sun is intense, the ice melting quickly, Dad urging his dog team forward in travelling conditions that no dog would dream of. Our passage slow and treacherous, there are times when we float—it takes us five days to get to our destination, an island some two square miles in size named Dewdney.

13

Turning east, we round this bend and enter what looks like a river but turns out to be a channel that separates two islands substantial in size, a sheltered refuge from the fearsome whitecaps of open water. Dewdney itself is the island to our left, Dad tells us. The island where an enterprising *Moony-ass* from Lynn Lake has built his dream lodge, some fifteen cabins form its nucleus. Bark-stripped logs of spruce their hallmark, the cabins are scattered in random fashion from the shore up a slope and into the forest, the land they stand on, as is obvious, just cleared of trees. And the soil is sand-golden and wondrous with earth-hugging cranberry bushes lying helter-skelter like carpets strewn across its surface. As for the other island, not only is it void of buildings and is, in effect, a virgin forest, it has no name. Which is why we give both islands one name only: Doodneek, "where Dewdney is," in the same sense that Companeek means "where the company is."

The fishing season has not yet started, so neither island shows signs of life, at least for now. As we penetrate further this no-name channel, however, we discover that the no-name island does, indeed, lodge one family: Zebedee Zipper, Mom's youngest uncle, his wife, Ice-keemee Minette, and their four young children. It seems they have moved here; from Brochet? From Southend? They are, like us, forever on the move so we can't keep track of them. The old man shouts to my father as we are pulling up to a landing for, God knows, Zebedee Zipper has always had a voice that can wake corpses. Though Zebedee Zipper will be our neighbour, if by half a mile, the situation will be temporary, for others will soon be arriving, he informs us, all from Southend. His hair snow-white and as fuzzy as a bush that's just been shaken, his face wind-blasted, his skeletal frame is taut and wiry; he moves like a puppet. Much younger than him, his wife, Ice-keemee Minette, is his second for his first died young, leaving him two sons who rival their stepmother in age. The first wife Cree, Ice-keemee Minette is Inuit, or Eskimo as we called them in those days, which is why we've dubbed her "Eskimo Minette" which comes out in Cree as "Ice-keemee Minette."

Ice-keemee Minette boasts two claims to fame. The first is that she is fluent in her native Inuktitut (the language of the Inuit) and Cree, two tongues so unrelated they could be dog and spider. The second is that she has the voice of a country singer. Whatever the quality of the woman's vocal cords, Zebedee Zipper and Ice-keemee Minette's four children—and there will be more—are living proof that we, the Highways, have cousins who are half Inuit, that's how far north the land we come from.

And true to Zebedee Zipper's ardent abstractions, within five days, over one hundred people, all from Southend, live on the island that persists in being nameless, prominent among them my Uncle Eelee with his wife, Rosie, and their eight children (of the twelve they will have within ten years). Like his elder brother Joe, Uncle Eelee likes acting silly, a trait I will inherit with vim and with vigour.

Because the southern half of Reindeer Lake was already open water in the week just past, its northern half still submerged ice, says Uncle Eelee, travel for the "southerners" has been conventional. No canoes perched like *jeerees* (cherries) on Inuit *komatiks* and dogs wearing moccasins. For them, they have used canoes "like normal Indians." Which is a pity, I brag to my cousin, Uncle Eelee's third daughter of six, Dorothy, for she has missed out on all the adventure. Six like me, and as chubby and as sweet as a *lapwachin* (pudding), I love Dorothy Highway with all my heart. Why? Because I can tug at her pig-tails and run to the bushes where a rabbit wouldn't go, she after me. *Iskwi-yaanees*, we call this game, which means "the last one." In English? "Tag."

Whatever the names of the games we play that golden summer—and we have playmates; from twelve families each with ten children on average? Scads—American tourists begin to arrive by Otter from Lynn Lake soon thereafter. In fact, within days, there are thirty. And Lockhart is there to receive them.

14

"Arctic Lodge," this *Moony-ass* from Lynn Lake known as Lockhart has chosen to anoint his fledgling enterprise, this tourist fishing lodge that will catapult Americans to trout Nirvana. Only rarely do I see him, for he flies in from Lynn Lake perhaps once weekly to count his money, Dad says. Balding and paunchy and pink of flesh, he looks ordinary but he must be something if he can pull this off. Like a picture in a catalogue his kingdom rises from the sands of Dewdney Island, dazzling all who lay eyes upon it. The building near the dock will serve two functions, explains Zebedee Zipper: an office on one side to accomplish business and a store on the other where one can buy such basics as flour, tea, and *kimsow-neegin* (toilet paper). Then there is the house for cooking, the house for dining, the house for throwing darts and drinking beer, the house for laundry, the house that will lodge the Lockhart family when they are in residence, the house for this, the house for that until, scattered like wood chips into the forest, stand fifteen cabins where will sleep Americans exhausted from fishing for trout the live-long day. All this Zebedee Zipper elaborates on in rapid-fire Cree, his delivery so impassioned that his lips foam over and we are convinced that he owns the establishment hook, line, and sinker.

On the shore, meanwhile, stands a boathouse with a gas pump from whose door juts a dock so capacious it can accommodate the ark built by Noah with all its *aya-weeya* (creatures), brags the voluble Zebedee Zipper, or, at the very least, two dozen speedboats of the kind the *Moony-ass* enjoy. In fact, four of these vessels are there already, poised on a dime to spirit Tom, Dick, and Harry from the plains of Texas off to the depths where lives King Trout, the question being: Who will drive them when they have never seen the lake? When they don't know it from a hole in the wall? The answer? The "Indian guide"—a man who knows it, says Zebedee Zipper, "like I know the Holy Scriptures." Thus the presence in Doodneek that golden summer of Zebedee Zipper, Eelee Highway, Apaag-waachees (Bat) Mooraah, Chaggy-wat Mooraah, Chi-Pierre (Little Pierre) Mooraah, William Clark, Zoowazay (Joachim) Gunpowder, the Syllables, the Birds, the Olsons, the list goes on. And, of course, us, Joe Highway's family. And to enable them to serve as these "Indian guides," Lockhart has equipped them each with a speedboat complete with a twenty-horsepower Johnson outboard motor.

And "speedboats" we call them as opposed to canoes because, up to that point in sub-Arctic history, Native people have known only the latter. The C-shaped bottoms and narrowness of frame, of course, make canoes tippy; one wrong move and "topsy turkey," as says Zebedee Zipper. Speedboats, by contrast, are three times as wide and have flat bottoms so they don't tip. Canoes, moreover, are limited to motors with ten horsepower. With speedboats, the sky is the limit. Thus are speedboats propelled to velocities where the *oopas-choosoos* can surface ten entire feet behind it where, with canoes, the *oopas-choosoos* is a joke, if they even have one. And to think that this Lockhart owns an entire fleet of these streamlined watercraft.

Just past sunrise does Dad drive his speedboat across the narrow channel to Dewdney Island to pick up his clients. I beg him to take me with him but he can't—Lockhart's rule: no guides' children. He will tell me the stories, says Dad, to appease me. Middle-aged men for the most part, these clients come four to a boat. And they are dressed to the nines in their uniform of rubber, rubber, and yet more rubber, even down to the hat—"sou'westers," the *Moony-ass* call them—in case it rains.

They also carry all their fishing equipment, their rods and reels, their tackle boxes filled with hooks, lures, pliers, knives, every knick-knack conceivable to help them wrestle with writhing, slippery, slime-covered *kinoo-seewak* ("fish" in the plural). As they load this baggage and themselves into the boat, together with, of course, their ever-present cameras, Dad rushes up the hill to the kitchen building for the box containing all the ingredients for a shore lunch—a northern tradition where one eats fish that's just been caught and cooks it over an open fire on a lakeshore—together with, of course, all the cooking equipment and eating utensils. Once all is ready, Dad reignites the motor and off they go up the channel, around the western curve of Dewdney Island, and into the vastness of Reindeer Lake.

Occasionally, a curious American sitting at the back near Dad shouts at him over the roar of the motor with questions about this island and that river and this bay and that bird (they have never seen an Arctic tern, a freak incident, in any case, as this is too far south for them) or that rodent (they have never seen an otter). They are amazed that you can drink lake water "just like that" with your cupped hand. "You do that in the Ohio River," says a codger with a belly the size of a tent, "and you burst into flame."

So rounding island after island after island, Dad seeks out and finds the larger and deeper sections of open water where thrives this fish so coveted by Americans that the very mention of its name makes them incontinent. And there, ten miles from Dewdney, Dad slows down to a cruise so his clients can cast their lines and, with Dad's gloved hand controlling, as always, the stick-handle of the mighty Johnson motor, they putter at the speed of a three-horsepower Champion motor, that is, a speed meant for trolling.

At first, the trolling is quiet, uneventful, calm, even meditative. But then, suddenly, a fisherman is startled into a frenzy by a tugging at the far end of his line and he shouts to announce the blissful event and a struggle ensues that is terrible to watch, says Dad. The nylon line criss-crosses the water this way and that, the fisherman reeling it in and reeling it out and reeling it in and reeling it out, following, evidently, instructions from a book he has read in some library in

Atlanta, the other fishermen shouting their encouragement with words like "pull it to the right" and "let go a little" and "don't give the bastard an inch." And pandemonium rules, the faces of the tourists all phantom-white, their eyes racoons' eyes. And so goes the morning. Until a trout is caught that meets all the credentials of size, heft, and beauty and the Americans exult with joyful noises unique to their species. And they pose for pictures with the biggest, fattest trout in the history of the world, according to the narratives these fishermen are rehearsing in their heads already for their friends down in Saginaw. The dead creature, meanwhile, hangs from a hook attached to a scale whose arrow points to some number bordering on mythical. For all Dad knows, the trout is the same weight as Elvis.

Towards noon, they break for lunch, a splendid affair by a hot campfire. And resume post-meal their ardent expostulations. Until the sky turns pink, the sun now approaching the islands in the distance towards Tate Island. And it is time for the journey back to Arctic Lodge and dinner for the tourists in their dining room, dinner for my father with his wife and children. And the exercise is repeated the next day. And the next and the next, the turnover of tourists occurring every six days or so. Most leave their "Indian guide" with tips that are generous, others not so generous. And at least one sour-faced, cantankerous old tightwad from a town called Fargo leaves not one penny. Still, through the course of that summer, my father meets some one hundred tourists. Giving him the fodder with which to regale us when he gets home in the evening. In fact, those stories of his that I've just shared are as colourless as mud when compared to some others.

Like the day a man from a city called Denver is stricken with a particularly nasty case of diarrhea yet insists on going fishing: "Business as usual," as he puts it. These holidays, apparently, cost some ten thousand dollars per person per week in today's currency and he isn't about to waste one penny of it because of some bug. As for my father, even if he'd known of the poor man's condition, which he didn't, what could he have said? The best he can do once they are out there trolling again is to keep snapping his motor from cruise to

full throttle at the slightest sign of movement in the man's lower regions and racing for the nearest shoreline where he rams into the
beach with the force of a bull moose at rutting season, giving the
victim just the time he needs to leap from the boat, drop his pants,
squat, and explode something terrible. Right there in the sand. In full
view of everyone. Ten times that day.

"*Eegeep-stowsoot?*" says Mom quizzically. ("He hit himself acci-
dentally, as with a gun," our way of saying "he shit his pants.")

"*Eegeep-stowsoot,*" confirms Joe Highway, then chortles, his wife
and children joining in the general hilarity.

"*Eegeep-stowsoot, eegeep-stowsoot,*" I sing all morning next day,
not so much for its meaning as for its rhythm, and dance tight circles around my cousin, the chubby and adorable Dorothy Highway.

"*Keetha ooti kigeep-stowsoon,*" she growls. ("It's you who shit
his pants.") And punches me, hard, in the nose.

15

The problem for Father Cadeau as resident priest of Brochet is attendance at his church. Much as he would like to, it is impossible for him to keep us corralled in Brochet just so we can live up to our good names as Catholics. The reason? Ours is a culture that is intrinsically nomadic—we are always on the move, out on the land following the caribou, the fish, and the *saagweesoo* (mink). That's who decides where we go when we go, not some priest from far-off Quebec, as handsome as Chaggy-wat Mooraah as he may be. Thus it is that he will often find himself sitting alone in his mouldy confessional, masticating reflectively on pink *pawpilly-cum* while waiting for customers who never materialize. Or wailing away with his nasal *Dominus vobiscum*s in a mostly empty church to unresponsive pews, the question being: How to solve the problem?

He buys a speedboat and points it southward. The vessel cuts quite the figure as it zips across the waters of Reindeer Lake. The reason? It differs markedly in two ways from Lockhart's. The first is that, though the hull is identical to those of Lockhart's, its steering mechanism works not with a handle that juts from the motor at the stern but rather with a steering wheel at the prow, as with a car. The second is that his boat has a cabin with a roof, windshield, and wipers that cover the front half of the vessel so that one can drive it without exposure to the elements. Thus shielded, Father Adrian Cadeau is free to battle wave, wind, and rain while cruising the islands looking for Indians, his liturgical equipment—surplice, maniple, stole, thurible, chalice, incense, hosts, and sacramental wine—all packed in a suitcase and stashed in his "cockpit," as Zebedee Zipper refers to the structure.

As for his quarry, meaning us, the Indians of Canada, there we are on some island or other on a given Sunday morning engaging in Sunday morning activity when attendance at church is out of the picture, meaning to say that we are moving slowly and with great pleasure. Dad, for example, is relishing his day off by shaving in the sun among tweeting chickadees while whistling and humming his favourite tune, "Hey, Joe." His mirror? A looking glass the size and shape of a saucer that he has borrowed from Louise and has hung from a branch just outside the main tent. Apart from sleeping, we live outdoors. We cook, eat, wash, brush our teeth, wash our dishes, wash our clothes, play outside and, in Dad's case, shave outside; rainy days, in any case, are rare, so why not enjoy?

Preparing for breakfast, Mom is kneading dough for bannock on a slat of plywood raised to waist-level by stakes of wood that act as table legs, her hands, forearms, and apron all white with flour. Now eighteen, Louise is washing dishes by the fire and seething at Florence who, home from school and aged fourteen, is *not* washing dishes but rather sits perched on a stump strumming her guitar and singing country. Also back from school and aged ten years, Daniel is carving the frame of a slingshot from a Y-shaped branch of willow. And Rene and I are playing in the water by the shore some ten yards down the slope with little wooden boats of Daniel's making. When, out of nowhere, a certain drone insinuates its way into our range of hearing. And grows and grows until, sure enough, a speedboat-with-cabin bursts like a bullet from behind Dewdney Island and into the channel that divides it from No-Name Island. So fast is Father Cadeau's speedboat advancing it is almost airborne. Spraying froth to both sides, its *oopas-choosoos* is so far behind it that Chaggy-wat Mooraah, who loves speed dearly, is sure to get jealous.

"*Eye-mee-gimow!*" ("Priest!") Rene and I drop our toys and scurry up the slope to the family encampment, yelling all along. "*Eye-mee-gimow! Eye-mee-gimow!*" At this announcement, Dad drops his razor, Mom her dough, Louise her dishes, Florence her guitar, and Daniel his knife and slingshot-in-progress.

Forgetting, as always, where she has put "the blasted things"— meaning her rosaries—Mom runs around the tent like a puppet gone insane. Once having found them in the place most obvious, generally her bedpost, she throws things in order, yelling at us to make our beds, sweep the floor, put our toys away, clean the yard, change our clothes, comb our hair, "Louise, take those damn things off your head and make yourself look human." And it's true, at that moment, Louise's head looks vaguely simian.

As with so many products of the modern world, curlers are unknown and thus unavailable to girls up north. All born with hair as straight as uncooked spaghetti, they thus have to be inventive if they want to look like their goddess, Marilyn (whom they've seen in movies and, of course, magazines). The kerchief which Louise wears like a pirate with its knot at the nape of her neck fails to mask a carnival of curlers of her own making, odd little gadgets that look quite ghastly.

Used Carnation milk tins scorched free of their paper-covering in the flames of a fire are but the start. Popped free of their tops and bottoms from the heat, they are then plunged in cold water and hung out to dry. Next are they cut open down one side so the metal, which is tin thin as paper, can be opened and then flattened out, the sheet that results then cut into strips a half-inch in width. Each strip is then wrapped in parcel paper. Wetting her hair, Louise takes it a lock at a time and wraps it around these strips to form balls with the strips of tin wrapped in brown paper knotted through and around them. The result? Some thirty balls of wet hair the size of thumbs, imprisoned in paper-wrapped tin. Last, she covers the final product with a kerchief. All quite the production, it usually takes her two hours to accomplish. Then she goes to bed. By morning, the hair now dry, she takes off the strips, a process that takes, by comparison, perhaps ten minutes. Then she brushes the hair out and, poof, she is Marilyn.

Except on a morning like this. With a priest walking up the slope from the shore—already!—with a suitcase, yet, filled to the brim with holy weaponry, she has no time for leisurely grooming. Ripping the curlers off one after the other, she throws them in the fire from whence they came. And without benefit of mirror, she brushes her hair out. Teeth exposed, lips snarling, face twisted with fury, she is frightening to watch. By the time she is finished, our tent is a church, a sheet of plywood balanced on two sawhorses and covered with a bedsheet its altar, our ten-year-old brother, Daniel, pressed into service as an altar boy. And having gotten wind of the blessed event through the moccasin telegraph, people from other parts of that island and on nearby islands arrive to take in the service. As the weather is generally agreeable, the front of the tent is pinned open so that, while one-tenth of the congregation kneels inside on bare ground—there are no pews or chairs for that matter—the other nine-tenths kneel outside in front of the tent where always lie scattered in scads wood chips from firewood. All the above is generic; it happens perhaps three times a summer on whichever island we are living of any given year (on the lakes up north, it never happens). But here's one instance in specific . . .

It is August of 1958 and we are living in Doodneek. Aged three and six, Rene and I are sleeping in the bed that we share in our parents' tent when, all of a sudden, we are woken by a howling that sounds like wolves baying at the moon.

The thing to understand is that, when Cree and Dene people sing hymns, they don't so much sing as wail in major-seconds. Untrained as they are in elocution, moreover, you can never quite make out what they are singing about. All I remember is the line "*Keeeeeespin kisagee-hee-heenaaaaaaan*" ("If you love us . . .") that Samba Cheese Weetigo used to sing with such passion at St. Pierre Church in Brochet that it gave you moose bumps.

"*Neeeee, keegway ooma*" ("What the . . ."), I say to no one as I drift out of sleep. I open my eyes. It is daylight. All I see is a white surface. Have I died and gone up to heaven? But no, it is not heaven. It is merely one of Mom's white flannel bedsheets, the one with the pink stripes across top and bottom. Hanging from the ceiling, it is acting as a curtain meant to block my view of the entrance to our tent here in Doodneek. When I finally emerge from the miasma of sleep, I know—Father Cadeau has arrived unannounced in his speedboat and is conducting a Mass on the other side of that hanging sheet. Mom, God bless her, has divided the room so we can sleep in uninterrupted. What was she thinking? Uninterrupted by visuals, yes, but no bedsheet on Earth is soundproof, so I hear the congregation singing as loud as day, Ice-keemee Minette's chesty contralto piercing through the moo as with a drill. Then they finish and Father Cadeau takes over.

"*Dominus vobiscum*," he chants, his voice, as usual, quavering, uncertain of the key.

"*Et cum spiritu tuo*," responds Ice-keemee Minette, another forty voices (or what sound like forty) now, in essence, her back-up chorus.

"*Oremus*," quavers Father Cadeau. I can picture him in his surplice and stole standing behind his makeshift altar facing his flock, raising the chalice with one hand, the Host with the other above that chalice, showing, in effect, the body of Christ to the faithful.

"*Ninootee-sigin*," says Rene ("I need to pee"), his three-year-old voice rising from his pillow like an Arctic tern. I put my hand over his mouth. The tussle that ensues is packed with movement. Duck feathers from our pillows fly this way and that. At one point, I swallow one and choke but dislodge it, just managing to stifle the resulting gasp. By this time, the congregation is praying in unison.

"*Aya-yaa!*" ("Ouch!") I yell. My little brother has just bitten my finger and is now crying at full volume. Fortunately, the general murmur behind that curtain masks his voice.

The word "*Nasigit-soon!*" ("I'm going to pee myself!") bursts from his mouth. Like a descant, it now carries clearly over the praying. Which only encourages the people to incant with even greater verve, even greater volume, even as Mom throws the curtain open and comes charging up to Rene with her rosaries jangling in one hand, a pee can glimmering in the other, her lips still muttering something about "*Kichitaw Maaree*" ("Holy Mary," our name for the Virgin) and some blessed fruit she apparently has swallowed. Obviously, Mom has just woven her way through the rows of kneeling suppliants with the can now empty of its former contents, stewed tomatoes, her objective to save her bedsheets from being peed on by a little boy of three. She gets there just in time. And as Rene tinkles happily away, Father Cadeau starts serving communion. Not five feet away on the other side of that hanging sheet.

Now, as who doesn't know, empty tin cans when tinkled upon by a small jet of liquid make music that is, well, tinkly and pretty, which is precisely what this one is doing at that most sacred of Catholic moments. All as our brother Daniel holds Father Cadeau's silver patina (a sort of tray with a handle, as with a mini frying pan) under people's chins, one after the other after the other, to catch falling fragments of God's raw flesh—thus affording him a view of hanging human tongues available in no other manner. As I myself am now peeking from the side of the hanging bedsheet, I see all this.

"The body of Christ," says Father Cadeau. "Amen," responds each person, one after the other after the other, as Rene's little *chak-sees* (penis) goes *tinkle, tinkle*. "The body of Christ." "Amen." *Tinkle, tinkle . . .*

16

Then one day at the end of August that same summer, we leave for Koowap (which rhymes with "to what"). A village on the east shore of Reindeer Lake at about its midriff, its original name was Koowap Point because, of course, it stands at a point of land, but people, for some reason, have shortened it to just "Koowap." A *Moony-ass* word, it is really just the way we Cree pronounce the word "co-op" which, in turn—as who but us non-English speakers didn't know—is an abbreviation of the longer English word "co-operative." A "co-operative" of Cree fishermen, indeed, is who founded it. And though Koowap, whose population is seasonal, later changes name a second time to Kinoosao, which is Cree for "fish," it is known, when I am six, as Koowap which, to this day, is what those of us who know it from that era still call it.

The first endeavour undertaken by this "co-op" of fishermen was the construction of a plant where fish caught and brought by its dues-paying members would be processed and shipped off to markets in far *maameek*. As an exercise in economic development, it worked; there was employment. So people flocked to it in numbers extensive. If the settlement's population in winter is barely a dozen, as Zebedee Zipper who knows such facts says, then, as with Doodneek, it skyrockets in summer to about two hundred which, for sub-Arctic Canada even today, with one of the sparsest populations on Earth, is a virtual metropolis. And, again, as with Doodneek, all come from Southend.

Koowap is located fifteen miles east of Doodneek with, of course, the obligatory half-dozen islands between them. The former, however, sits on the mainland though across from an island, meaning that the site was chosen for its sheltered position from the intermittent violence of the waters of Reindeer Lake. As with Doodneek, a channel is the upshot. Barely fifty yards inside Saskatchewan, it is as pretty as a postcard when seen from boats.

Jack pines well-spaced one from the other, sandy footpaths wind their way between and among them, while carpets of wild cranberry bushes sit scattered willy-nilly across ground covered with golden sand. If you run through its fineness, which I love doing, clouds of powder puff out behind you. White canvas tents line an elongated hill, a plateau, in effect, that slopes down to the lake across whose shoreline sit, beached and waiting, a row of boats—speedboats, canoes, skiffs— many with crates filled with nets curled up inside them. *Moony-ass* use reels when they fish for trout, Indians nets, says Zebedee Zipper, who knows Koowap, where fish Indians, and Doodneek, where fish *Moony-ass*, in equal measure for the reason that no man on Earth has crossed Reindeer Lake more often or with greater energy than he, the adventurous and daring Zebedee Zipper. A tent village in effect, the only buildings in Koowap are a corner store made of plywood that sells gasoline and the usual staples and, mere yards beside it, the fish processing plant downhill from which juts into the channel a dock made of planks held up by posts of spruce shaved of their bark. This is where all "co-op" fishermen deliver their catches of trout, pickerel, and whitefish. This is where, as well, a Norseman lands at least once daily to pick up this fish ice-packed in crates and fly it to Lynn Lake from where it is shipped by train to Winnipeg, albeit, of course, in refrigerated cars, at least so says Zebedee Zipper. It is also where the plane, perhaps even this self-same Norseman, will come to collect me, tomorrow, to fly me to *maameek* and school for the winter. Which is why we've come here: to meet it, to drop me off, and say good-bye. I am excited.

On the last day of August in the low sub-Arctic, nightfall comes at 6 p.m. After an uneventful albeit scenic crossing from Doodneek

with our family—and setting up camp at the far end of the village—
Rene and I, with Louise between us holding our hands, are walking
down a trail. As a consequence, we pass the rear of one tent after
another, each one of which has a campfire dancing before it. And as
we stroll, Louise keeps getting recognized by former schoolmates
from her residential school days at Sturgeon Landing, Saskatchewan,
most of whom she hasn't seen in at least two years. She thus is invited
to the fronts of tents for tea and chats in, of course, this most clown-
like, joyful, and musical of languages. Like her, these friends are young
women aged eighteen to twenty, some already married, some already
mothers. All entranced by the doll-like beauty of my three-year-old
brother, their girlish chatter releases, as with jets of water, an intermittent salvo of "*oo*'s" and laughter that glides across the glass of Reindeer
Lake and skyward, sparks from campfires their faithful escorts.

Still, because of the darkness, all Rene and I see are their faces,
masks illumined by flames and, behind them, their shadows splashed
against the walls of the canvas tents and against the stands of stately
pines. And because the flames of those fires are dancing, then so are
the shadows, so are those masks. Northern Manitoba is dancing farewell to its favourite son. A stump our seat, my little brother has fallen
asleep leaning against my flimsy left shoulder.

Status Indians are the descendants of Native people who, in the late
nineteenth and early twentieth centuries, signed over the rights to
their land, if under duress, to the Crown of England via the agency
of the Government of Canada. The documents signed are called
treaties. Though some are unnumbered and known instead by
names such as "Robinson-Superior," in the east in particular, others
are numbered. And of these numbered treaties, there are eleven, each
applicable to a different part of the western provinces. Treaty One,
for example, covers southern Manitoba. In our region, my forebears signed an adhesion to Treaty Five in 1908, the original of which
was signed in 1875. These, together with the way the Indian Act of
1876 is worded, are what have consigned us to plots of land called
Indian Reserves.

Non-status Indians, by contrast, are the descendants of Native people who did *not* sign treaties. *Or* who signed their status away so they could vote in federal elections, leave the reserve for reasons of employment or post-secondary education, join the armed forces, or drink alcohol, all things forbidden to a status Indian by this Indian Act. Until 1985, moreover, status women who married non-status or *Moony-ass* men lost their status, while a *Moony-ass* woman who married a status man became, in the eyes of the law, a status Indian. Go figure.

We, the Highway family, are status Indians who belong to an Indian Reserve. The name of our band—or reserve or First Nation; the terms are interchangeable—is Barren Lands. It covers an area of seventeen square miles at the northern tip of Reindeer Lake. As its administrative capital, the village of Brochet, with its population, when I am six, of about eight hundred, stands at the southern edge of this irregularly shaped rectangle of land. Barren Lands, one concept; Brochet, another. Ultimately, however—and as says old and crusty Zebedee Zipper—"the same damn thing."

The law that defines reserves, however, is only one of many contained in this Indian Act. Another applies to the matter of education. According to this section of the document, all status Indian children are to be taken from their homes and sent to residential schools, there to be transformed into *Moony-ass*.

The schools are funded by the federal government. The federal government, that is to say, bought the land that the schools are built on, and it hires and pays the architects, engineers, carpenters, construction workers, electricians, and plumbers to build them; equips them with furniture, appliances, pots, pans, and dishes; and pays and houses the staff who work there. The transport of children is covered by the government, which charters the bush planes that fly them to the schools and back from their communities that are, in some cases—as with Brochet—among the most remote on Earth. The federal government buys the children's clothes, their books, their pens and paper, their chalks and crayons, their food, their hockey equipment, even their Christmas presents which, in our case, take a small army of nuns to wrap till three every morning in the month leading up to Christmas. Health care, eye care, dental care, all are covered.

And speaking of nuns, if the government funds these schools, then the churches run them. Catholic, Anglican, Methodist, it varies with the region. In our case, it, of course, is the Catholics. Opened in September of 1958, the new Guy Hill Indian Residential School was built to replace the old one in Sturgeon Landing which used to stand in Saskatchewan just south and slightly west of Flin Flon which, in turn, stands on the border just inside Manitoba, if by mere feet. Victim to an electrical short circuit, it burned to the ground in September of 1952. As for its replacement, the new "Guy Hill" stands on the shore of this stunning, emerald-coloured body of water called Clearwater Lake, twenty-five miles north of a railway town in west-central Manitoba called The Pas. Which means that, for the nine years that I will be spending at this school on Clearwater Lake, I will be living ten months of the year some four hundred miles south of the land I was born and raised on, some three hundred south of Brochet, and four hundred north of the city of Winnipeg. And some forty east of Manitoba's border with Saskatchewan. Always that border lives inside us.

One should note, however, that there already exists a school in Brochet, one that has stood there for at least two decades by the time I am six. A one-room affair that is run by the Government of Manitoba as opposed to the church or the Government of Canada, it stands ten yards west of and down the slope from St. Pierre Church. It is meant for non-status children who, unlike status children, are ineligible for attendance at residential schools. Some status families, however, do, in fact, keep some of their children at home and send them, instead, to this non-status school. Of his eighteen children, for example, Alec Fitzhenry has sent eight of the fourteen who survived to adulthood to this school, thus sending six to Guy Hill. His third son, Isaac, has grade four only, that's how briefly he went to Guy Hill. As for Isaac, he himself kept fourteen children away from Guy Hill. My mother's sister, my Laughing Aunt Margaret Kipawm, together with her husband, Man Kipawm, sent but three of their seven, and that but briefly.

The problem for successful hunters and trappers like Dad is that they are out on the land with their families for the bulk of the academic year which, ironically, is what makes them successful—they are always working. And as people in Brochet generally already have fourteen children each to care for, lodging other people's children while they go to school in Brochet is impossible. In homes where already sleep five children to a bed? Forget it.

Besides, the difference, even for a man who never went to school, is obvious. A one-room school with one teacher teaching all eight grades at once is a recipe for an education that, at best, is sub-standard. Half the time, moreover, kids are pulled out of the classroom by their parents in the middle of the day to go out and cut firewood or go out hunting to feed their families, with the result that they miss half their classes and are thus lucky if they make it to grade four. If his world is on the cusp of leaping five generations in one, something Joe Highway knows is about to transpire, then his people *have* to be ready. As no transition transpires easily—some have cost millions of lives, he knows. He has heard the stories from Father Cadeau—he knows, implicitly, that we, the youngest of the seven surviving Highway children, none of whom went past grade seven, will have to make certain sacrifices and contribute to the easing of that transition, will have to contribute to saving their people. And now the chance presents itself—a brand-new school near The Pas with seven grades, seven classrooms, and seven teachers of the very highest order, at least so has said Father Cadeau. And Dad is excited. He is optimistic.

He is excited, for one thing, because he himself never had the chance. The second of thirteen children, only nine of whom survived to adulthood, his one elder sibling, a boy named Samba Cheese, had drowned in an accident at age sixteen, leaving Dad, at age thirteen, the eldest, and therefore the leader, of eight children. He always remembers: while he watched his father send the others to the first Guy Hill Indian Residential School in Sturgeon Landing one after the other after the other, he had to stay at home to help with chores and care for the youngest, that is, those not yet at school. The fact that he couldn't even write while his younger brothers could made him resentful. He hid it well but it was there, a boil that festered. That's one point. The second goes deeper.

By the time Rene and I are born, Mom and Dad have seen so much death among their progeny that they are willing to give their lives to save their last two, in particular, from dying. Rene and I are the pearls at the end of the necklace. We are special, we are cherished, we are loved in a way no child on Earth has ever been loved and we will go to a place where death won't get us. It has taken much reflection but Dad has decided.

In the south, all one has to do to get grade one is walk two blocks down the street and be home for lunch. For high school, all he has to do is walk ten blocks. For university, all he has to do is ride a city bus for an hour and be home for dinner. In sub-Arctic Canada, where three hundred miles is equivalent to a mile in the south, that is impossible.

With Vi, their eldest, who was born in 1929, Mom and Dad had to paddle—not motor but paddle, as there were no motors up there back then—the six hundred miles from Windy Lake on the Manitoba–Northwest Territories border to Sturgeon Landing. That boreal forest having no roads to speak of, not then, not now, it took them a month to traverse that distance. Then, after dropping her off, it took them another month to paddle back north to Windy Lake, which is where they were living that year. This was in autumn. Come June, same thing except, of course, in reverse, making for a total of four months of travel, and back-breaking travel at that, just to get their first child to grade one *and* her first word of English. The fifteen portages that they had to cross going in either direction, one of them twelve miles in length, would kill most people; with that kind of cargo, they wouldn't last a mile. Vi made it to grade two.

For the next child, Swanson, who was born in 1931, Mom and Dad didn't even try, with the result that Swanson, like Dad—and Mom for that matter—had grade zero. With their next ten children, it goes like this . . . Born in 1933, Marie-Adele Highway died at nine. Sylvia Highway, same thing, born in 1936, dead at age seven. By the time Louise came along in 1939 and reached school age in the late

1940s, the bush plane had arrived in Canada's north, which enabled her to get to grade seven. Born in 1941, Jeanette died as an infant. Born in 1943, Florence achieved grade five—though not until age sixteen, thanks to the school fire that robbed her of three years of schooling (she, Louise, and Daniel eventually went to interim facilities the school had rented in The Pas, some fifty miles east, while the new school was under construction twenty-five miles north of the town).

The next one in line was Weezoo. Named after Mom's father, he died as an infant. Then came Daniel. Born in 1947 and of school age in the mid-1950s, he could take planes that were faster and could fly greater distances; in addition to which, the railroad had come, ready to whisk him, if need be, from Lynn Lake to high school in Winnipeg. Next came Hermeline, who died as an infant. And then came me. Born at the end of 1951, I was fifteen years old when the first jet arrived at the newly built Lynn Lake airport, enabling me to fly all the way to Winnipeg in three mere hours for high school and then university. The first person in all Brochet to achieve both a high school diploma *and* a university degree, I was a freak, a case to be studied. And last, in 1954, came Rene, who also finished high school but then went on to dance school and, against all odds, the world of dance. And even then, these distances gave us no choice but to stay separated from our families for ten months each year. Beautiful as it is, the north can be brutal.

The first of September, 1958, dawns bright and crisp in the village of Koowap. Cool yet warm, a breeze from the south ruffles the water of Reindeer Lake. To my child's eyes, that lake is joyful. And so, that morning, is Joe Highway's heart. He walks with a bounce so, thus inspired, *I* walk with a bounce, for that's what we are doing—walking down the footpath that leads from our tent through the forest to the dock at the fish plant: Mom, Dad, Louise, Florence, Daniel, Rene, and I. All as the Norseman that is coming to get me buzzes the treetops above us as it banks in for landing. I *love* planes; I can't wait to ride one.

Off to school in far *maameek* with our brand-new (though empty) suitcases, Florence, Daniel, and I are dressed like models in brand-new outfits Louise has ordered, like the luggage, through the Eaton's mail-order catalogue. White cotton shirts, black pants and jackets, and black canvas runners with white shoelaces for me and Daniel; for Florence, a pastel sky-blue, light wool sweater with white plastic buttons down the front, a blouse of white poplin with embroidered collar, a flouncy pink skirt also of poplin, and, on her head—the style back then in north Cree culture—a floral-patterned silk kerchief to match her skirt, tied loosely under her chin. Why loosely? Because of her "country-star pouffe" of a hairdo, a frothy concoction Louise has sculpted with her burnt-in-charcoals-and-cut-into-strips Carnation-milk-tin curlers.

We arrive at the fish plant. At its dock, moored already and waiting for us, floats the silver Norseman. With its dark blue stripes encircling its midriff horizontally, it sways slightly in the inch-high waves. People stand clustered on the dock beside it and under its left wing, the crush so intense it's a wonder the wooden structure doesn't buckle. There is excitement, a festive environment. The crowd spills out onto the slope that climbs its way to the fish plant and beyond and yet more appear emerging from the bushes. All have come, it is clear, to bid their children a fond farewell—their sons and daughters, their sisters, brothers, nephews, nieces, aunts, uncles, cousins, friends, even lovers. And how we know this is because Mom, Dad, Louise, and Rene are there for the exact same reason.

When we get to the dock, we have to practically elbow our way through the throng to get to the plane. The pilot, a young blond man with bright, white teeth and a print cotton shirt, stands on one of the plane's two pontoons, engaged already in the act of loading children and their suitcases. He lets Daniel, who is ten, jump from the dock down to the pontoon from whence he scrambles athletically, like the other boys of similar age, up the four rungs of silver steel ladder and hence to the door and the plane's interior. To Florence, who is fourteen, the pilot gives a hand, like a prince with a princess, first with her suitcase and then her person. With the breeze on her flouncy pink skirt and pink silk kerchief, Florence Highway flutters up the ladder like a monarch butterfly and into the plane. As for the younger ones, the fathers pass them from the dock to this pilot ten inches down on the plane's pontoon who then heaves each child the two feet up to the open passenger door of the aircraft, each from there to take their seat. Rene wants to come with me but can't, says Dad; he is too young. He cries.

Finally, it is my turn. For Daniel and Florence, this is their third and fifth time respectively flying off to school in far *maameek*, for me my first. I am not scared, however, nor am I nervous. And I am not shy either. Rather am I gung-ho. Evidently of like mind and spirit, Dad kneels on the dock before me. Placing his hands on either side of my bony waist, he looks into my eyes. I look into his. The joy inside them is palpable; I could reach in and touch it. Then again, it is hard for Dad not to be joyful. No matter what happens, he always finds a way to laugh his way out of it. If the expression "finding the silver lining behind every cloud" was invented for anyone, it was for him. He just has this gift for turning disaster into something spectacular. And when disaster happens, which, of course, it does from time to time, he laughs his trademark laugh that goes, "Ho-*ho*!" Rhyming with "the hoe!" it sounds like a trumpet announcing the entrance of Chief Chi-Louie at a major event. The classic story of his finding that lining goes like this . . .

17

Eleven years prior to my birth, my family is passing the winter on Nueltin Lake, the lake that straddles the Manitoba–Northwest Territories border and is so vast that it makes Christ's Sea of Galilee look like a duck pond, says Father Egg Nog who knows these things as he is a *Chaariman* and has seen Nueltin Lake. Dad is thirty-two, making Mom twenty-nine, Vi eleven, Swanson nine, Marie-Adele and Sylvia still alive at six and three, and Louise still a baby. As for me and Rene—and Florence and Daniel, for that matter—we are unborn, dreamt of only.

Nueltin Lake lies a hundred miles long and fifty at its widest—except that its shape is whimsical. When seen on a map, it looks like a bloodstain, thanks to glaciers of times long past that have gouged all these craters for lakes to thrive on. And though its wealth in islands knows no limit—some parts could pass for a mangrove swamp when seen from the air, there are that many—it also features four wide-open stretches that know no land. And it is on the eastern shore of one such section that Dad has chosen to establish camp that winter. Why? He knows of an abandoned trapper's cabin that stands there. As with so many others in his sub-Arctic wanderings, and as he has always had a way with saw and hammer, he transforms the cabin in a matter of days to make it habitable. One-room shelters of the genre, in any case, are willingly co-shared by northern adventurers; no rent is charged; if unoccupied, all passing travellers are welcome to use them. Northern hospitality. That's what it's called.

And the reason some enterprising hunter or trapper has built the cabin on this location is that a Hudson's Bay fur-trading post stands almost directly across, the distance at that point in the curve of the north–south shorelines more like twenty miles as opposed to fifty. Once a week on average, Dad drives his sled from this cabin across this stretch to this trading post to trade in his furs, returning with groceries such as milk in cans, tea, lard, flour and, of course, a packsack holding his trusty sleeping robe.

Finished doing business this one fine day, he emerges from the post at half-past noon (he says) just in time to spy in the distance a gathering storm, clouds roiling and churning. A blizzard of the kind that kills and maims is on its way. Normally, with an empty sled, an experienced racer like Joe Highway can cross twenty miles within two hours if he goes full tilt. With a practised eye, he measures the distance between himself and the clouds. Will he make it or will he not? Always a gambler, he throws his box of groceries into the sled, unties his lead dog—Rich, at the time; Kip was yet to come; from the fence post she is tied to, jumps on the footboard, grabs the handle-bar, and, to the ever-ready, ever-enthusiastic, and handsome Rich, snaps his whip. "*Marches!*" he shouts, and off they go. (The French word from which comes "mush," the canine directive that means "go!" and is now used by all dogsledders. And it's always *marches* as opposed to *marchez* because the verb is singular and so is meant for the lead dog only.)

Eastward he races. And races and races. He races like a madman, he races like a wind, he races like no man in the north has ever raced before, not even when Oos-eye Naapao (Yellow Man) Hatchet, the great Cree shaman, fled from the *Weetigo*. Always determined, sure of his destiny, Joe Highway will make it to the eastern shore, his dear *weegi-maagan* (wife), and his five children by 4 p.m. that day. Nothing will stop him, not storm, not hell, not even *Machaa-is*.

Unfortunately, he is wrong. With a wallop and a bang that sends stars flying inside his head, the storm hits, boom, and he is blind. He can't see his nose let alone Mistik, the last dog in his team. That's what blizzards in Arctic and sub-Arctic regions are like: white-outs, they're called, because, of course, all one sees is white. And all one hears is a terrific roar, a monstrous whistling. At this point, most people panic. They give up the ghost. They lie down and die. Of exposure. Not Joe Highway. Joe Lapstan Highway of Brochet, Manitoba, is made of different material. With a crack of his whip, he yells "whoah" at Rich, who stops on the spot.

Struggling against the gale-force wind, barely breathing, blinded, he claws his way from behind the footboard to the front where sits, rolled up inside its packsack, behind his groceries, his saviour—his cherished sleeping robe. All by feel, he extracts it from the bag, unrolls it lengthwise, and lays it across the sled's wood bottom in two thick layers like a hotdog bun might be made ready to receive its wiener. The north wind doing everything it can within its power to blow him all the way to the North Pole, he clambers in. His plan? He will have a nap, the kind that Lazarus of Bethany was reputed to have had before Jeezoos raised him from the dead. And the last thing he does before he shuts himself in is snap his whip one final time at Rich. (Attached to the handle, which is made of spruce carved finely and beaded artistically, the whip's ten-foot length is made of a hundred shotgun ball-bearings tied tightly together by strips of hide braided in three. Which is why, when snapped, it curls out dreamily over the animals and comes to a *snap* just over the lead dog's nose.)

The sled inches forward. And inches forward and inches forward, each snail-like advance a titanic struggle for the beasts of burden. Inside the sled, the north wind's roar has been contained, muffled to a murmur by piles of goose down which, acting in concert with the sled's soft rocking, lull my father to babe-like sleep. And dream . . .

Here in Koowap, Saskatchewan, I am ready for adventure of the kind Joe Highway is known for. On this crisp, bright morning on the first of September, 1958, on the border between Saskatchewan and Manitoba, Joe Highway takes his fourth son, his eleventh child, and second-last born off the fish plant dock by the waist and lifts him high. Seen in the hands of this taut-muscled hunter, this world-champion dogsled racer, I am tiny. Aloft, I am his trophy, lustrous, golden, glittering in the light of a mid-morning sun. His brown skin glowing, his white teeth flashing, he beams with pride and says, "*Keegwaathoo itigwee paaskach igootee kaawee-naatak*" ("What on Earth is he going to get down there?"), the question rhetorical, asked of no one. But the answer is implicit, and all there know it; it scintillates between each word, syllable, consonant, and vowel. That answer? "Marvels, marvels, marvels . . . he is going down there to accomplish marvels." Whisked by the breeze to far *keeweet'nook* (the north), the echo tapers.

"Yes"—the voice inside me climbs that echo and rides it, rides it, rides. "I am travelling south to dance with marvels." Dad hears it clearly, I know, feels its vibration inside his blood—"*keetha kichi, paapaa*" ("for you, Father").

"Ho-*ho!*" Joe Highway trumpets. And puts me in the hands of the princely pilot who, in turn, lifts me easily on to the plane. I don't even remember his hands or his presence. I am too busy floating . . .

Back at Nueltin Lake, seventeen years prior to this late-summer morning in Koowap, Saskatchewan, Dad wakes up. In his goose-down sleeping robe. The sled has stopped. The wind has stopped. All is silence. For days on end, perhaps even years, so far as he knows at that point in time, he has slept through the blizzard. Or has he died and gone up to heaven? When he peeps out the sleeping robe, he sees clear sky and hears child-laughter, Sylvia Highway's tinkly voice ringing above it, "*paapaa, paapaa.*" He sits up. Only to find his adored three-year-old facing him by six mere inches. And smiling so hard she hurts his eyes (four years later will she be dead). Behind her appear his four other children, Viola eleven, Swanson nine, Marie-Adele six (to die in three years), and baby Louise cradled in the arms of her elegant mother. Standing at the door, she waits for him. Three full hours after he has sunk into a sleep as deep as death, his lead dog, Rich, has found her way through the white-out. On the sense of smell.

The moral of the story? Many is the time sled dogs in the Arctic have saved the lives of their masters. Yes. Perhaps. But more important: When disaster strikes, you don't take fright, you don't panic. You just lie down and take the most beautiful nap the world has known. And when you wake up four hours, two years, or three decades later, you will find yourself at your destination . . .

As a boy/girl of six, to be seven in three months, I am sitting on that Norseman with eleven other children and adolescents. Now airborne and leaving Koowap, I see my parents far down below, still standing on that dock waving at me. Dad holding Rene in his arms; tiny Rene, too, is waving. And he is crying, I know he is crying because I, too, am crying. But I'll see him again, I'll see him in June. And through the wash of tears, the sky takes over, sky that fades into a surface of white and yet more white. And, in that white, I see Dad crossing Nueltin Lake. And a voice inside me whispers, breeze-like: "I think I'll take a nap."

18

I am sitting in the trailer of a truck that is rumbling down a road. The road of gravel, the vehicle leaves in its wake a swirling cloud, making it a trick to breathe at times. The trailer being open to the air, what is there for us to do but try our best, "us" being the twelve young passengers who have just disembarked from the plane from Koowap? Built into the walls like shelving units, the benches they have given us as seats afford us leg room while the walls of the trailer serve us as backrests. Our destination a school somewhere out there, all I know is that we have just left the floatplane base on the outskirts of a town called The Pas. The vehicle rattles. A half-hour later, we turn a curve and there it stands, this building that reaches to the sky by three whole storeys and sprawls from the forest to the lake behind it. I must stand up so I can see better.

Never have I seen a house so huge. Constructed out of brick pink-orange in colour, its windows just go on forever to the right and left, three entire rows of them, in fact, one row on top of the other on top of the other. It looks like a cake. As we get closer, I see that the parking lot in front is a seething mass of black.

"Nuns," explains one girl who is much older than me, "nuns and priests all dressed in black." Priests I have seen, nuns never. I am curious. "They belong to an order called the Sisters of St. Joseph," my new friend adds, "from a convent in far-off Quebec." Greek to my ears but I like her anyway.

The truck comes to a stop. Like a gate, its back door opens. We hop off nimbly (though Daniel helps me). Glad to have our feet on ground that is solid, we are attacked. Hands reach out to touch us, white faces beam, voices both male and female cluck like ptarmigans, the words they utter a general babble, a monstrous moo.

It can accommodate three hundred people, says the older girl who has shared our journey from Koowap and whose English, it is clear, is good enough for her to interpret what is being said. In this case, that language is being spoken by the priest who is chief here; that much is evident by the way he talks *and* by his presence, which is forceful, as he waves his arms about explaining his fiefdom. The number three hundred beyond my reach, I merely nod. It even has a church, says my interpreter, a teen from Southend whose name is Hilda. *And* two gymnasia. To me, the word sounds threatening. Like Mom's TB, it might be fatal. I must take care that I am breathed on only by people who don't have gymnasia.

"*Nimantoom*" ("My God"), I whisper, more to breathe out anxiety than to express my awe of this building. Awe and anxiety colliding inside me, I stand there reeling, the gravel of the parking lot against my soles. Back home, the ground was caribou moss *with* my soles, not against them; the difference is minor but, to me, significant. Dwarfed by this edifice, I feel like an ant but hear Dad's counsel-by-action: The silver lining, *nigoosis* (my son), always look for the silver lining. Eyes unblinking, shoulders squared, I persist in my absorption of this avalanche of fact, of smells, of faces and voices, of odd sensations.

Built to replace its predecessor, the burnt-to-the-ground residential school at Sturgeon Landing, Saskatchewan—where went Louise and Florence—and after Daniel spent his first two years of schooling, along with Florence, at the burnt school's interim facility in The Pas, the new Guy Hill Indian Residential School is opening today, September the first, 1958, and it gleams accordingly, the floors so clean they look like mirrors. Kindergarten unknown in the north back then, we grade ones are thus, in a sense, its first crop of residents. Florence and

Daniel, too, of course, are here, but they don't count; in advanced grades already—three and five, to me stratospheric—they're practically fossils when compared to us neophytes. In a sense, therefore, *they* are moving in with *me*. And this *misti-waaska-igan* (big house) is my palace. There, Dad. How's *that* for positive thinking?

The building has its back to an emerald-watered lake, its front to this gravel-covered parking lot with room for a dozen vehicles of one sort or other including the truck we've just pulled up in. Dogsleds? I somehow doubt it. Spreading out beyond this lot lies a field with grass and tufts of flowers; beyond it the road to The Pas, the one we have just navigated. Escorted by the nuns in single file—and there are twelve, explains this Hilda—up the central staircase that leads to the entrance, it strikes me as odd that, shrouded in black, full-length robes with veils that look heavy, only their hands and faces betray them as human. Oversized black rosaries that hang from their waists go *clickety-clack* as they trundle up the stairs.

The building's facilities too numerous to describe, suffice it to explain that there are, at one end on the upper two floors, three dormitories for a hundred boys, at the other, three more "dorms" for a hundred girls. In between and on lower floors are situated gender-divided dining rooms, washrooms, and playrooms—what, in the last case, my tour guide, Hilda, called "gymnasia"—though the classrooms, at least, will be mixed in gender, she assures me. Also on this floor are one-room sleeping quarters, dining rooms, and lounges for staff both lay and clergy. Then there are the laundry facilities, the sewing room, the infirmary, the storerooms, the church which the nuns call "chapel," a boiler room the size of Companeek that controls, apparently, the water, heating, and electrical system for the entire facility. Still, the most impressive, at least for me, is the kitchen that can feed over two hundred people, says my friend, Hilda, with ovens so immense they could each roast a moose unbutchered, antlers and all. The place is a labyrinth, as I am soon to discover, a kaleidoscope: for me, a kingdom of magic. There, Dad. How's *that* for a silver lining? No one here—*no one*—will ever think of calling your second-youngest child sentimental or cowardly, not when I have Hilda, Florence, and Daniel.

The size of the building and its contents impresses me, yes; its complexity of structure makes my head spin; the number of students, once all have arrived from reserves across northwestern Manitoba and northeastern Saskatchewan, excites me, for I will learn to love them just like Dad loves everyone, I am sure of it. But all three impressions pale by comparison to those that enter my bloodstream via my three other senses: taste, feel, and smell.

That last is unnatural. Having lived my entire life to that point in time steeped in smells that come from nature—spruce, pine, willow, caribou moss, muskeg, fish, campfire smoke—I am perplexed. As it turns out, I find out at my first meal that that smell comes from plastic, something then foreign to northern cultures. The dishes in the dining room, the bowls, the saucers, the cups, all are of plastic (back home, ours are of porcelain or metal). Hospital-gown green and canary yellow for the boys, steel blue and orangey pink for the girls, there are hundreds of them. The bedsheets smell of plastic, our clothes smell of plastic, the nurse in the infirmary, a *Chaariman* woman whose name, apparently, is Nurse Kratzen, *she* smells of plastic, even the food we eat smells *and* tastes of plastic. In this room they call a "refectory" they feed us potatoes and bread and small green beans called "pees" and other delicacies, even *oochak-seesa* ("small penises," our word for macaroni) with melted cheese. Many other boys appear to dislike them. Me? I am hungry so I eat them with gusto. The meat, however, is suspect.

It tastes like steel. Like the dishes it is served on, there is something of plastic about it. Or soap or chemicals. Maybe they soak it in Lysol before they cook it, I sit there thinking at my table, one of ten, each with places for ten. I have heard of Lysol from my sister Louise. Having used it to wash floors, walls, and toilets at Sturgeon Landing School, she says it is poison.

Whatever the flavour of this so-called *weeyaas* (meat), the animal it comes from is called *kookoos* (pig), according to my brother Daniel, who does take time to talk to me if all too rarely. *Kookoos*? I have never seen one much less consumed one. Maybe it's related to *ateek* (caribou), except, of course, for the antlers (for Daniel tells me these animals have none). Is the flesh of this *kookoos*, after all, not every bit as chewy and rubbery as *ateek*'s? Does one not have to *maamaa-g'waachi-gee* (chew) just as long before one swallows it hook, line, and sinker? Whatever the animal looks like, this meat is not *ateek*, it is not *amisk* (beaver), it is not *wachask* (muskrat).

The reason I have never eaten pig is, of course, very simple—it is not a northern animal. Like the cow, the skunk, the cat, and the snake, it stops at latitude fifty-four, which, in essence, is where sits Guy Hill, and then turns back to southerly environments where it doesn't stand a chance of freezing to death; so says my father, whom I dream of a lot. In fact, in one dream, he tells me a story that, over the years, has become one of my favourites.

One winter, a Cree community somewhere in the north decided to conclude its annual winter carnival with a pig roast, something the Chief of the village had seen in a movie at his residential school. "After John Wayne slaughters the Indians," claimed this Chief, "he celebrates his victory with a pig roast and corn." As there are no pigs in northern Canada, however, or corn for that matter, the community had to order both from Winnipeg. Pig roasts, though, involve young animals—piglets, that is to say, as opposed to adult pigs—this for reasons of time and volume (and probably of money). The Chief explained it this way: an adult pig would take one week to roast on a spit over an open fire, "which is the way of the pig roast in *Moony-ass* culture," and, a) the winter carnival lasted three days only, and, b) such a beast would feed three thousand people. For a village of three hundred people as this village was, it would take a year to eat it. "A piglet, by comparison," said the Chief, who was as eloquent as Moses reading the tablets, "will, a) take just twenty-four hours to cook, and, b) feed three hundred people nicely." Closing off his bestial expostulation with a chiefly flourish, he added: "There is no need for anyone to make a pig of themselves." *Ergo*, the piglet that arrived, live, on the Norseman the day before the carnival opened.

Four months of age according to estimates by Elders, band councillors, and the resident Anglican minister—for this was in northeastern Manitoba near its border with Ontario, where rule the

Anglicans—it was as cute as a button on an old man's coat. Never having seen a live *kookoos* before, much less a *kookoosis* (piglet), the people hadn't realized how cute they are. So cute, in fact, was this specimen that the entire community fell in love with it and thus couldn't bear to kill it much less cook it much less eat it. Instead, they decided to keep it as a pet, a sort of village mascot.

Accordingly, they put it in a shed where a bitch had given birth to eight puppies and a rabbit had survived two glacial winters. If it was warm enough for newborn puppies, went the theory, it was warm enough for piglets. It was not. The next morning, the beast was found frozen as hard as a piggy bank, said one eyewitness. He knew. He had "pinged" the rotund little corpse with a hooked index finger to prove his thesis. *Ping*, went the piglet, said this person. That's what happens to southern animals when they dare come north of the fifty-fourth parallel, says Joe Lapstan Highway inside this dream, there, in my dormitory bed at Guy Hill School.

Which is why I, Tomson Highway of Brochet, Manitoba, have never eaten pork to that point in time; bacon, yes, but roast pork, never. Or beef, for that matter. I will miss moose dearly but, from that day onward, *kookoos*—even if it has been slaughtered in Winnipeg and come north as chops—will be my diet.

19

One hundred boys and one hundred girls have now been installed as full-time residents at the Guy Hill Indian Residential School. I, of course, can't speak for the girls as we see them in class and at church only, two places not conducive to extended chatting, but the boys are divided into three categories, Small, Medium, and Big, a keeper keeping watch over each ("supervisor" too big a word for us, we call them "keepers"). Small Boys are aged five to eight, Medium nine to twelve, and Big thirteen to eighteen. The dormitories are organized accordingly. At my age, which is three months short of seven, I sleep in the Small Boys' dormitory on the second floor at the west end of the building. The Medium Boys, too, have their "dorm" on the second floor, though at its east end; that's where Daniel, aged ten, sleeps. As for the Big Boys, theirs is on the third floor right above the one for the Small Boys. With thirty-three boys in each dormitory, dreams will run amok—the thought excites me, for I love dreams.

But eighteen-year-olds in grades so low? At a school that teaches seven grades only? Because of the distances and nomadic lifestyle up north, starting school at age twelve is par for the course at this time, *if* one is even lucky enough to get to a school in the first place. Thus does the eighteen-year-old, hulking, glowering, and terrifying George Peter Buckskin of Pelican Narrows, Saskatchewan, to cite one example, tower over the grade seven classroom like Kinaws-koo Sophie Yazzie, back in Brochet, towers like a giant over her husband, Meat Toss.

Four-foot-high lockers line the entire back wall of the large, square room. One per boy, this is where we are to put our day clothes at night, our night clothes in daytime. Dressers unknown in our culture—as nomadic peoples forever on the go, we keep our clothes in packsacks—this will take some getting used to. The walls on both sides, meanwhile, are lined with windows the size of doors. From the perspective of us "Small Boys," they rise from our heads to a ceiling twelve feet high and stand so close to each other that they might as well be one continuous surface of glass and curtain mint-green in colour. If you stand on tiptoe, you can see Clearwater Lake in the near distance. To me, its emerald waters at night are a lullaby. Finally, little single beds lie like cookies on a cookie sheet in six rows of six with their bedspreads white, their pillowcases white, and their headframes of steel painted white. White, so omnipresent—walls and ceiling are also white—radiates a mix of enticement and menace, the former because those beds look inviting and I, when I first see them, am tired; the latter because the colour imparts to the room the air of a hospital—Mom said that everything at hers in Ninette was white—and all that stands for, death not least. Luckily, the sunlight beaming in anoints my spirit, thus dispersing to the elements such sombre thoughts.

We are given numbers, Boy Number One to Boy Number One Hundred. Boy Number One is the oldest and largest, Boy Number One Hundred the youngest and smallest. From what I understand, this is done for the purpose of keeping track of each and every item of clothing and sporting equipment that belongs to each boy: shoes, socks, underwear, pants, shirts, jackets, parkas, mitts, tuques, skates, hockey sweaters, hockey pads, hockey sticks, not to mention beds, lockers, chairs in the dining hall, desks in the classroom, pews in the chapel. Each number hand-printed in black ink on a white cloth label the size of a stamp for sending a letter, it is then sewn on by the kind Mrs. Rasmussen and her resident sidekick, this dwarf-sized nun we call Sister Tiny. If I try, for example, to identify which pair of socks or underwear belongs to me when Gilbert Hell (Small Boy Number Ninety-five), Chally Canoe (Number Ninety-four), Jericho Zah

(Number Ninety), and a dozen other boys wear the same size and colour, I need that number. If I don't have it and I end up wearing Boy Number Eighty-nine's underwear (Michael Mitaas of South Indian Lake), I risk catching gymnasia. Even our names are impossible for staff to remember, especially at the start of the school year. All this by way of saying that we are given numbers not because we are criminals in prison or beasts in cages but because we need them to identify our socks of which, of course, there are two per boy making for a total of two hundred socks.

One keeper's bedroom abuts the Big Boys' dormitory on the third floor while another stands flanked by the Medium and Small Boys' dormitories on the second, tray-sized windows with curtains giving them eye access to the respective sleeping quarters for which they are guardians. Having no night-watch duty, the third keeper apparently sleeps elsewhere; where that is, I don't know.

That September of 1958, I am given the number Ninety-nine which means, of course, that I am the second smallest *and* the second youngest boy in the line of one hundred. Only one boy is smaller and younger. Freddy Begay is Dene, comes from Churchill on the Hudson's Bay coast, and looks like a doll with his porcelain skin, his coat-button eyes, his turned-up nose, and his tight black curls, as if Louise has just done his hair with her Carnation-milk-can curlers. Sleeping in the bed next to mine at the far end of the very back row, he thus qualifies as Boy Number One Hundred. And as he is Dene, Freddy Begay speaks that language only. Fortunately, I, though Cree, speak some Dene, grace of my parents and their network of Dene friends and neighbours such as Henry Beksaka and Adoo-naazay. Meaning to say that this Freddy Begay and I are able to speak to each other after a manner.

"*T'laa-nit-heh?*" ("How are you?") I whisper to him under cover of moonlight across the foot-wide aisle that separates his bed from mine which, now that I think back to it, is not much bigger than a cradle.

"*Asawn-ti-leh*" ("Fine"), he answers. "*Koona-aan?*" ("And you?")

"*Sits-yay-nay*" ("My friend"), I answer, and smile shyly. As neither of us speaks one word of English—or French or *Chaariman*, for that matter—this language-in-common is a god-send.

And normally, I sleep well. I have, after all, my own bed, am not squished in with Rene and Daniel on a single mattress with their stinky feet on either side of my head. With the crisp clean sheets and central heating, I am in heaven; no bannock frozen rock-solid in the morning, no freezing outhouse to go to. Lights out and I'm gone. Tonight, however, I'm not. No matter what I do—counting caribou as they leap over a rock, naming Alec and Geraldine Fitzgerald's eighteen children over and over—I toss and turn. I am upset. I am unhappy. Even in the dark, my face glows red with embarrassment, I am sure of it. Why?

In class that morning, Sister St. Louie de Montfort gives me a box the size of a deck of playing cards and a magazine—"scribbler," she calls it—with pictures on its pages drawn in ink, black with the insides blank, what the *Moony-ass* would call "pen-and-ink" drawings. The box contains eight paper-wrapped sticks of wax all different in colour. Never having seen such *maameek* wonders, I sit there thinking—*What now?* Fortunately, every member of that grade one class is likewise perplexed—all have these sticks, all these books. Finished handing out her school-marmish bounty, the nun swishes her nunnish way back to the front of the classroom and tries to demonstrate her vaunted scenario. No one understands. All sit stumped. One breath from angry, the big, black rosary that hangs from her waist like a skipping rope clicks and clatters as she zooms to each desk one after the other, illustrating her instructions with clucks and waves of her pale thin hands, her black robe rustling, her white skin smelling like laundry soap.

We get her message. Pick one page from the colouring book, for colouring book this apparently is, and apply these sticks—"crayons," she calls them—to the drawings. Grabbing a crayon from Kipoots McDonald of Pelican Narrows, Saskatchewan, Sister St. Louie de Montfort slashes one of his pages with a blood-red streak and raises it for all to ogle. Cowed, embarrassed to the quick, Kipoots McDonald starts colouring a house. Red. Opal Mobster of Nelson House, Manitoba, picks a flower and starts colouring it purple. Freddy Begay picks the sun and starts colouring it yellow. I can see them all from my desk. So I, Tomson Highway, pick a dog. Or rather, Sister St. Louie de Montfort picks him for me.

"Cat," she says, putting her index finger on it.

"Cat," I say. What an interesting name for a dog, I say to myself; I have never heard it. Nor have I ever seen a dog that looks like this, with its pointed ears and its long, thin tail deprived completely of curly *oopee-waya* ("hair," of an animal as opposed to a human). She pulls a crayon from the box and puts it in my right hand. I take it. I hold it uncertainly between my thumb and index finger. Guiding my hand, she applies the tip of the crayon to the creature.

"Cat," she repeats. And mumbles something. If I understand correctly, I am to apply this crayon to this animal and start colouring it like the other students are colouring their houses, flowers, and suns.

This dog named Cat wears a collar. I know what I'll do. I will use two different colours on either side of the collar thus revealing my colouring instincts to this nun who, it seems, is blind to my angst. She will be astonished. She won't know what hit her.

I go to work. From the collar up, I apply the black crayon, the one she has given me. From the collar down, I apply the brown. This will be a two-toned dog, I decide. Then, putting my elbows on my little wooden desk, I study my handiwork. It looks wrong. Dreadfully wrong. Who on Earth has ever seen a dog with a black head and brown body? I ask myself. Would a dog not then be as upset as I am?

I am mortified. The last thing I want is for anyone to see my freakish-looking *atim* (dog), least of all the teacher. I will be the laughing stock of the class. Worse, with the woman's twelve-inch ruler sitting so visibly across her desk, I will be spanked. Furtively wetting my right forefinger with a gob of saliva, I apply it to the dog's head and start rubbing, try to undo its ghastly blackness my objective. It looks worse. The colour runs. I take the brown crayon and try to overlay the black with its stain so that the animal's body and head will match. It is even worse. Wax in black and brown and sticky saliva mix and mingle and run and splatter this way and that with the result that, horrors, the dog has transformed into a *Weetigo*, the man-eating monster of Cree mythology. My first encounter with visual art and I want to die, right there in that classroom.

In bed that night beside Freddy Begay, I finally find sleep but it is a fitful one, one just inches from waking. And in that space between sleep and awakeness, the disembodied heads of fifteen dogs who are actually cats, as I learn later, are lunging and lunging at me, their white teeth flashing, their claws extended.

And that, my friends, is my grade one.

20

Ours, by and large, is a net-fishing culture, doubly so in the two months of summer when I am home from school and reunited with Rene. And, oh, what joy that is. It thus makes sense that our diet should be governed by the lifestyle and industry. In July and August, that is to say, we eat fish. And lots of it. Dad might kill a moose—a chance encounter as one, for example, is swimming across some channel, he motoring by on his way home from his nets; Swanson might shoot some ducks, if he happens on a flock while cruising for a spot that teems with pickerel. And Daniel might get a ptarmigan while out woodcutting. But such happenstances are rare, so fish on the menu is a daily reality.

An overkill on fish, some might say—but not us. And this for three reasons. Reason number one is the sheer variety. Not only do we have recourse to whitefish and pickerel and trout and pike and even the lowly sucker; they come—reason number two—from the clearest, cleanest waters in all God's Kingdom one mere hour before we eat them. Meaning to say that the flesh of the fish we eat is pure, untouched by toxins. And reason number three? Balazee Highway's genius with fire.

Never have you seen a human being, male or female, work with fire in a manner so unbuttoned, so fiercely inventive. Once it's going, she tends it with a stick not much bigger than a twig. She pokes this piece of wood, she pokes another and another until the flames are moving, *and* of a size to her satisfaction. One size of flame, for example, is for the boiling of fish, whole or in sections with, of course, the obligatory condiments. Another is for grilling it on a stake made of willow until the skin snaps and crackles; another for poaching, for frying, for smoking, for baking bannock "the outdoor way." For this last, she waits for the flames to die completely so all that remains are coals, red-hot and glowing. If you try to bake your bannock in any other way, she insists to us children, it will burn to a cinder, "pitch-black, inedible."

Still, there is a problem—how to feed very young children all that fish without their choking to their deaths on a bone for, as who doesn't know, hundreds of bones make up the skeleton of God's good creature. And that's precisely what happens to Rene one day the summer he is four, I seven and home for the summer following my first year at residential school.

Barbers up north, like hairdressers, are non-existent; regardless of their skills in the cutting of hair, people cut each other's. That summer I am seven, for example, we are living on an island in Zangeza Bay, some thirty-five miles behind Brochet and that spectacular, mile-long, wild-raspberry-strewn sandbar called Thigh Daddy. So if Louise has proven her skills as hairdresser-at-large with something as simple as Carnation milk cans, it only makes sense that she take on the role of barber-at-large to the Highway clan. This one day, Mom has decided that it is time for Rene and me to get our haircuts. From Louise. I go first.

Perched on an aluminum water pail turned upside down three yards from the main tent's entrance, an errant square of cotton on my shoulders and around my neck to serve me as cape to catch cut hair, I sit there poised for the onslaught. Mom's sewing scissors gleaming in her right hand, her large, pink plastic comb clutched in her left, Louise starts snipping. *Snip, snip, snip. Snip, snip, snip.* My hair is getting shorter. Tufts of hair fall on my cape and on the ground around me. *Snip, snip, snip.*

Meanwhile, Rene and his toy-like salt-and-pepper yapper, Itchy, are running tight circles around our feet. Rene's objective? To catch Itchy. Itchy's objective? To catch Rene. No one will win, so much is evident. I have no mirror so have no way of telling just how my hair-cut is progressing. But, within ten minutes, Louise snips off the last of what she feels is unwanted hair then whips off the cape and shakes it, commands me to stand, and tells me I look like her hero, Elvis Presley. My patience, she adds as a footnote, has been impressive. For a Cree boy of seven? Worthy of mention in books, she adds, perhaps even movies.

Not so with a certain four-year-old named Rene Highway. He sits on the pail, gets draped with the cape, and grits his teeth—he hates haircuts. *Snip, snip, snip,* go the scissors. He shifts and twists. He moans. Sitting on her rump at her little master's feet, Itchy watches him with mounting concern. *Snip, snip, snip.* Louise continues. Rene shifts slightly. He moans. Itchy whimpers. Louise continues. *Snip, snip, snip.*

"*Igwaani naa?*" inquires the victim after three minutes. ("Is that it?")

"*Neeee,*" says Louise, bemused. "I just got started." Rene moans. Itchy whimpers. *Snip, snip, snip.*

Two minutes later, Rene inquires, "*Igwaani naa?*"

"*Neeee, maati keetha!*" ("Oh, pul-leaze.") Two more times, Rene asks the question. Louise's response to both inquiries? "*Maati kaatha waskawee,*" said very sharply, almost barked. ("Will you please not move!")

Finally, Rene can't take it. He hops off the pail. Cape or none, he doesn't care. He just goes running, first into the main tent and out—running circles is his favourite activity—Itchy at his heels like an *oopas-choosoos.* With the right side of his head just shorn to a brush cut, the left still sporting a mop three inches long, the four-year-old fugitive looks utterly ridiculous. As with a Raggedy Ann doll, "lop-sided" is the word. He doesn't see, he doesn't care.

"*Aastam,*" barks Louise. ("Come here.")

"*Waapaagi n'si,*" answers Rene. ("Tomorrow. We'll finish tomor-row.")

"*Seemaak!*" barks Louise. ("Right now!")

"*Waapaagi!*" repeats Rene. And, the cape still hanging from his neck and billowing like a comic-book superhero's, the little Superman flies into the forest to throw sticks at squirrels, Itchy yapping after him. Swearing bloody murder with her scissors, Louise pursues him. Twice she catches him in the brambles but both times loses him to writhing and wriggling of a genre not seen east of Thigh Daddy since the night Zebedee Zipper married Ice-keemee Minette and begat the first of what would be twenty-one children. And the brown boy disappears, swallowed by the forest as by a spirit. All we hear is the cawing of crows, Itchy's intermittent yapping, and that forest sighing.

At dinner that night, Rene squatting between me and Mom, we are eating fish. Trout caught that evening in Reindeer Lake. An *arababoo* of trout poached with years of experience in a broth with onions and peeled potatoes and rice and salt and pepper and, tonight, small chunks of bacon, it is spectacular. The conversation is convivial if somewhat sparse, silence, after all, having always been a part of North American Indigenous verbal communication.

"Did you like school?" asks Rene.

"Yes," I answer. "But I missed you."

The *arababoo* is being served from its pot inside the main tent on a bed made of spruce boughs spread out on the floor, we, the diners, all kneeling or squatting around it. In fact, there are two trout, enough for seven people and one dog: Mom, Dad, Louise, Florence, Danny, me, Rene, and Itchy. Cleansed of their entrails, Mom has cut them into eight and served them accordingly. The boiled fish itself sits on the spruce boughs, the soup served in bowls on the side. Mine has the head because Mom knows my weakness for trout cheeks, Rene the tail because it is the smallest piece, his the smallest stomach.

"What did you learn?" asks Dad.

"I learned to count," I say, "in English."

Using thumb and forefinger like we all do, Rene plucks small pieces of flesh from the fish, puts them in his mouth with ginger agility, and munches away. In Cree culture, we use no forks, not in those days. His cute half-haircut bobbing up and down and shimmying back and forth from left side to right, Rene is enjoying himself most royally, Itchy sitting on her rump to his left, wagging her tail like one would a feather.

"*Agee-taasoo*," says Mom to me. "*Eeya-gatha-seemoo-yin*." ("Count. In English.")

"*Aahow*," I say ("okay"). "One, two, three . . ."

"Ho-*ho*!" goes Dad, impressed quite rightly. I beam proudly.

Rene, meanwhile, is on the point of dropping a morsel on his dog's pink tongue which hangs anticipating delights from heaven when, suddenly, he chokes, falls back, and starts caterwauling.

Squatting to his right—strategically positioned, that is to say, in case something of the sort should accost her baby—Mom leaps into action. She grabs him, clamps her left hand on the nape of his neck, and pulls him forward. Forcing his mouth open with her right hand, she holds her fingers together so she can plunge them as deep as she can into his throat. Which she does with fearsome dexterity. Once down the passage, she roots around inside it as if she were Itchy digging for bones.

Rene, meanwhile, is choking and gurgling and gasping and hyperventilating, incapable of breathing, turning all sorts of colours. His arms akimbo like a Norseman taking off, they shake and tremble and thrash and gyrate, Itchy going lunatic with her barking, right there at the dinner table, such as it is. Finding the bone her sworn objective before her son dies, Mom pulls it out in two seconds flat, throws it to the side of the spruce-bough table (it and everything on it biodegradable), and throws Rene back as if he were a piece of *machig-wanaas* ("dirt," a common expression in Cree).

"Next!" you can almost hear her say. Hey, if *you* had twelve children, you would do the same. Like Balazee Highway, you would have no time for beating around the proverbial bush.

Then, wiping her hand on a moistened dishrag, she goes back to eating. The incident takes seconds. Rene, meanwhile, kneels there reeling, the breath knocked out of him. His eyes glazed over, he looks transformed, as by a vision.

And *that*'s how Balazee Highway deals with fish bones. She did it with all of us when we were small, Vi, Swanson, Louise, Florence, Daniel—for they tell the stories—including, later, her grandchildren of whom there are dozens upon dozens; I remember well my own such experience at age four years.

As for Louise, she takes it all in stride. But remarks politely that this is poetic justice, punishment for Rene for his having refused to let her finish his haircut. The lesson well learned, our adored baby brother with the coat-button eyes, the tan complexion, and the cupid-bow lips lets her finish her job early next morning. But refuses to eat fish for the next three days.

21

Natural forces such as wind and water betray their own rhythms, their own personalities. Those of sub-Arctic Canada are no different. As with humans, their moods are volatile: friends one day, killers another. In fact, we can never tell which mood they will bless or blast us with from one day to the next. So what are we to do but roll with the punches? Here's one mood . . .

The first three weeks of August are known for their beauty. No wind, no rain, no mosquitoes, the temperature exquisite. By its last week, however, the fall winds have come and the temperature plunges. Augurs announcing the advent of autumn, they whip the water into waves so gigantic they look like churches coming to get you for not confessing all your sins to Father Cadeau, they are that scary. On the wide-open stretches of Reindeer Lake where there are no islands to paddle to for refuge or hide behind from such Leviathans, you risk losing your life.

As with all cultures that live with water, drownings are as common as is death by car in urban realities. Alfoos Zipper (my mother's younger brother, one of six), Stanley Kamaa-magoos, Paul Peter Beksaka, John Kipawm, Pierre Fitzgerald, Isidore Hatchet, then eighteen, and his bride, Marianne, then sixteen and pregnant with their first child, the list goes on. Even one September, Dad's entire team of sled dogs, all eight of them devoured by insatiable, omnivorous Reindeer Lake, their bodies never found. In the case of Stanley

Kamaa-magoos and Paul Peter Beksaka, who were fishing together this one summer, their bodies were discovered washed up on a beach behind House Point some fifteen miles west of Brochet. Stark-naked and frozen rock-solid, they had swum ashore and tried, in vain—in October? in the midst of snow flurries? with no dry matches?—to dry their clothes. And to think that, even with such lessons, no one— not us children, not the elderly—wears a life jacket. The life jacket? Lockhart brought it to Reindeer Lake for his Arctic Lodge guests in the summer of 1958. Strictly for *Keechi-moogoo-maanak* (Americans), we don't even have a word for the object, not in Cree, not in Dene.

At camps, on the other hand, such winds have been known to blow tents down. Seasonal family domiciles the size of small houses, the main tent especially—where sleep our parents and, when it rains, where we eat—is sometimes as much as ten yards long, six yards wide, and six feet high, virtually a tent that can accommodate a circus, if a small one. The men out minding the nets on any given day, it is generally just us children and the women there to tend to home fires. Which is what we're doing when, out of nowhere, a wind appears and, like a starving animal, attacks our tent. Suddenly, the canvas dwelling is trembling to the point where we, its occupants, believe it is perfectly capable of being ripped from its moorings and flying to the barrens. Which is all Mom needs to leap into action.

Flinging aside the moccasin she is chewing to make it pointy, she jumps to her feet and grabs, at its middle, the central beam that serves as spine to the structure. An unpeeled spruce log propped up by two other spruce logs standing vertical at the tent's front and back ends, this beam hovers just short of six feet above ground level. At five foot three and standing on tiptoe, Mom can barely reach it (and Rene and I are as yet too short to help her). At eight inches thick and ten yards long, the beam also has a weight that matches its bulk. For one small woman to withstand its might is one tall order; if it falls, the whole tent collapses, and Mom well knows it. Worse, if that beam falls on someone's head, especially boys of four and seven, it kills them. To lose her sons to this bastard of a current of sub-Arctic flat-ulence? Out of the question.

The wind now grown to tornado proportions, it swoops and screams. And that beam shakes and trembles something terrible and the canvas material shakes and trembles something terrible and Balazee Highway shakes and trembles something terrible. Her arms held up above her head, her wiry frame vibrating like a string on a fiddle, she clutches that beam like no beam on Earth has ever been clutched before. And as she does, she shrieks at us, "*wathaweek, wathaweek*" ("get out, get out!"). Accordingly, Rene and I (and Itchy) go stumbling our way out the one door, our hands held over our heads as protection.

Once safely outside, we stand there buffeted and lashed and torn like scraps of paper, clinging to trees, to branches, to whatever object we can get our hands on, the roar infernal. All as we watch our tent engage in a dance that rivals in athletic virility the one danced by Satan and the archangel Michael on that dreadful day.

Fortunately, the stakes of willow that anchor its borders are sunk so deeply into the soil that they don't budge.

We watch that structure shake and shake and shake and shake. Until, like a punctured balloon, it all comes down, tent, beam, and mother. And the whole structure lies there with the stove (unlit, thank God) and bed and grub box and, yes, Balazee Highway betraying their shapes like lumps in pudding, those shapes, for now, eerily inanimate. All that moves is the canvas of the tent, which flaps and ripples in a wind that will not stop. What now? Is Mom dead? Killed by the beam she has fought so bravely?

But no, there is movement. Like Sylvester the Cat (I will think some two years later) crawling under a carpet to sneak up on lunch, the songbird Tweety, Mom's cat-like form comes snaking and weaving its way through the crumple of flapping and rippling canvas until her head pops out the only door. Alive, unbowed, her hairdo a mess, she looks at us with an expression that says, "*Cheest?*" ("You see?") "I told you I could do it." Her eyes crossed slightly, she is seeing chickadees flying little circles around her head (she tells us later).

———

Then there are the times when the wind strikes a medium between such violence and calm inviolate, and boats rock like cradles on three-inch-high waves. No risk here of inundation, capsizing, or some such ghastly, undreamt-of disaster.

It isn't every summer that we live in such a way, where a bush plane comes to get our fish and flies it to Lynn Lake. That happens, for the most part, only when we live on a lake away up north. But when we don't, when, that is, we live on Reindeer Lake, we sometimes use canoe transport to take our fish to this little depot on an island just off the mainland on its east side. Called Jack Pine Island, it floats halfway between Brochet and Kinoosao and, again—as with everything in our northern lives—just inside Manitoba from its border with Saskatchewan. A tiny village of perhaps one hundred—though in summer only—Jack Pine harbours a summer business owned and operated by a pot-bellied *Moony-ass* named Ingmar Stoleberg. Enamoured of the north and liked by his customers, this Stoleberg buys fish from Native fishermen on Reindeer Lake then has them flown on a bush plane to Lynn Lake daily. Some of these fishermen live with their families, in tents, of course, right there at Jack Pine. But most live on islands scattered hither and thither. We, the Highways, are of the latter persuasion, at least that summer. So, living as we are at our own encampment some two dozen miles west of Jack Pine, Dad takes his fish there at least twice weekly. And normally, he takes Daniel as his assistant. Sometimes, however—and for whatever reason—he takes me instead.

The trip to Jack Pine is always fun. For one thing, you get to see Stoleberg's little store and buy a chocolate bar. Our business with Stoleberg finished this particular day—our fish sold, our payment collected (in cash), our groceries bought—Dad and I start for the unnamed island on which we are living that summer. For some reason that I don't remember, we get held up at our starting point so we leave late, so late, in fact, that it is dark by the time we are halfway home. The boat now bare but for empty fish crates, a box of groceries, and sundry items, Dad stops the boat somewhere in "mid-flight" and rolls a goose-down sleeping robe out on the floor at the bow and puts me there well-wrapped and warm. Then restarts our ten-horsepower outboard motor.

So there I am at age seven years, enveloped completely by piles of goose down, gazing sleepily at a cloudless sky with its trillion stars and faint pulsations of silver light, a hundred stripes standing parallel and reaching to Orion, the lonely hunter. It is *waawaa-steewak*, the northern lights, the north's great miracle. Being sung a lullaby by the drone of the motor accompanied by the sibilance of water lapping at the boat, the rocking cradle I find myself in that August night bestows on me a sense of security that will last me a lifetime.

When I think back to it, even the fact that I am a "girl" does not faze Dad. He sees me playing "girlie" games—putting on Mom's apron, for example, and pretending it's a skirt—but, to him, it makes no difference, even when he sees the "macho" Fitzgerald boys at old Brochet's Companeek store mocking me. Where too many men would beat the woman out of their effeminate boys to turn them into "men," thus destroying the lives of those boys, the lives of their families and, most blindly, their own, the world's most athletic, most masculine man, world-champion dogsled racer Joe Lapstan Highway, loves me even more.

And here's a third mood, Reindeer Lake at its most stunning at this, the most spectacular month of the sub-Arctic year, August.

If travel by dogsled in Canada's north is slow and exquisite beyond compare, then travel by canoe is not much faster and just as beautiful. Even with the Johnson ten-horsepower outboard motors that everyone has on Reindeer Lake in the 1950s, crossing one hundred miles in just one day is unheard of. When you factor in the loads we pack those boats with—four to eight children (depending on the family), worldly belongings from tents to mattresses and pots and pans and stoves and axes, sled dogs, guns, you name it—we are lucky if we cross one-quarter that distance in that time period. In such circumstances, it is not all that much faster, when one thinks of it, than the paddled canoes that served our forebears.

Attached to the stern of our sawed-off canoes, those little red-and-white Johnson *peewaap-swka* (motors) chug merrily along like toys in bathtubs, thus giving us the pleasure, if inadvertently, of a panorama unrivalled in beauty as in detail. Each swirl in the water challenges visual intelligence, each *waaskee-choos* (cone) on each pine tree on each island we pass a possible participant in some narrative as yet to be written. The point here being: with those motors, crossing the seventy-five miles from Brochet to Doodneek or Koowap may take two days, but they are days of pleasure that make, for example, an overnight stay on an island obligatory. In tents. For us small children—in fact, for everyone, Dad including—it is adventure of the sort seen only in dreams.

But what can confound a situation already snail-like in speed to begin with is the rare occasion when our little runt of a motor breaks down somewhere. A spark plug goes, an air valve clogs up and the tool to unclog it goes somehow missing. Sooner or later, it happens to everyone. (Even Chaggy-wat Mooraah of Southend, Saskatchewan, a man much admired for his insight into and instincts about mechanical dyslexia, is smitten by the curse on two known occasions.) In which case we are forced to cross the remainder of whatever distance by dint of paddling. In which case, it can take us five or six days to accomplish the crossing from Brochet to Koowap. Which means that we have to camp out on at least four islands one after the other after the other, islands that we would otherwise never have stopped at, *and* that we have so much time to feast our eyes on the movement of water, our ears on the music of birdsong, that we could write books on the subjects and sell them in bookstores. We even see *kinoosees-sak* (minnows) glimmering like pinpricks of light just under the ripples set off by our paddles. It is more than adventure, it is meditation. It is a miracle. And it is just such a crossing of Reindeer Lake this one night that illustrates in spades this salient point. And that gives me one of my most indelible, and precious, of childhood memories.

It is late August just before the winds and the waves of September arrive. Late this one night, the stillness of both air and water is such that one can hear the leaves of birch trees breathing, fish fins plying through water. I don't remember the details but our motor, for some reason, has broken down and, whatever he does, Dad can't fix it. So here we are, caught in the middle of Reindeer Lake in the middle of the night without motorized propulsion: Mom at the bow, Dad at the stern with, in a row between them, Rene at four, me seven, Daniel eleven, Florence fifteen, and Louise nineteen. Having been home for two months from my first year at school, Florence, Daniel, and I will be leaving in two days to go back, I for my second year. And, though I love my Reindeer Lake with a passion, I hunger still for a new year of learning. I hunger still to live out Dad's dreams for me.

We are paddling, in any case, across that much-feared five-mile stretch of wide-open water that divides Boundary Island in Manitoba from Porcupine Point in Saskatchewan. Not one island far as the naked eye can penetrate, certainly not at night. And as the sky is clear, the stars out in numbers so extreme they blind people who look at them beyond five minutes as once happened, claims Masky Jimmy Perkins, to an old Dene woman named Chooch Sag-way Marie Antoinette Inik Win-aaree Rogers (who had married a *Moony-ass* from *maameek*, which is why her last name).

Rene and I are sleeping like teddy bears at the bottom of the boat, cushioned *and* covered more than amply by a goose-down sleeping robe, duck-down pillows under our heads. And we are dreaming. At least I am. In fact, I am dreaming about none other than the star-crossed Chooch Sag-way Marie Antoinette Inik Win-aaree Rogers who, in my dream, is just getting her eyesight back by means of some unprecedented technique of eyeball-transplant operation somewhere down in far *maameek* from whence comes her husband, Roy Rogers, and his twin brother, Ray Rogers, when, suddenly, I hear a voice.

"*Anima n'si*," says this voice. "*Iskootao*." ("Look. A fire.") I wake up. It's Florence. I open my eyes. Her silhouette to me, she is sitting upright a foot in front of me. And she is looking out into the distance and pointing a finger through the wash of starlight at some campfire on some far island. It might even be that of the shaman, Oos-eye Naapao (Yellow Man) Hatchet, conducting a ritual to honour the eagles, the bears, and the spirits. Louise likes to mutter about the hoary old codger for Oos-eye Naapao is not exactly her favourite person, certainly not her favourite shaman. As for Florence's posture, movements, and voice, I am only vaguely aware of them, the light being dim, I still on the threshold between child-sleep and dream.

What catches my eye hangs high above me. There, ten trillion miles into that night sky shine ten trillion stars, the arc of the dome they hang from flawless in its roundness, the only sound a ripple—paddles dipping in Reindeer Lake, water swirling in response to their movement, then sliding back out, dipping in, swirling, sliding back out . . . As by a magnet, the silver light that is that sky reaches down for me, grabs my heart and, by such means, pulls me up to a sitting position. And there in the water all around the drifting canoe and stretching out into infinity is the exact same dome of ten trillion stars, a perfect reflection of the night sky above . . .

But for that moment when I, in essence, am still half-sleeping, still half-dreaming, we are floating, my family and I, through the heart of this gigantic sphere made exclusively of the purest, most perfect of silver lights, Wynken and Blynken and Nod sailing off in a wooden shoe to some far country, as a song I learned in grade one last spring goes. And I know then, at age seven, that no matter what happens to me in life, I will float through the "orb" of that privileged life, float, that is, through the heart of the universe in a little magic boat illuminated by *achaag-wak* a trillion strong. (*Achaag-wak* has two meanings: "stars" and "spirits.")

22

A typical day at the Guy Hill Indian Residential School goes like this . . .

We rise at seven. Though most keepers rouse us in a manner considerate enough, Mr. Laflamme has this infuriating manner of turning the lights on and singing at top volume, a song that starts, "Oh, what a beautiful morning!" He thinks he is being funny but I don't. I might enjoy it if his voice were pleasant but it isn't. I groan but rise. Together with the other thirty-two boys for whom the Small Boys' dormitory is home for the year, I shuffle to my locker and grab my towel, then cross the corridor to enter the washroom, of which there are two: one with the toilets and urinals, the other with the sinks and mirrors. With a quarter of the boys, I line up at the toilets, of which there are four, while the second quarter lines up at the urinals, of which there are two. As for the two other quarters, they go to the washroom with the sinks, of which there are eight against one wall, with mirrors above them, and eight against the wall facing opposite. All thirty-three boys having accomplished their morning ablutions, the two halves switch and, bingo, I am ready for the next step in life *schooleek* (at school). As for the shower room, which is situated between the room with the toilets and the room with the sinks, we use it twice weekly only, in the evening, in shifts of eight.

I walk back to my locker to change into day clothes. An institutional uniform of sorts, our clothes are long-sleeved plaid flannel shirts in red, blue, and turquoise, blue denim coveralls, and canoe shoes. Canoe shoes? Commercially manufactured, commercial-leather, moccasin-type slippers as comfortable as they are practical and which look like canoes. Hence the name we give them. Finished dressing, I return to my bed to make it, then follow the line downstairs to the "playroom"—our word for gymnasium, much kinder for a Cree, so we have decided—where we have twenty minutes of free time. Wrestling like puppies is a favourite for the Small Boys; the Big Boys prefer to read the comic books they have found somewhere, loafing on gym mattresses, ten or so of which are piled in a corner. But I play tag with Chally Canoe, a boy from Nelson House, Manitoba, whom I've taken a liking to, as he to me. But then the keeper-on-shift blows the whistle that all three keepers, when on duty, wear suspended from a shoelace around their necks, to catch our attention. At this time of day, that whistle means breakfast. Responding to the summons, I jump into the queue for the grade two boys at the centre of the room (for there is one queue for each of the seven grades).

This year, an American man serves as one of the Small Boys' keepers. Come to Canada following a stint in his country's armed forces (he tells us), he takes great pleasure in passing his training on to his charges.

"Ten hut!" he barks and I, with one hundred boys, snap to attention. "At ease," he says, and I stand at ease, my feet splayed out, my arms loose and hanging behind me with left hand wrapped around right wrist. "Ten hut!" he barks again and I snap back, rigid. He blows his whistle—for the fourth time that day, far from the last—and off I march together with another hundred boys in one straight line as Ten Hut counts, "Hup, two, three, four." My arms swinging and my legs moving like scissors, I march down the corridor and into the dining hall where waits my breakfast. I never do learn what the words "ten hut" mean and why he says them, but with my non-existent English, how could I? All I know is that in no time flat, the man earns the nickname "Ten Hut." To this day, I don't know his name, first or last.

Just inside the entrance to this second enormous room that is our dining hall but which, for some reason, is called a "refectory," stand six tall structures of stainless steel with shelving units and wheels the size of Oreo cookies. Actually trolleys for holding trays, we call them "trucks." Like the boys in the line before me, I take one tray and inch my way on.

Next comes a counter made of four parallel, ten-foot-long, stainless-steel cylinders, across which I slide my empty tray. Behind that counter sit industrial-sized pots steaming with porridge. Big Boys dressed in white cotton aprons serve it with ladles. As condiments? Scoops of brown sugar and milk, and bread with margarine and jam and an orange. And off I go to my numbered seat at the rows of tables to eat in silence. No longer the smallest or youngest, I am, this year, Boy Number Eighty-six. As for Freddy Begay, he has disappeared. Quit school? Stayed in Churchill? I don't know.

For now, I am too busy missing Rene to miss this Freddy. Again had I said good-bye to my little brother before leaving home in September, but "next year, you'll come with me, I am sure of it," I said to him on the Companeek dock as I wiped off his tears, as he mine, and got on that plane.

Then come chores. Each of the four higher grades gets one that lasts one month and then rotates on to the next. Collecting used dishes in the trucks and wheeling them into the kitchen, there to be washed by the older girls, sweeping the floor in the refectory, sweeping the floor in the playroom. The most coveted chore is serving the food, the one least liked cleaning the toilets. For now, however, the first three grades are absolved of chores; we are too small.

While this is going on, we grades ones, twos, and threes have just enough time to rush to our lockers in the playroom, jump into our winter clothing, run outside, and fight with snowballs or, on tobog-gans provided by the school, slide down the slope that connects the level of the parking lot at the front of the school to the boys' play-ground, which lies some three feet lower. Or, in autumn and spring, I like playing marbles with Chally Canoe in the gravel that the entire yard, which is as large as Moomoos Island and enclosed by a steel mesh fence, has for cover, as with a carpet. I will win all of Chally's marbles from him—for this, in essence, is a gambling game we play—and save them for Rene. Then Ten Hut blows his whistle for the tenth time that day and off we rush, Chally and I, back into the building to whip off our winter apparel and jump back into the grade two line for yet another march, though this time up the stairs that lead to the classrooms.

From nine to ten, I receive instruction in spelling. My grade two teacher is this kind woman named Miss Menard. She comes from a farm near Winnipeg. Single, in her twenties, heavy-set, she is homely, with black hair curled and bobbed and wrists so chubby they hide her watch so that, when she needs to see the time, she has to tweak the folds of fat apart and squint. Still, she loves us.

"D-O-G," she prints in large letters with chalk on a blackboard that stretches from one end of the front wall to the other, ending at the long row of windows that look out to the waves of Clearwater Lake. Finished, she points at the first of the three letters with a pointer made of wood. "Repeat after me," she says, "Deeee." Greek to us but we try. Mimicking the movement of her lips, teeth, and tongue, we manage. Or seem to.

"Deeee," I say in unison with another twenty-nine students, both male and female, aged seven to ten. She makes us repeat it until we get it. Satisfied, she points at the next letter.

"Owe," she says.

"Owe," I say. And again I practice, "Owe, owe, owe."

"G"—Miss Menard goes on to the next, and last, in the line of three letters.

"G," I say. And I practice. "Jee, jee, jee." Then she leads us through the pronunciation of the word formed by these three letters.

"Dog," she says, helped, of course, by her pointer on the black-board. *Chip, chip, chip,* goes the pointer.

"Dawg," I say with the others, though I am stumped. A letter Miss Menard has just told us is pronounced as "owe" is, all of a sudden, pronounced as "awe"? I don't get it. And then there's the "g." We have just pronounced it, several times, as in "jeep," and now it's pronounced "gaw" as in "god"? Unfortunately, the language barrier stops me from asking why there is such contradiction.

"Dog," Miss Menard soldiers on unbowed, unapologetic.

"Dawg," we follow, as docile as fish, for that's how we hear it.

"Dog."

"Dawg." Then she makes us scrawl the word into our "scrib-blers," as she calls the books she has given us, which, for us, is a tall order. In fact, it takes me twenty minutes—seven minutes and twenty seconds per letter all told. And all through a process where we squeeze blood, sweat, and tears out of our pencils and wrists, the question that rings inside my head is: What on Earth is a "dawg"? *Kichitaw Maaree* must have heard me for, at this juncture, Miss Menard waddles to her desk at the front, plucks from its surface a large sheet of paper, and shows it to us. Wonder of wonders, it is a picture. Of a dog.

We encounter the same problem with "see." "Ess" as a letter; "sss" when used in a word. "The," surprisingly, is easy, for it sounds like the "th" in *kaatha* (Cree for "don't").

The complete sentence Miss Menard has just printed out with chalk on that blackboard? "See the dog," whose meaning we will learn the next day as, at just that moment, Miss Menard reaches into her desk and pulls out a bell as shiny and silvery as Father Cadeau's chalice at St. Pierre Church. And she rings it and rings it. And it is recess. The girls march out one classroom door of two, the boys out the other.

Back in the playroom, I play tag with Ernest Kipawm. Half Cree, half Inuit and from Brochet—his aunt, in fact, is Ice-keemee Minette—he runs faster than me. We run here, we run there, we run and run and run, all over the room, whooping and hollering, until Ten Hut blows his whistle and recess is over.

Back in the classroom we do reading with Miss Menard. For this, we have books with pictures, called "readers." The first page shows a white dog with black spots. His name is "Spot," says Miss Menard. I have never heard a name so ludicrous. I want to guffaw but the lan-guage barrier prevents me. I wouldn't know how to apologize for such rudeness.

We get to that point in the lesson where Miss Menard asks if anyone can count the spots on Spot's fur. No one volunteers. How could we? In Cree, I can count to twenty, but in English? Five, perhaps? Chally Canoe, too, can count to five; I heard him once. But Cordelia Kamaa-magoos can count to nine! In English yet! Apparently, her father has achieved the towering height of grade eight where mine has grade zero. Cordelia Kamaa-magoos's father can thus speak some English as can his daughter, so this Cordelia Kamaa-magoos has an advantage over me. And wouldn't you know it but the very clever daughter of Alfred Kamaa-magoos of Island Falls, Saskatchewan, is able to count the spots on Spot's fur—Spot has nine. Someone's chest puffs out with pride. And mine it isn't.

"See Spot run," in any case, is the sentence from which comes the name. And we practice it. And practice and practice until our cheek muscles hurt.

"See David come." David, evidently, is Spot's master. A boy our age, which is eight, he has hair that looks like straw. I have a friend here from Brochet named Gilbert David Hell so that helps.

Minutes later, Susan Yazzie, a large-boned Dene girl from Brochet, manages to mumble "Ran, Spot, ran" for "Run, Spot, run," then bursts into tears. As kind Miss Menard bends over to staunch her tears with a handkerchief, she sees a stream of liquid on the floor under Susan's chair—the nine-year-old has just wet herself. Mortified, the girl leaps from her seat, pushes Miss Menard aside, and runs out the door. The language barrier, again, has prevented her from asking for permission to go to the washroom. When she doesn't reappear some ten minutes later, Miss Menard goes out to fetch her. And when she re-enters, escorted gently by Miss Menard, she is so embarrassed that she can't look up.

Dinner is the same basic routine as breakfast except for the menu. Today, we have vegetable-and-macaroni soup followed by a square of shepherd's pie; as drink, a glass of milk made from powder; and, for dessert, raisin pie. The meal finished, the chores recommence, leaving us with half an hour of free time in the playground before Ten Hut again blows his whistle. A virtual stampede for the entrance erupts. And another whistle. And another queue. And another whistle. And another march to the classrooms for the afternoon session cut in half, like the morning, by a recess period of fifteen minutes. Printing, arithmetic, arts and crafts, religion, we are taken through the steps of each subject one after the other after the other. Poor Miss Menard. The experience must exhaust her. But she soldiers on. As do I.

At the end of the school day, which comes at four, Miss Menard rings her bell for the final time and we march back down to the playroom where Ten Hut takes over with his whistle and army commands. This time, however, it is for a snack called "lurnch." At least, that's how I pronounce it. A sandwich cut in half, of ham with cheese, does the job for I am always hungry, taken, of course, with a glass of milk. And we have, moreover, a whole twenty minutes to enjoy it.

Then, at five on Mondays, Wednesdays, and Fridays comes PT which, on Tuesdays and Thursdays, is replaced by choir practice. Another hangover from Ten Hut's army days, PT stands for "Physical Training." We do our exercises in our everyday clothes. The routine? Stretch this way and stretch that way, squats, sit-ups, push-ups, touch your toes, jogging-on-the-spot, swing your arms this way, swing your arms that way, and so it goes for twenty minutes, by which time I am panting. Twice a week, to vary the routine, and only when it's nice in autumn and spring, Ten Hut leads us in a jog down the gravel road the two miles there and back from the boys' yard to the stop sign, where a right turn takes you to The Pas, a left to a beach on Clearwater Lake called Pioneer Bay. Of the hundred boys engaged in this marathon, I usually finish last, which is when Samba Cheese Fitzgerald of Puck, Manitoba, tells me that I run like a girl. Memories of the Fitzgerald boys making fun of me at the Companeek store sting me. But I can't do anything. Samba Cheese Fitzgerald is older than me. And bigger.

As for choir—and here's another instance where boys and girls spend time together—we rehearse in the boys' refectory with the ruddy-faced Sister St. Clare as conductor and Matilda Mitaas of South Indian Lake, Manitoba, Sister St. Aramaa's star student, as piano accompanist (Sister St. Aramaa is the school's piano teacher). Surely still in her twenties (for she looks like a girl), Sister St. Clare is an angry woman. She stands on a chair waving her arms this way and that as if casting spells, her exaggerated sleeves waving and flapping. Fortunately, all I have her for as teacher is choir. As for Matilda Mitaas, she is my hero; I want to play the piano like her when I grow up.

"There's a Bluebird on Your Windowsill," "The Bells of St. Mary's," "The Happy Wanderer" with its "Valderee" and "ha-ha-ha-ha-ha-ha" which I enjoy immensely; hymns like "Be Joyful, Mary" and "Heart of Jesus"; at Christmas, Christmas carols; at Easter, hymns such as "Christ the Lord is risen today, *A-a-a-a-a-lay-i-loo-oo-yaa!*"—this is our repertoire. And even if I have no idea what I'm singing about, I love the music.

Then we break up. The girls file through the giant kitchen into their refectory while I line up with the boys to take our trays from the trucks to be served supper. Roast beef with peas, carrots, and potatoes, and bread with margarine and a chocolate pudding for dessert are regular features. Or roast chicken. Or roast pork. Or beef stew. Or, this being a Catholic school, fish, if it's Friday. Apparently, says Father Grew, our religion teacher, Jeezoos did it so we, too, do it. (Spelled in its native French as "Groulx," for he comes from Ste. Agathe, a town near Winnipeg, we spell it as we hear it, that is, without the "x."). Which is followed by chores for the older boys followed by more free time followed, at 7 p.m., by a return to the classroom for an hour of "study period." And here I spend, in complete, rigidly enforced silence, the entire hour memorizing facts and figures until the inside of my head vibrates and clangs. But the nuns and the principal—the stern and rather frightening Father Picard—and such lay-teachers as Miss Menard and, in the years that follow, Miss Demark (grade four), Mrs. Babchuk (grade five), Miss Crispy (grade seven), and Mr. Manning (grade nine)—are right: what preparation for exams. What preparation for future success. In fact, Father Picard, who comes from France, tells me one day that if I keep working as hard as that, I might go to Paris to this school he knows and enter the priesthood. The thought excites me.

Then we march to the dormitories and prepare for bed where the last act is prayer. Pacing up and down the aisles between the beds fingering his rosaries, the keeper—Ten Hut, Mr. Laflamme, Mr. Tremblay, it depends on whose shift it is—takes us through the rosary. Kneeling on the grey linoleum floor in my blue-and-white flannel pajamas with my elbows on my bed, I talk to God, I talk to Jeezoos, I talk to his Mother, I talk to the Holy Ghost. I talk to my parents. I talk to Rene and Itchy who, I think, should be declared Saint Itchy for taking such good care of my little brother, or so Louise informs me in a letter (yes, she sends me at least four letters a year, all, of course, handwritten). And then comes "lights out" and blissful sleep in crisp white sheets and warm, wool blankets. After a hard day of work. Just from the run to the stop sign alone, my whole body tingles. Still, I dream of Dad—always, always—crossing Nueltin Lake in his dogsled, giving chase to caribou a thousand strong . . .

23

The choir at the Guy Hill Indian Residential School is progressing by the week—grace, for good or for bad, of the angry and ruddy-cheeked Sister St. Clare who is our musical director. The problem for some is that participation is obligatory. Even if you sing like a dog being strangled, you are a member. For me, it's a pleasure—I love music *and* I have a voice, a "boy soprano," as this Sister St. Clare calls it. The school being Catholic, the primary purpose of this choir is to serve "the glory of God," as Sister St. Clare reminds us time and again. So we sing hymns mostly. Though we sing one in Cree and four in Latin, most are in English. Barring the Cree, which we sing at Christmas only anyway, we learn the hymns phonetically. We stand in our rows in the middle of the boys' refectory with our eyes trained rigidly on the crow-like figure of Sister St. Clare as she stands on a chair gyrating away. And Matilda Mitaas plays the piano.

Fifteen at the time, Matilda Mitaas is skinny and as tall as the flagpole in front of the school. As such, she sits to the side, thumping away at that rickety upright piano as if it were nothing but a lump of dough for all she cares about the music she is playing. At least that's the sense I get from sneaking fleeting glances at her hawkish profile and not once seeing her smile or grin. Still, it isn't her performance that gets my attention so much as it is her instrument. I love that sound. In fact, I am jealous—why has Sister St. Aramaa, the school's piano teacher, picked *her* as a student and not me? *I* care about that music. When it comes to a dirge such as "O Sacred Head surrounded by crown of piercing thorns . . ." I would play it to the point where trees would weep.

The choir's repertoire changes with the liturgical calendar. There is October, which is devoted to hymns in praise of *Kichitaw Maaree*; there is Advent, which are the four Sundays that lead up to Christmas; there is Lent, which is a mourning period that leads up to Easter and where the hymns are dark, even tragic; there is Easter itself where the hymns are joyful; there is Ascension Day, there is Pentecost. But my favourite is Christmas; *that* has the best music. "Joy to the Whirl," "Oh Cum all Yee Fateful," "Away in a Ranger," and "Silent Knight," I sing them with gusto, I sing them with verve. All as Matilda Mitaas pumps that piano like no piano on Earth or in heaven has ever been pumped before, her glare at the score before her so enraged, for some reason, so accusatory, that I half expect it to burst into flame. *That* is the first sign of Christmas—when we hear, through the wall of our classroom, Matilda Mitaas start practicing "Away in a Ranger" in the "lie-berry" next door, which is where Sister St. Aramaa has chosen to conceal her rotten-toothed brown instrument.

The second sign is when the teachers, lay and clergy, start rehearsing their students in their routines for the Christmas concert. Boys and girls with singing voices are taught certain solos. I, for example, am taught "Suzy Snowflake." Others are coached in the art of reciting poems such as "The Owl and the Pussy-Cat." Sister St. Aramaa's piano students are taught special pieces. Students such as Sally Saagweesoo of South Indian Lake and Charlotte Zipper of The Pas who are good at jigging are encouraged to practice their jigs to the record player in Miss Menard's classroom. Others rehearse pageants, others pantomimes, others dances. The point here being: such fevered preparations are the second sign that Christmas is coming.

The third sign is Mr. Babchuk. When the tall, large-framed but wiry Ukrainian with the Adam's apple so pronounced that it bobs like a yoyo when he says "good morning" starts building the stage for the Christmas concert, we know that something is cooking. If the girls take home economics, then the boys take "shop," as Guy Hill calls what in other places is called "woodwork" or "carpentry." And as this Mr. Babchuk's "shop" is located in a building apart, behind the main school structure towards the lake and the houses where live the lay staff with children, we never see him on the boys' side of the school. Except at Christmas. Or rather, two weeks prior.

Out of the blue does he surface at the entrance to the boys' gymnasium carrying his toolbox and electric saw and wearing the white-paint-blotched beige canvas apron that holds his tools. Stacks of plywood and two-by-fours follow, carried in by "Big Boys" like Man Fitzgerald of Puck, Manitoba, Ferlin Wachask of Beaver Lake, Saskatchewan, and Michael Mitaas of South Indian Lake, Manitoba, cousin, apparently, to Matilda Mitaas, the Cree piano player, I learn that day. I try to help the Big Boys carry the wood but get pushed away. Why? I am a girl, according to the manly Ferlin Wachask. I, of course, am hurt to the quick but show no sign of it as they place this wood in stacks at one end of the boys' gymnasium. All while I walk to a corner and stand there crying. At one point, I see my brother Daniel and hope he comes to put one arm around my shoulder but he ignores me. Angry at him, I stop crying.

Once all is ready, Mr. Babchuk dives into work. And one busy beaver he is for days. He measures, he saws, he hammers, he pauses to assess his progress. He measures, he saws, he hammers, he pauses, the aforementioned boys his gung-ho helpers when classes are over and they are free to engage in extracurricular activity such as "shop." And wonder of wonders, the stage they are building rises before me. Two feet above ground does it float, as though on stilts, with beams that rise around it to form a support for the backdrop, the cloth for the wings, the curtain, and the lights. And there, of course, are steps for us to mount it from both sides, left and right. So huge is the structure that it fills the entire back quarter of the playroom with its sky-high ceiling, and so solid that old Brochet's Seagull's Little Poop with her great big bum could dance on its surface and it wouldn't budge an inch. Mr. Nick Babchuk, husband of Mrs. Sonia Babchuk, the grade five teacher, is an artist worthy of comparison to a man named Michelangelo, according anyway to Father Grew.

The fourth sign that Christmas is coming is when the kind and humble Brother St. Arnaud who works as an all-round handyman to the school in general, troops off into the forest that surrounds the school with an axe and rope accompanied by four more Big Boys. I try to join them but I am pushed away; I cry in private in the downstairs toilet between the playroom and the refectory. But rally. Fortunately, Brother St. Arnaud reappears two hours later resembling a snowman. Just having wrestled a tree the size of a church down from its rigging, his teenaged assistants come dragging their quarry out of the forest, across the yard, and into the playroom where the entire team erects it, a task not easy considering its size.

Fortunately, the nuns come bustling in with stepladders and cardboard boxes exploding with lengths of crepe paper, ribbons, tinsel, wreaths, garlands of tiny red berries they call "holly" (which turn out to be made of plastic), umpteen wires of Christmas lights, and umpteen boxes of balls and bells, all decorations for Brother St. Arnaud's gigantic Christmas tree. By the time they are finished, with the angel at its summit—the installation of which has given the frail and sylphlike Sister Marie Zepherin a case of vertigo so acute that she reels for an hour—the tree is a miracle. Never have I seen anything like it (for Brochet people don't have such customs); I stand there transfixed. Next is the stage just built by Mr. Babchuk. For the front, two more nuns climb two stepladders to hang red curtains of what looks like velvet and, for the wings and back, lengths of ink-black cloth. At the very top and at either end of the curtains, the much more athletic and ivory-complexioned Sister Ann, standing on the same stepladder that gave such an acute case of vertigo to the frail and sylph-like Sister Marie Zepherin, staples huge bells made of white crepe paper that fold like accordions, to contrast dramatically with the red of the curtains. Sister Ann, God bless her, lets me help; I climb four steps of the ladder to hand her the bells. And boom. The boys' huge playroom is a theatre, a concert hall.

The fifth sign that Christmas is coming is when these nuns, who give the impression of sleeping three hours nightly, start constructing a Nativity scene in the chapel. Six spruce saplings of various heights sprinkled with artificial snow, tinsel, Christmas balls, and twinkling lights form the backdrop of a tableau so rich in detail it makes my eyes hurt; I swear the entire population of Bethlehem is here represented. The shepherds, the sheep, the cows, the donkey, the wise men in the distance, the angels above, the hills, the trees, the rocks, the stars, moon, stable, hay, *Kichitaw* (Saint) Joseph with his staff and halo, his wife, *Kichitaw Maaree*, in blue with her halo, the cradle, the baby in "squabbling" clothes with his halo, all are there in miniature, *and* in chicken wire, construction paper, paste, and paint. And the tiny little lights that twinkle and wink in all sorts of colours! That is the fifth sign. I sneak in one evening to take in the sight. And kneel at the communion rail in front of the "*crèche*," as the nuns here call it, to tell Jeezoos that certain boys are torturing me and will he help me. "Yes," I hear him say, though I think it is just my imagination playing tricks on me.

Then comes the sixth sign—the Christmas concert. Under supervision from a keeper such as Ronald Simpson of far Alberta, we have set up twenty rows of chairs, rows that fill up the back three-quarters of the boys' gymnasium which is where we, the audience, are to sit to watch the show. With white-haired and portly, cigar-reeking, stern Father Picard, the school's elderly French principal, sunk into an armchair that looks like a throne in the front row, the grade ones dance a dance called "the Tot Dance," a kind of *skweetaas* ("square dance," mangled by the Cree tongue) for five and six-year-olds. Then Lady Beksaka, a Dene boy from Brochet who is so effeminate the Big Boys torture her by calling her "Lady," sings "Jinger Bells" with Elizabeth Gunpowder of Island Falls, Saskatchewan, accompanying him on the piano. Then the bony and gangly Onyx Mobster of Nelson House, Manitoba, leads her class in a foot-stomping, stage-rattling rendition of a dance called "the Bunny Hop." Then Charlotte Zipper jigs. Then Tomson Highway sings "Suzy Snowflake." And though he has no idea what a "snowflake" is, he is accompanied by his cousin, the indescribably pretty six-year-old Melinda Kamaa-magoos, on the piano. Then Ann-Adele Ateek of Puck, Manitoba, plays an angel in a scene where she comes down from heaven to announce to *Kichitaw*

Maaree that she is "with child." Unfortunately, standing on a table masked as a rock, the hefty young woman with the thighs of a caribou trips on her robe which is full-length, falls with a crash on top of *Kichitaw Maaree* (played by petite, nut-brown Sexy Sally Bacheese, as we call her, also of Puck) thus crushing her, quite literally, with the news of her pregnancy, *and* breaking one wing. Still, the show must go on. And this one does. Thus it is that, with the Virgin and the angel still hobbling off in hysterics, Matilda Mitaas strides on stage and attacks the piano with a terrifying solo about pirates raiding a village. Why this piece for a Christmas concert, only her teacher, Sister St. Aramaa, knows. But she plays it with vim, she plays it with fire.

Still, the performance that steals the show is when the grade two class, which is us, performs a quadrille called "Dance of the Butterflies." There we are in all our splendour criss-crossing the stage in an elementary shuffle repeated over and over. The girls in white cotton blouses, the boys in white cotton shirts, strapped to our backs with white silk ribbons hang these wings that dwarf us, wings of crepe paper in magenta, saffron, scarlet, turquoise, midnight blue, purple, luminescent orange, luminescent green, the wings of each student different in colour. Each wing bordered with tinsel, they sparkle in Mr. Babchuk's overhead lights as we turn this way and that. (Miss Menard says not a word so I learn only years later that not only did she make these wings with her bare hands late into the night for weeks—thirty pairs of wings in total!—she shopped for and paid for the material herself. In Winnipeg.)

Having started school late, Arabella Beksaka, a Dene girl from Brochet, is two years older than the rest of us, so is taller; in fact, she towers over us like her cousin, Bad Robber Yazzie, used to back in Brochet. Which is the criterion Miss Menard has used in selecting her as queen of the butterflies (that is, her height, not her relation to Bad Robber Yazzie). Sinuous and elegant Arabella Beksaka thus has the biggest wings of all, so big that she looks like she is dragging a tent around. While mine are "goldenrod yellow" (as Miss Menard calls it), hers are purple. Lined and criss-crossed by strips of tinsel, they match her tiara which is also made of tinsel and crowns her head with its thick black hair in a manner befitting, for she holds a wand that matches her wings in colour as in magnificence *and* is tipped with a star the size of a cake. As leader of the squadron of "flying" insects and as dignified and grand as the great constellation Queen *Kaaski-pichi-gan*, she waves this wand hither and thither, her brown face radiant. As is mine. Basking in the nods and smiles of Father Picard and his staff in the front row as well as the 170 students behind them, how could they not be? The applause is loud, sustained, insistent. I am smitten.

And then there is midnight Mass on Christmas Eve at which I, with nine others, am an altar boy. Dressed in crimson cassock, white starched cotton surplice with red-thread embroidery, and a scarlet silk bow the size of a kite at my neck, I feel like an angel (and look like one, for I see myself in a mirror "backstage"—that is, in the sacristy, where we change from our street clothes into our "uniforms"). The ceremony is spectacular, filled as it is with sights, sounds, and smells that make one's heart puff out with joy—the Christ child is born and the whole world knows it.

And then there is Christmas morning. Someone has taken the trouble to go out and buy two hundred toys. Someone has stayed up till all hours, for a month, wrapping them with Christmas wrapping paper, complete with bows, then labelling each gift with the name of one of two hundred children. And someone has stayed up till five in the morning bringing them from their hiding place in some storage room and piling them with love under Brother St. Arnaud's two-storey-tall Christmas tree. For there they are when we come downstairs the next morning. Even *Saanchi Giloss* (Santa Claus)—the athletic and husky engineer, Mr. Van Dyke, dressed in red suit, black boots, and absorbent cotton—is there after our breakfast of bacon and eggs, a rare treat indeed, to greet us and hold the smaller boys on his knee as Mr. Simpson, our keeper that morning, hands him presents from the huge pile on the floor to give to each child. All one hundred boys stand in line. Some get toy guns with child-size holsters, some toy boats, some toy soldiers, some multi-coloured tops that whirl and whir when you pump the little piston that crowns their tops, some board games such as Chinese checkers and Snakes and Ladders.

We have no *Saanchi Giloss, or* Christmas trees for that matter, in old Brochet. Before the arrival of the missionaries, we *had* no Christmas—so all this is new. Our transference to a Christian culture is still, at this point in our lives, in development.

I stand in line awaiting my turn on the old man's knee, before me ten then eight then five then three boys; I actually count them. And, finally, here I am laughing like a loon with *Saanchi Giloss* as he holds me on his knee and hands me a box wrapped in crimson paper a-splash with snowmen and tied with a ribbon complete with bow, snowmen and bow both white in contrast to the red of the paper. I have never seen anything so pretty. In fact, I am scared to touch it in case I break it.

I walk as fast as my eight-year-old legs will carry me to a corner of the playroom, there to tear like a puppy through the wrapping. I hope for a doll but am disappointed when out comes a truck, yellow, steel, the size of a brick. Its back container tilts up and back. Still, I rally and decide on the spot that I will use it to dump snow outside this morning. Which is when Brother St. Arnaud enters the room with a cardboard box the size of a suitcase and starts distributing its wondrous contents to us all. Inside that box? One hundred socks. Inside those socks? Peanuts packaged in miniature plastic bags, candy canes striped in alternating spirals of red, white, and green, yet more candy, and, my favourite, Japanese oranges. I decide on the spot: I will save the candy for Rene. Our eyes on fire, we dive into play, our new toys whirring and popping and pinging and clanging.

And then we eat a huge turkey dinner complete with trimmings and Christmas cake and ice cream, prepared with love through the course of three twelve-hour workdays in a row by the saintly, apple-cheeked Sister Remy St. Joseph and her kind Ukrainian assistant, Darlene Sawchuk. Miss Sawchuk will tell me in time that she peeled six hundred potatoes for that meal, starting at five in the morning. Then I jump into my boots and parka and run outside to romp in the snow. I have, after all, ninety-nine brothers to play with—not one, not four but *ninety-nine*—more than any boy on Earth can dream of. And I love dearly each and every one of them, especially today.

And to think that Hallowe'en and Valentine's Day, to name but two, are just as spectacular if not more so, the first an explosion of the colours black and orange, the latter of red and white, the former a graveyard of ghosts and goblins, the latter an overkill of hearts and cupids.

24

"Loons fear red," is Balazee Highway's heartfelt conviction. Which is why they avoid it. For white, on the other hand, they feel "quite warmly." So if they flee from the former like mice from bats, they swim to the latter like trout to a lure. Where she gets information so abstruse, she never tells us; she simply leaves it to wild conjecture as, indeed, she does with so many others of her pearls of wisdom.

. She believes, for example, that if you put a shoe on the wrong foot, you will meet a bear. For kids who know moccasins only, this is hard. Even if a right-foot moccasin eventually does take on the shape of the right foot and the left the left, a) this can take months, and, b) they are still not easy to tell one from the other. For a four-year-old, which is what Rene is this summer? Impossible. Because we are, moreover, a forest-living people, the possibility of meeting a bear behind our tent is real. As kids, therefore, we are terrified of putting the wrong moccasin on the wrong foot.

If you drink tea in the evening, you will wet your bed that night. If you play with food, your children will starve. If you step on human blood, you will stop growing. If you kill a spider, it will rain.

Our favourite, however, is that, according to Mom, thunder and lightning are scared of rosaries, their crucifixes especially. Which is why, when these elements strike, she runs out in the downpour to hang hers from a tree or a pole on her *agoo-wanis* ("smokehouse," a tepee-shaped rack for smoking fish, meat, and even drying socks), getting soaked in the process. Which explains the fact, she insists with pride, that not once in her life—"*maw pee-yag'wow*"—has she been struck by lightning.

As for loons, the normal scenario, of course, is that the men are out minding the nets the live-long day, thus leaving us children and women at home on whatever island we are living on of any given summer. It happens every year but let's make this the summer I am seven, Rene four, and we are living on an island in Zangeza Bay, on the northern side of the stunning mile-long sandbar called Thigh Daddy. To this day, we call that summer "the summer we lived with Obert Gunpowder" because that's what we do. We live with him, his wife Apwee-tigwee—she of the gramophone which at this point she no longer has—and their now-eleven rambunctious thugs (of an eventual fourteen). Also resident are sundry Dene including, among them, Keeyaas-koomay-is (Seagull's Little Poop), the old Dene woman with the great big bum.

Rene and I are playing around the trio of tents that constitute the Highway encampment, turning sticks and stones into characters, naming them, engaging them in tragedies, comedies, and musicals. Mom, meanwhile, is busy some fifteen yards to the side of the main tent, scraping away at a moose hide stretched out on a rack of her husband's making, the first in a series of steps that will transform the *paageegin* into tanned hide for moccasins. At age nineteen and single still, Louise is sitting on the floor in *her* tent, which stands to the side of the main tent and whose front and side flaps are pinned up like kites, its interior thus exposed to sunlight as warm as pie. Genuine artist that she has developed into over the years, she is stringing beads on a miniature loom to make a beaded belt for Swanson, our beloved elder brother who is off somewhere engaged in work. Florence, on the other hand, is sitting on a rock playing her guitar and singing, as always, country songs. At age eleven, Daniel is off with Dad replacing a worker for the day so now is gone the proverbial live-long day.

"*Mawg'wa!*" ("Loon!") Rene and I shatter the silence.

"Shhhh," goes Mom.

"*Mawg'wa!*" we whisper back. "There's a loon out there."

"*Taantee?*" ("Where?") she hisses back, for the last thing she wants is to scare the bird away if bird there is. We can also tell by the way it moves that her mouth has already started watering—she *loves* loon *arababoo*.

"*Neetee*—" ("There!") And we point. She looks. And lo and behold, there it is, this large black bird some thirty feet offshore floating on the water like a giant rubber duckie, except, of course, with that elongated neck and the speckles on her back. If anyone is wearing red, Mom snaps at them to take it off *seemaak* (right away) and replace it with white; offenders both, Louise and I jump to the order. Living on *terra firma* and wearing moccasins as we always do, we have no need to tiptoe to sneak from point A to point B; we simply walk, on a carpet of, need it be said, reindeer moss. Which is what Mom does, too. Dressed, as always, in her floral-patterned cotton granny smock, blood-streaked white cotton apron, and, of course, moccasins, she strides into the main tent and, five seconds later, strides back out with, in one hand, a white pillowcase and, in the other, a twenty-two-gauge hunting rifle of the kind meant for game such as rabbits. And loons. Trying her best to be invisible, she sneaks to the shore so the loon won't see her. Which we think is redundant, as she is wearing blue and loons, according to her, are blind to the colour.

Once arrived at the spot she deems best for vigilance, she hangs the pillowcase on a clump of willow branches which, as always, droop over the water, drops to one knee beside it, and aims. The gun's butt pressed against her thin right shoulder, her cheekbone against it, her right eye shut and her left pressed hard to the viewer, she bends her right index finger into a curve and wraps it around the little metal trigger. To wait for the *mawg'wa* to approach the white lure of her pillowcase her vaunted objective, she prays in silence to *Kichitaw Maaree*. And lo and behold, the Virgin responds in no time flat and the bird floats nearer, if slowly.

Loons have not white but blood-red sclera, a feature that makes them unique in the avian world, at least in the north, so only once she can see "the reds of its eyes" (as opposed to "the whites") does Mom pull the trigger and, *bang*, the bird is dead. One second basking like a *manchoos* (bug) in the bright light of day, the next floating on the water like a length of driftwood. Balazee Highway could have been a sniper in World War Two.

Paddling off in a canoe to claim her prize would seem a foregone conclusion. We have none. They're out with the men. Getting me and Rene to jump in the lake and swim to the loon is also impossible— we are not swimmers; no one in the north is. Besides, the last thing Balazee Highway wants is to have her two youngest children drown or, worse, die of hypothermia, for we speak here, of course, of sub-Arctic waters which, even in summer, are cold as ice. Which leaves her with two options: a) wait for the loon to wash up ashore, which could take hours, or, b) send a dog to fetch it.

The sled dogs on "work leave" for the summer, they are living unleashed and running wild on an isolated islet some two miles off, so we see them only at day's end when Daniel and I drive over to feed them fish offal and suckers. Besides, being almost as wild as the wolves they resemble and, in fact, are related to, they would run off with the loon the second they clamped their jaws on it and devour it. Which leaves Itchy as the only option.

There are two kinds of loon, says Balazee Highway: *mawg'wa* and *achi-mawg'wa*. The first, of course, means simply "loon." As to the second, I still don't know and she never does explain. The closest I can get to the "*achi*" part of "*achi-mawg'wa*" is that it might mean "dog," as in *atim* (rhymes with "a gym"). When we give the word a child-friendly tweak—as in, "puddy cat" for "pussy cat"—it comes out as "*achim*." A puppy, for example, is an *achim-oosis*, that is, a "small dog." Meaning to explain that *achi-mawg'wa* is possibly a "dog loon," not quite up to the standards of a "human loon." Humans, after all, eat *mawg'wa* only, not *achi-mawg'wa*. The former is vegetarian, it eats plants only, but the latter? Not only does it eat fish, it steals them from nets, *our* nets. *Achi-mawg'wa* is a thief, a mangy scoundrel, not worth eating.

Once the bird here in question is safely in hand, grace of Itchy who swims like a muskrat, off goes Mom with her pots and pans, her knives and forks. Shouting orders this way and that, she grabs her most lethal-looking butcher knife and sharpens it with another, the two blades flashing in the sun like bolts of lightning. Chop the wood, make the fire, fetch the water, boil it, snap boughs off spruce trees in the ever-present forest for the making of our tablecloth—that is to say, prepare everything for the cooking of a bird unlike any other, that is our job, Rene and I. For my part, I like stirring the sauce for Mom. And at six that evening when the men are back, the entire family, including Itchy, sits in a circle on the ground in the main tent. A carpet of spruce boughs freshly snapped our banquet table, the glow from a setting sub-Arctic sun as seen through the walls of our canvas shelter our only light, we feast on *arababoo* of loon and fresh roe-bannock (bannock made from dough infused with roe, that is, the eggs of whitefish, that is, caviar, which is orange, making for a bread with a golden crust but an orange interior).

Their meat aside, loons are beautiful. Just as with lambs, calves, and rabbits, we don't think twice about their beauty before we eat them. A goose's grace in flight, for example, has precious little to do with the fact that its liver is one of the world's great delicacies. Known as *pâté de foie gras*, we just eat it. So it is with lamb, whose meat is delicious but whose source is as cute as a puppy. So it is with veal. And so it is with *mawg'wa*.

The same size as geese, their shape is similar. Elongated necks with C-shaped curves topped off by heads the size of duck's eggs, the bulky, football-shaped body that looks too large for a neck that thin, the foot with its toes in triplicate connected by a web that looks like leather but isn't, the short stubby legs that waddle—the resemblance ends there. For geese are grey for the most part, grey and brown touched off by black, on the neck, for example. Loons, by contrast, are black for the most part, black marked boldly with white. On a full-grown bird, six rows of bright white speckles line the back in a curved row of eight, ten, or twelve. It looks, in fact, like someone threw a cloak made of shells onto the creature's back. The more rows of these "shells" a bird has, the older he is, and therefore the wiser, says Mom.

An old blind man was so grateful for having his sight given back to him by a loon that he yanked the necklace of shells from his neck and threw them on the bird's back, which is where those white shell markings come from, is how legend has it in some Native cultures.

The other part of the loon that is white, and this time pure white as opposed to speckled, is its breast and the lower part of his neck which, for the most part, is black right up to and including the head except for a white band that, too, looks like a white-shell necklace encircling it at its halfway point. Last, as has earlier been noted, he has a sclera that is red, as if his eyes are bloodshot, as if he is forever recovering from a bad hangover.

Geese live in flocks, or skeins, as the *Moony-ass* call them. Loons, by contrast, are solitary. Even if they do, apparently, mate for life and do, in fact, live in pairs and, more than likely, live on the same lake in the same general area, they are rarely seen together. Which is not to say that, away up in sub-Arctic Canada, they have not been known, on occasion, to approach an encampment at sunset in flocks of twenty. From a safe distance offshore, say ten feet, they will float up *en masse* to face you. And they will look at you as though they are curious as to who you are and what you are doing on their territory. And, just as the sun sets, which up there, in July, can be as late as eleven, they will burst forth with song, a plangent chorus, their way, one can only imagine, of wishing you a fond "goodnight."

This call, of course, is what they are known for. Haunting, a lilting airborne la-la-la, a pentatonic tremolo that cuts to the heart, that makes men weep inside their beings, it, in the end, is Canada's sonic signature, as indelibly Canadian a sound as the two Cree syllables that make up the name "Quebec."

Still, the most amazing thing about them is their diving, which can go on forever. Like *wachask*, the muskrat, or *amisk*, the beaver, they are amphibian. They walk clumsily on land on their webbed feet and short, stubby legs, *and* nest on land, but are happier on and in water. Even airborne—because, of course, they do have wings—they don't seem all that happy, for they don't do all that much flying. You are paddling along, in any case, in your little blue canoe on the glass-smooth water of a sub-Arctic lake of a sub-Arctic evening when, suddenly, you see one floating some thirty feet before you. As quickly as you can so you can have a better look, you paddle towards it. But you don't get close. You can't. For the second it senses your non-loon presence, it dives. And is gone for what seems like five minutes. You stop paddling and float. And look around and look around, hoping to see it again somewhere out there, but it doesn't re-surface. Two minutes pass. Three. Five. Won't its lungs burst? Or has it drowned? Imperceptibly, your canoe shifts position. And, suddenly, you see the bird, there, some thirty feet *behind* you, just popped from the water like a mink from a hole. How did it get there? It dove. And, using its wings as propellers, it swam and swam and swam underwater right past your *cheemaan* (boat) some ten feet under—and for five minutes—that's how skillful their diving is, that's how powerful their lungs and wings.

Then there are the babies . . . Even if we have our outboard motors attached to the sterns of our outsized canoes, we often paddle, and this with three scenarios in mind: 1) when we have a breakdown or run out of gas, which is rare, 2) when our boat has to negotiate narrow passages that are too shallow for our motor to navigate; when, that is, its propellers hit bottom and we have to lift the tail out of the water and prop it against the gunwale, in which case we pole our way through with our paddles as with a barge, 3) on evenings when the lake is tranquil, we simply enjoy the act of paddling; we simply enjoy listening to the size of the sub-Arctic silence. And the cry of Arctic terns, the cawing of crows, the loon's ululation which, when borne by water with not one ripple, has its own special resonance. The very sky itself will echo in kind.

When the men are out moose-hunting as opposed to fishing, something they do every summer, even when the rutting season is nowhere in sight, they will leave one boat at home. In which case, the women and the children will use it to go blueberry-picking on a nearby island—though, to conserve gas for the fishing enterprise, they paddle. All day do we pick that juice-filled fruit and have shore lunches and pick more berries until we tire and, at day's end, start paddling home. Which is when we see the infant loons.

Our little blue canoe slices through the water in complete silence, which is what gives us license to get closer to the loons than usual. I don't remember where Florence and Daniel are but Mom sits at the stern steering the vessel, Louise at the bow, paddling steadily. And Rene and I are kneeling in the middle, our knees on padding that cushions them against the hardness of the wooden corrugated bottom. Some thirty feet before us and a little to the left, a loon drifts into view. Rene and I are the first to notice that she is not alone. Mom steers to the left. The boat veers accordingly. Glancing back, we can see from the expression in her eyes that she means to amuse us. As we get closer to the loon, Rene and I can see that its travelling companions are babies, *her* babies, and that they number six. So excited are we that we want to scream, but control ourselves, for the last thing we want is to scare them away. Louise paddles faster. She, too, means to amuse us. We get closer. And closer and closer. Which is when, of course, the mother dives. Her babies follow suit. But because their wings are so unformed—an inch in length and not much wider—they can't dive deep or swim very fast, certainly not enough to match their mother's velocity. Which is why they end up chasing frantically after her a mere four inches underwater. Which is what makes them so visible and so easy for us to catch up to them. Propelled, of course—and on purpose—by Mom and Louise, we do, thus giving us the benefit of watching them swim right there beneath us. At that age, they are brown, not black or speckled like their mother; that comes later. And, not much bigger than a songbird, their tiny little wings flap, whirl, and wiggle like desperate propellers. You can almost hear them crying, "Wait for me, Mommy, wait for me!" And they are swimming and swimming and swimming and swimming like they have never swum before in their young lives. All while, at ages four and seven thus making Louise nineteen, Rene and I are leaning over the gunwale cheering "our babies" onward: "*how, soogi, soogi!*" ("go, go!")

Those little baby loons are our stuffed animals, our wind-up toys.

25

A rattling of metal attracts my ears. It sounds like pails, empty but for some metal object scraping a bottom. It takes me a second but I recognize the sound. It's Keeyaas-koomay-is (Seagull's Little Poop), the old Dene woman with the great big bum, waddling her way down the hill behind our tent rattling her pails suggestively, the dipper inside one making that unholy racket. Her way of telling Mom that she, Balazee Highway, is to get her lazy sons out of bed and walk down to the lake to get her some water, she stops at the entrance to our tent and drops her pails. Very loudly.

"Too damned lazy to get it herself," I mutter (in Cree, of course). I'm in bed, Rene not with me, and it's only seven. Seagull's Little Poop always does this, which drives me crazy. It drives me crazy because we have no choice, Rene and I, but to do Mom's bidding which, in reality, is the old woman's.

"She is almost ninety," says Mom to plead her friend's case. "She can hardly walk." When I open my eyes, I realize I'm not on Mariah, Robinson, or Reindeer Lake but in my bed at the Guy Hill Indian Residential School, and it is Saturday. Morning. Yes! I can sleep till eight. And it's September, not May or October, the two months devoted to *Kichitaw Maaree* when we have to rise at six every morning from Monday to Friday to go to the chapel and pray to her glory. In the eight other "non–*Kichitaw Maaree* months" that we are in residence here at school, we can sleep till seven. But Saturday is special. On Saturdays, whether "Virgin month" or "non-Virgin month," we can sleep till eight, unheard-of luxury if it weren't for this woman who haunts my dreams, this Seagull's Little Poop and her great big bum. Reality and dream collide inside me; I lose my footing.

"Good morning, boys," booms Stumbo the Giant, our keeper that year, as he flicks on the lights. A pink-faced *Moony-ass* so large and tall it gives us vertigo to look up at him, we have named him thus because he looks like the character in the comic books. I squeeze five seconds from this precious time of day to squirm with comfort in my white sheets, on my white pillowcase, my entire body as warm as toast. I can see the sky through the ceiling-high windows that line one wall of this large chamber. Unmarked by clouds, it is blue.

I slide out of bed. I walk down the hallway with thirty-three boys aged five to ten all headed for either the toilet or the washroom, that is, the room with the sinks. Soon to be eight—and Boy Number Eighty-six—I am bent over a sink washing my face with piped-in water. I thank my stars—we have taps here! One for hot water, one for cold, technology unheard of in the cold white north. Meaning to say that I don't have to battle my way with Rene up a hill with pails that weigh a thousand pounds in the freezing dead of winter and then chop wood for a fire to heat it to the point where I can wash my face, all of which takes one whole hour. *And* takes the strength of a whole team of huskies. Here it takes two flicks of a wrist and I am done in three minutes, giving me the wherewithal to savour the prospects of my favourite day.

I can play all day. With my ninety-nine brothers (though not Rene, not this year). Unfortunately, when I get back to the dormitory to dress for the day, I look once more to the windows and see, with sadness, that clouds have come. Writhing and churning, grey with anger, they look like smoke. Within minutes, it will rain. Why does September always have to be so rainy? I can't go outside. I can't play marbles. I can't ride the slide or the seesaw. So what will I do? Stumbo will think of something, I am sure of it. Stumbo is smart. Stumbo may look like a giant but he has a heart.

After breakfast and chores—I am still too young to have any—we learn that Stumbo has made the decision. In consultation, of course, with the keepers of the two other dormitories—Norman Dubois of Medium Boys and Danny Tremblay of Big Boys—he has decided that we, indeed, will stay inside, all day if need be, and play a game called "bollyboll." I've never heard of it but it sounds like fun. How can something with a name like that *not* be? To me, it sounds like "Happy Doll," the Dene hunter who once entered a *Weetigo*-lookalike contest and came in last because he was too pretty.

Thirteen to eighteen years old and thus Big Boys, Man Fitzgerald of Puck, Manitoba, Ferlin Wachask of Beaver Lake, Saskatchewan, George Peter Buckskin of Pelican Narrows, Saskatchewan, and David McMillan of South Indian Lake, Manitoba, are working hard. Setting up the stands and the net for the game to be played in the middle of the boys' gymnasium—that is, our playroom—none can hide the fact that the tall steel stands are heavy, the bases in particular. Their faces are contorted, maps of grimaces. As they labour, Stumbo divides us Small Boys into four teams of six. The boys left over too small and young to play, they are relegated to Snakes and Ladders and Chinese checkers on the floor at the far other end of this gigantic room, where Rene would be, now that I think of it, if he were here except he's not, a fact I regret. Myself, I may still be a Small Boy but I am well past the stage of Snakes and Ladders. By the time Stumbo is done his divisions, the stands are up, the net hanging between them as if ready for the passage of trout and whitefish. A large rectangle spreads out below it across the linoleum, sweeping to both sides by a good ten yards. Marked off with tape of the kind and colour used by Nurse Kratzen to conceal wounds, it is meant to define the game's parameters. If the ball goes beyond it, says Stumbo, the game must stop and a new round be started.

Next he names us. He calls one team the Wolves, another the Hawks, a third the Cougars. And I, Tomson Highway of Brochet, Manitoba, am a Mink. The four teams are to take turns of a half-hour each on what Stumbo the Giant calls "the court," that is, the taped-in part of the playroom floor. Dressed in our normal weekday attire, we stand there waiting: What next? Simeon Kamaa-magoos, a Big Boy from Brochet, Manitoba, will be the game's scorekeeper, says

Stumbo the Giant. And with the ever-present whistle attached to his paunch by means of a shoelace that hangs from his neck, who better to fill the role of referee than him? says Stumbo humbly. The word "referee" shoots from his mouth like a swear word but means nothing to us. "*Keegway itigwee paskach anima* referee?" ("What on Earth is a referee?") I whisper to Chally Canoe of Nelson House, Manitoba. We soon will know.

All of a sudden, the keeper is tossing a ball from one hand to the other as if playing for time. Where he got the object is anyone's guess; this Stumbo the Giant is full of surprises. This must be the "boll" of bollyball. The circumference of my mom's bannock, it is obviously as light as air, for it floats, balloon-like. Or seems to. And it is white. The great big keeper explains the rules to be followed. Even though we don't really get it, we nod sagely. The clouds break open, the rain comes down. We can see and hear it through the ceiling-high windows.

For the first game, the Wolves will play the Hawks. The teams take their places. In two rows of three well-spaced one from the other, they face each other from opposite sides of the net. Stumbo throws the ball at Wilfred Gunpowder of Island Falls, Saskatchewan, captain of the Wolves, who catches it deftly and stands there waiting. He is not to move until he hears Stumbo's whistle. Stumbo blows his whistle. Like a whip, athletic, tough-muscled Wilfred Gunpowder snaps to life. With a leap engaged in only by rabbits and perhaps grasshoppers, he lances the ball over the net at the other team. Machaa-is Bacheese of Puck, Manitoba, captain of the Hawks, leaps in kind and hits it directly with the palm of a hand, thus sending it flying back over the net where another boy leaps to attack it. In the next half-hour, the ball flies back and forth and back and forth a hundred times in this manner, ten Cree boys (and two short Dene) who are the spectators leaping this way and that and this way and that just outside the delineated court yelling encouragements at their teammates when things are going well, curses when they are not. *That's* why the windows in this room are placed so high, just under the very high ceiling, I say to myself, because it is a boys' playroom—a gymnasium, in effect—because games not glass-friendly are played here. Some boys move well across that court, others not so well. But when the cavey-nostrilled but fast-on-his-feet Marvin Mitaas of South Indian Lake, Manitoba, misses the ball and it goes flying outside the taped line and hits a wall with a bounce—it *is* made of rubber—Stumbo the Giant blows his whistle and the game stops dead. Only to begin with another round of leaping and throwing and hitting and leaping and hitting and leaping and hitting.

A group of boys from the Medium and Big divisions, meanwhile, has joined the spectators present already to wait their turn. It is obvious from their impatient shifting that they can't wait. Each to last half an hour, we Small Boys will take two hours in total to finish the tournament. As the rain is of the kind that lasts all day, says Stumbo the Giant, the Mediums and Seniors will have all afternoon to play. For now, half the spectators applaud the Wolves, the other half the Hawks. The Wolves win neatly. Wilfred Gunpowder puffs out with pride. They exult, their fans with them. And now it's the Mink against the Cougars. I freeze with terror. I will not be good at this game called bollyboll, I can tell you right now.

The teams take their places. Our captain, Rufus Skylark of The Pas, Manitoba, puts me in the front-row middle. On the other side of the net, Samba Cheese Fitzgerald of Puck, Manitoba, takes his place as captain of the Cougars. Samba Cheese Fitzgerald does not like me. He thinks I'm a girl and says so as loudly as he can as often as he can. With him, "You look like one, you talk like one, you walk like one" is a mantra. Me? It hurts. It hurts like hell but I have no choice but to take it and soldier on. Where would I run to? Brochet?

He glares at me. He has plans, so much is obvious. He is also athletic and macho and he knows it. Not only that but he is older than me by two years and thus bigger and stronger. I am vulnerable. I have no way to protect myself. As he paces like a lynx from right side to left and back to right, he fiddles with the ball, tossing it from one hand to the other and back to the other with quick little jerks. He is waiting, I know, for the perfect moment. The glint in his eyes says it all. Stumbo blows his whistle. With a leap on legs that seem made of rubber, Samba Cheese Fitzgerald's feet leave the floor by a whole yard, I swear. And he hovers, a virtual demon with eyes of fire. At least, in my terror, that's what I see. And then from up there, he holds the ball high up with his left hand and aims it. With his right, he punches it. So hard is the impact of his fist on the rubber that it sounds like a bullet. The ball hits my face. It knocks me out. And that is my first experience with the game called bollyboll. And I wish it to be the last but it isn't.

Same thing for basketball, same thing for floor hockey, same thing for track and field, same thing even for Ping-Pong. I am terrible at all of them. I am the laughing stock of all Guy Hill.

Girl, girl, girl. Girl can't play is the constant chorus that haunts my ears. And the worst is yet to come. For winter arrives and, with it, a sport called hockey. *Ice* hockey this time, the "game of champions," has said my nemesis, Samba Cheese Fitzgerald.

Well before the first sign of snow, Mr. Babchuk, the shop teacher, builds a structure out of planks three feet high to one side of the boys' Moomoos Island–sized playground. The structure is rectangular though with corners that curve and could accommodate a hundred people; a "rink" they call it, which rhymes with "stink"; the English language persists in confounding a Cree boy of eight. Then the first snows arrive and the kind and humble Brother St. Arnaud sets to watering the ground inside this structure with a large hose connected to a fire hydrant that stands nearby. It takes him an hour but, by next morning, that water has turned to a solid sheet of ice. Every day for the next few days does he do this until that ice is as thick as two layers of plywood and strong enough to carry the weight of one hundred boys. The stripes all painted in red and blue with a circle in the middle, the goals installed, the rink is finished.

While all this is happening, we receive our uniforms from the keepers. Skates, socks, pants with their elastic suspenders, protectors, knee pads, shoulder pads, sweaters, gloves, even sticks, all brand new (helmets won't come until the 1980s). And all grace of the school's sports programme, meaning to say that not one penny do our parents have to pay for all this equipment. And because each age category is divided again, as in bollyball, into four teams, these uniforms come in four different colours.

Our sticks are made in a small city some hundred miles east of Montreal, says Brother St. Arnaud. Called Victoriaville—which is what the sticks are called, "Victoriaville Hockey Sticks"—it happens to be the birthplace and hometown of Brochet's resident missionary, Father Adrian Cadeau. It seems that his family owns the factory that makes these sticks, says Brother St. Arnaud, sticks that are admired by professional hockey players across our country. A man not known for kindness or generosity, Father Cadeau does break that mould on this one count—he pulls strings at his family's business to have a yearly supply of its hockey sticks shipped to Guy Hill for use by its boys, a fact that translates, when you factor in breakage, into some four hundred sticks. For us? Free.

Held after school hours, the practice sessions demand great effort. Skating back and forth and making sudden stops, thus making shavings of ice spray out like fountains (a sight I like), skating in circles small, large, and medium—sometimes right around the rink—skating figure eights, skating crossovers, passing the puck, receiving the puck, slap shots, positions—left wing, right wing, centre, defenceman—we do it all, learn them all.

And, of course, there are those who love the game and are good at it. Simeon Kamaa-magoos of Brochet is one. So is Wilfred Gunpowder of Island Falls, Saskatchewan. Gregory Crumple of The Pas, Manitoba, is a star in the making, swears Alan Manning, a teacher who is also a coach. William Peeskwa, Andrew Kapee, Toby Crumple, Chuck Fitzgerald, they form the lineups to watch.

As for the coaches, only in one case is he a teacher, the aforementioned Alan Manning of Winnipeg. Most in their twenties, the rest are keepers. Erik Laporte of Gilbert Plains, a farming community just east of Dauphin in south-central Manitoba, is one. Butch Bouchard of St. Anne, another farming village, this one just west of Winnipeg, is another. Even Stumbo the Giant is no slacker (Stumbo never tells us where he's from so I don't know). They give their all to their charges.

Still, when it comes to ice hockey, no one can hold a candle to Daniel Highway of Brochet, Manitoba. At this point in his life, he may be fourteen only and a Big Boy, but he is already showing signs of greatness, says keeper Erik Laporte. Not only does he skate like Rocket Richard, the greatest hockey player who ever skated this planet (says Erik Laporte), he handles his stick like his father, Joe Lapstan Highway, handles his whip for his sled dogs. Once on that ice, he is one hundred percent male. That muffin-sized black puck cradled securely on the blade of his sleek pinewood stick, he zigzags his way in and out of the lashing, flashing sticks of the opposition players in such a way that they start hallucinating—did they see that or did they not? I know because I see the expressions in their eyes, even from the stands. Having left even the defencemen of the opposing team grasping for air behind him, he makes his now-unimpeded way toward the goal with the terrified goalkeeper standing six feet before him with eyes so distended a raccoon could have been his Cree spirit animal. And he shoots. And scores, the roar of the crowd that surrounds him—all the students of the school, male and female—inviting comparison to thunder. Fodder for the National Hockey League is the general consensus among coaches and teachers.

As for me, I can't even skate. I fall on my bum at every turn. I try to get up and, like a drunk, fall again, splayed out like a glob. Instead of going for the puck, I flee it, try to get as far from it as I can. One day, I see Samba Cheese Fitzgerald of Puck aiming a slap shot at me and I close my eyes like a coward which, of course, is what I am. And cringe. I hate it. I hate every second of the experience. People boo me. They yell at me. They tell me to get off the ice.

"Girl, girl, girl can't play." The humiliation is total. I am not even human.

26

If we have pet loons then we have pet rocks, we have pet minnows, we have pet horseflies that serve us as kites, we have pet squirrels. Long-time residents of this gnarly old spruce tree in whose kind shadow stands our tent, they are our alarm clock. Rene and Florence once raised Arctic terns from age one day. Mostly owing to his age, which was four at the time, Rene lost his to an accident after one week but Florence raised hers successfully; it helped, of course, that she was fifteen that summer. The story of her pet's life goes much like that of two other birds who joined our family the summer that followed . . . on a lake called Seeseep.

June is at its end. We have just arrived home from boarding school, Daniel and Florence and I. Yet another one of those long, golden Sundays—being that close to the land of the midnight sun, we see this magical effect every year in late June and early July—it is Dad's day off from fishing. And as sometimes happens, once we have finished our picnic lunch of pike tripe grilled on a stake over an open fire, on the mainland in this case, we go walking on an esker. An esker? Picture a hill an eighth of a mile in height and some two hundred miles in length and which slopes its way from lake level up, up, and up to a ridge where the forest cover of spruce and pine gives way abruptly to a surface of sand, the meadow that results also, like the hill, two hundred miles long. The forest may begin its downward journey on the ridge's other side until it re-connects with land that lies at lake level,

but the sand ridge itself gives the impression that a mole of proportions gigantic has burrowed beneath it for it snakes its way and snakes
its way to the high sub-Arctic. Golf courses in the clouds, a *Moony-
ass* bush pilot once cryptically called them (for us it was "cryptic"
because we wouldn't see a golf course until years later, and that not
in reality but on TV) but that is an esker. A breathtaking sight, it was
carved by glaciers of the Ice Age receding northward as temperatures
rose, has said Father Cadeau. Today, as always when we scale one to
hunt for ptarmigan or pick cranberries, the Highway family has this
esker all to itself.

Our feet kicking up clouds of sand as fine as powder, we are walking. And walking and walking. The conversation spare, intermittent,
we prefer the whisper of the breeze as it winds its way through our
lives. And the chatter of squirrels and birdsong. We come upon a pine
tree the height of a church, rare for the north. And quickly discover
that, at its summit, sits a nest. An eagle's nest. There is, however, no
eagle in sight so it must be abandoned, is the general consensus. But
then we hear the cries of what we think are baby eagles. What on
Earth has happened to the mother? Off hunting for food? Killed in
battle with a predator, a lynx, for example? Or a wolverine? God
knows, it's been known to happen. Maybe *ma-chimes-chigoosoo* (the
bad *Moony-ass*) ate her, is Rene's speculation.

We wait. Five minutes, ten, perhaps fifteen. No sign of mother.
Whatever has happened, our cousin, John Joe Kipawm, our Laughing
Aunt Margaret's third son of four, is living with us that summer.
Thirteen years old and as fleet of limb as he is of foot, he scampers
up that tree, achieves its summit, puts one hand into the nest, lifts
one occupant, drops it to the ground, lifts the second occupant, and
drops it as well so that the birds come tumbling each in turn head
over talons over head with their winglets flapping and their small
voices squawking. Cushioned by branches thick with bush the entire
length of their downward trajectory, they remain unhurt—eagles, in
any case, are hardy creatures—and come to a landing at our rubber-
booted feet. The size of ducks and unable to fly, at least for now, we
bring them home.

One raised by Louise, the other by Daniel, Rene and I, too, have a hand in their feeding which is fish, fish, and yet more fish—uncooked, of course. And as with Rene's and Florence's terns, they start walking, if unsteadily at first, then hop then jump then fly small distances then further and further. Until, by the end of July, they are gone the live-long day hunting and surfing the currents of air like gliders. Their wings now spanning a good six feet—three feet per wing—the heights they climb hold us spellbound. But always do they end up coming home at sunset, double arcs in the distance, their cries songs of love for the Highway family.

For some reason that I can't recall, Louise and Daniel let Rene and me name them. "Waagichaan," I call mine because, like all birds of his species, his beak is crooked and Waagichaan means "the Crooked One" or "He Who Has a Hooked Nose (or Beak)." As for the second, Rene calls him "P'weegichaan," because it rhymes with Waagichaan and because we Cree, whose language is ridiculous to begin with and who, as we have seen, have an affection for names that have no meaning such as Lapstan, Peechoochee, and Chaggy-wat. Which is what P'weegichaan means: nothing. At the same time as which, based as it is on the verb *p'weegi-too* (to fart), it means something approximating "He Who Farts" or, better, "The Farter." So there you have it, our pet brown eagles, Hooked Beak and Farter. Only in Cree . . .

Now late August, there we are squatting in a circle on bare ground eating our supper, a carpet of spruce boughs, as always, our banquet table. Mom, Dad, Louise, Florence, Daniel, our cousin John Joe Kipawm, Rene, me, eating *seeseep* (duck) *arababoo* with, this time, macaroni and stewed tomatoes (canned), a stew to die for. And there they are, Waagichaan and P'weegichaan, perched on the ground beside us waiting for handouts. For all intents and purposes, they are sitting with us at the dining table, our kith, our next of kin. Adjusting their wings from time to time and purring enticements such as "*Kisaa-gee-itin*" ("I love you"), their eyes are yellow with small black pupils, eyes that somehow know your spirit, I am certain. Still, September looms and they will be leaving for the winter, soon, I *know*. Didn't Florence's Arctic tern leave us for Antarctica on the first of September last summer? Well, I will, too, in just one week, but not for Antarctica. I will, instead, be leaving for the Guy Hill Indian Residential School and my grade three. The difference this fall? Rene is coming with me (and, of course, Daniel, but no Florence).

Having no other way of getting us to The Pas, Dad puts us on the Norseman that comes twice weekly to collect his catch and fly it the one hundred and fifty miles to the fish depository in Lynn Lake. Being almost adult in size, Daniel gets to ride "gunshot," that is, beside the pilot. But filled to capacity with some fifteen corrugated aluminum tubs of trout and whitefish packed in ice but uncovered and smelling accordingly, where will Rene and I sit? Ever inventive, Dad takes two of these eighteen-inch-by-eighteen-inch, foot-high tubs and turns them into seats by covering the two at the front with double layers of cardboard slats from empty Campbell's Soup cartons; this way, our bums and our new clothes—ordered by Louise from the Eaton's mail-order catalogue—will be shielded from the slime and cold and wetness of whitefish and ice. As for seatbelts, I don't remember. So here we are, me perched in comfort behind the pilot, my feet just touching the floor, and Rene behind Daniel with his little kiddie feet in their brand-new runners swinging back and forth most merrily. Yes, one would think that this achingly pretty Cree Indian boy, still prac-tically a baby, would be scared witless to be leaving his parents— and his dog—for the first time in his life, but no. Rather is he excited, rather is he gung-ho, just like me when I first left home for school two years prior. Girlish we may be but we Highway boys are no shrinking violets; we are brave, we have guts. Rene's first ride on a plane, for one thing, he is going with his brothers to far *maameek* and who knows what he'll see there; maybe he will meet the man who makes *pawpilly-cum*, he whispers to me just as the plane's propellors whir to life.

For him, being an only child on their patch of the untold vastness that is Canada's sub-Arctic was a lonely experience. Coming from a family of five hundred cousins? And counting? (Today, pushing the age of seventy, I have over a thousand.) "Horrible." In fact, he was the one who begged our parents to let him leave for school one year early—so he could be with me. Which is why, if I left home at age six three-months-short-of-seven, he is leaving home at age five two-months-short-of-six. His argument surprisingly mature for one his age, he won them over with, "children should *never* be without other children."

One hour later, we land in Lynn Lake. Dad has made arrangements with the kind bush pilot (who, like everyone, loves Joe Highway) to lodge us at his home that night. At ten next morning, he and his wife drop us off at the station, from where we take the train the three hundred miles south to The Pas on the railway that our brother, Swanson, helped build some ten years prior. The slowest train on Earth, the kids from Puck who join us halfway to The Pas tell us, it takes ten hours to complete the trajectory. Meaning to say that, all told, it takes us thirty-two hours of arduous—though spectacular—travel to do what takes your average city kid fifteen minutes . . . which is go to school.

That September, I sneak into Rene's bed at the far other end of the Small Boys' dormitory at every opportunity. For the first half-hour, I doze with my arms wrapped tightly around him. Only when I am assured that he is asleep will I sneak back out. But in my dreams all that autumn and into the winter, he and I are sitting astride the feathery backs of Waagichaan and P'weegichaan, our hands clutching their necks. And we are soaring in the air in great wide circles, the wind in our hair, our faces white with elation. Our tents below us get ever smaller until they fade from view. The eagles' voices arcs of sound that soar first up then down, we look down at the Earth with eyes semi-paralyzed by permanent astonishment. There the thirty green islands of Seeseep Lake with their golden beaches, there the sandy eskers winding their way to Inuit country, there the Cochrane River long, blue, and sinuous winding its way south to Brochet, the bays, the beaches, and the five thousand islands of Reindeer Lake, the bears, the moose, the skeins of geese, the schools of fish, the beaver dams, the long-bodied otters sliding down the slopes of algae-covered granite into the blue of Casimir Lake, where Florence was born, the great herds of caribou, the Arctic, the North Pole, Greenland, Norway, France, Italy, the Vatican, the African desert and the African jungle, the Indian Ocean, the elephants of India, Australia's kangaroo hopping across the great southern outback, the coast of Antarctica, Antarctica itself, the South Pole, the human heart, its complex network of veins and blood, its million molecules, its pulse, its rhythm, we see it all . . .

27

Every Saturday for the nine years that I'm here, starting as early as late October when the first snow falls, we play hockey right up till April when the snow starts melting. Fortunately, Sundays come after Saturdays to save me from hell.

"The house of God," red-haired and red-eyebrowed Father Grew calls the chapel at the Guy Hill School (with the small, tight paunch that protrudes from his cassock, he looks pregnant). A room more church than chapel in the sense that it has room for over two hundred people, it is by far the building's finest. The floor, the walls, the ceiling that reaches to heaven, the pews, the communion rail, the altar, all are of oak cream-beige in colour, planed and varnished. So rarefied is the ambiance generated by this wood that a hush overtakes us when we enter. Abetted by organ music, the fragrance of incense, and mid-morning sunlight as filtered through windows stained-glass and oblong, I almost ache. At this juncture in my life, that is to say, and grace of my parents, I am a Catholic hook, line, and sinker. I even dream, at one point, of becoming an Oblate of Mary Immaculate like Father Grew, Father Picard, and Father Cadeau.

Sounding celestial as it always does, not least to the ears of a nine-year-old, this music comes from the balcony at the back where the school's piano teacher, the very earthly, wrinkled, and squat Sister St. Aramaa, plays an electric organ. She toodles around with notes that tinkle as the congregation enters and, three-quarters of the time, I enter with it.

The other quarter of the time, I arrive a whole hour early to change in the sacristy into my altar boy "uniform." The sacristy? A sort of dressing room behind the altar where are kept the officiating priest's liturgical equipment, his sacramental wine, and, of course, his ceremonial attire along with those of "his boys." I get there early because, as head altar boy, I have certain "pre-Mass" duties such as lighting the candles, a yard in height, white, that line the back edge of the altar. Besides this altar, they also line the aisles on both sides of the pews as well as sundry other corners; candles, candles, and yet more candles.

I love my "costume." A full-length black cassock just like priests wear and, over it, a surplice in starched white linen edged by lace-work that falls from neck to thigh level like foam in a river; I like the way it swishes like a skirt when I walk. In the mirror on the wall at the back of this "dressing room," what I see is a small-for-his-age nine-year-old boy who looks like an angel ready on a dime to engage in flight. At Christmas midnight mass, we are ten. Altar boys. Today, we are four; they're like that, these "ordinary" Sundays. With a cute little thump, Sister St. Aramaa arrests her performance.

Which is the cue for our entrance. Father Picard goes first. Looking spectacular in his purple silk chasuble—a sort of poncho "for popes and bishops" (as explains Father Grew in our catechism class)—with its gold trimming, he carries a gold-plated thurible that he swings this way and that. An ornately wrought urn that hangs from gold chains in triplicate, it contains burning incense so that smoke billows through the holes in its cover, thus spreading to the congregation like fog from a lake. And imparting to the room a perfume that soothes. All as he sings the *Asperges me* a capella—that is, without instrumental backing. Meanwhile, Nameegoos Kipawm of Brochet, Harold Mitaas of South Indian Lake, Victor Fitzgerald of Puck, Manitoba, and I follow his steps from the sacristy into the much more expansive sanctuary, that is, the part of the church between the altar and communion rail. As we boys walk, we carry lit candles one foot taller than Father Picard, who is squat to begin with, as he sings Gregorian chant. Gregorian chant? A kind of music, defines Father Grew, sung by monks in ancient Rome. A style most haunting, especially with its Latin delivery, it holds me captive.

"*Asperges me*," chants Father Picard in a quavering bass, "*Domine, hyssopo, et mundabar, lavabis me . . .*" ("hyssop" is a herb of the ancient world—Greece, Rome, Israel—whose fragrance, like sweetgrass, is deemed sacred; here, the priest is asking God to anoint him with hyssop-infused water). And he goes through the exact same motions, sings the exact same chants, and intones the exact same prayers as does Father Cadeau at St. Pierre Church in Brochet. And he does it, what's more, as in Brochet, in Latin—"God's language," explains Father Grew.

After the *Asperges me*, Father Picard goes on to the *Kyrie* then the *Sanctus*, the *Credo*, the *Confiteor*, the *Agnus Dei*, we altar boys either chanting along or responding to his "calls" at moments expected.

"*Dominos vobiscum*," he chants at one point, for example.

"*Et cum spiritu tuo*," we chant in response and in unison.

"*Per omnia saecula saeculorum.*"

"*Amen.*" The "*per omnia*" is my favourite. Every chance I get—in the yard while out making snowmen with Rene, for instance—I sing my own version. "*Per omnia saecula saecula saecula saecula saecula saeculorum,*" extending the *saecula* (forever) for as long as I can breathe. I sing it for him at his request because it makes him think of *choggy-lat* (Cree for "chocolate"). Which is all he needs for him to launch into his own version: "*Per omnia choggy-lat, choggy-lat, choggy-lat, choggy-lat, choggy-lat oolawroom.*" (The last word is nonsensical in this case; it means nothing.)

"*Amen.*" We will chant in unison. And laugh. He's also wearing, very proudly—no holes, no patches, no threadbare embarrassment!— the brand-new parka the school has given him as, indeed, it has to all one hundred boys and one hundred girls herein enrolled.

Another favourite is *Agnus dei qui tollis peccata mundi, miserere nobis.* I say it in my prayers at bedtime. "*Agnus dei qui tollis peccata mundi, dona nobis pacem . . .*" I can't believe it. I, a nine-year-old Cree Indian boy from the wilds of sub-Arctic Canada, am speaking Latin! A small group of us nine-year-old boys, after all, have learned all the chants and prayers from the stern but handsome Sister Ann in her classroom two evenings a week. In fact, at this point in my life, my Latin is better than my English, says Sister Ann, who was orphaned at age three years on her family's farm in southern Manitoba and so was raised in nearby St. Norbert by nuns at a convent that was known for its chickens. The other boys hate the lessons, but I love them. I love the feel of the syllables upon my tongue. I love the curve of the pentatonic melodies as they float like soap bubbles to the sky-high ceiling. The help this language will give me in my mastery of French and Italian—and English—later on in life aside, I love my newfound closeness to God. Why am I closer to him? Because I now speak His language.

Once Mass is ended, the best meal of the week is served downstairs. The main course this Sunday is roast beef with gravy, scalloped potatoes, and boiled vegetables. Rather than sitting in my usual seat with the Medium Boys where I belong, I sit with Rene and the Small Boys, even four months into the school year. Why? Because kind, bespectacled Brother St. Arnaud saw me once too many times scooting across the room to stand by Rene and help him cut his meat. Out of all the siblings in the room, and there are many, only for the Highway boys does he place an extra chair, for me, by my little brother's side. To this day do I give thanks, in my prayers, to this Brother St. Arnaud.

The prize plate, however, is the scoop of vanilla ice cream and triangle of chocolate cake that come at the end. Every morsel of this meal prepared with love by Sister Remy St. Joseph and her kind Ukrainian assistant, Darlene Sawchuk, it is scrumptious. With no electricity for freezers or fridges in Brochet, ice cream is unknown at the Companeek store, even in winter.

Then there is free time, where I play in the yard with Rene if it's nice—making tunnels in the scraped-off snow that has piled up two feet high around the ice rink is a favourite—in the playroom if it's not. This is followed, at one-thirty, by a second, though, thank God, much shorter service in the chapel. A mere recitation of the rosary as opposed to a Mass, it is called Benediction and, in the forty minutes it takes to complete it, the entire school recites all five "decades" of the string of beads called the rosary—meaning to say that we recite fifty Hail Marys, in English, punctuated after each ten by one Our Father and one Glory Be. Between the second and third decades, we pause to pay homage once more to the Host. This time, however, the sacred object sits inside this spectacular instrument of what looks like gold called a "monstrous." Buoyed by a base that holds it upright followed by a stem that serves as handle when raised up high, it looks like a sun with its rays exploding. At its heart—that is, where the sun itself would be—stands a Host clearly visible behind this small round glass door that will swing open on a hinge when comes the time for the priest to extract it. Indeed, at the climax of the service, the priest takes this monstrous by its stem in both hands, turns to the congre-taion—in those days, before the Vatican changed the rules in 1962, including changing Latin to English, priests stood with their backs to the faithful—raises the object, and chants the *Tantum ergo*. Which is the signal. Kneeling in our pews and singing with him, we put the palms of our hands together and pay tribute to "our Lord on high"— that is, the Host, though this time, while still paper-thin, it is larger: the circumference of, say, an oatmeal cookie. Thus are we, for the second time that day, filled with "the Spirit." (Only later will I learn that the "monstrous" is actually a "monstrance." Oh, my English . . .)

We do, that is to say, an awful lot of praying at the Guy Hill Indian Residential School, on Sundays especially. Then we have supper, after which comes my favourite part of the entire week: Walt Disney night on TV. Before my grade four, we had, of course, no television at Guy Hill School. But now we do. And how we huddle around that set on Sunday evenings in a corner of the boys' refectory devouring the pirate movies, dragon movies, Tarzan movies, princess movies, fairy movies, cartoons—all, of course, in black and white. When Rene sees Sylvester the Cat crawling under a living room carpet to sneak up on his supper, the songbird, Tweety—just like Mom did the day that terrible wind blew our tent down—he points to the screen and squeals, his little boy's voice a xylophone, "*Neeee, kimaa-maanow!*" ("Look, it's Mom!") All there laugh.

But then comes an even better treat, once monthly. Every fourth Sunday evening, Father Picard turns the boy's playroom into a cinema. He shows what he calls a "picture show" that he has ordered from Winnipeg for he, God bless him, has had the foresight *and* the kindness to buy us a movie projector as well as a screen that rolls up to the ceiling when not in use. Yet one more instance when boys and girls get to spend time together in the same room, we get to see our sisters, girl cousins, and girlfriends, even if we sit separated by two yards of aisle. Still not wide enough to prevent furtive contact, the older boys take advantage of the dark to share love letters. Hidden in crumpled balls of paper, they throw them at each other across the division like spitballs.

I am yours, Marius Wachask, signed Bertha Mistat (of Nelson House, Manitoba), says one for the last-born of Pitooria Wachask, the resident midwife of Brochet. I know because the studly, precocious Marius Wachask, who is three years older and sits next to me, shows it to me. And shows me, as well, the imprint of his massive erection through jeans so tight they might well burst.

I love you, Tomson Highway, says one for me, *signed Roseanne Bacheese* (of Puck). And we return the love messages in kind. The one pencil available to the boys going from hand to hand—as I imagine it does on the girls' side—we write furtively on the back of the piece of crumpled paper just received, scrawl the name of the girl it is meant for on it, crumple it back up, and throw it back across the aisle. And because it is dark, neither Father Picard nor our keepers nor the guardians of the girls who, of course, are nuns, see anything.

You are cute, I write back to Roseanne Bacheese. And she is. As pretty as a picture in the Eaton's catalogue as she may be, though, I can't say "I love you," because, at age nine years, I don't have feelings for anyone. Apart from parental and sibling love, and perhaps "puppy love" admiration for certain boys, I have no idea what love is.

Most of these movies Westerns (in, of course, black and white), they always feature thousands of Indians letting loose with arrows on flawless *Moony-ass* and burning their covered wagons in which they are crossing land that belongs to them—that is, the Indians, not the

Moony-ass. Until a cowboy named John Wayne—who apparently wears a girdle to mask his girth, I am to learn some ten years later—comes along and kills all the Indians with one bullet. We cheer him wildly.

The other funny thing about these nights is that, when a love scene comes along, Father Picard stops the projector and orders a keeper to turn on the lights. Which is what he needs to advance the film manually, thus sparing us the obscene act of kissing. Once certain that he has skipped it, he gives the signal to the keeper—Erik Laporte, this one night I'm thinking of—to plunge us back into darkness and the film continues. Killing we can watch, lovemaking we cannot, seems to be the rule. Thank God our movie diet consists not just of Westerns.

Father Picard also shows war films where killing runs rampant, where innocent people die by the thousands. There are comedies that feature the Three Stooges, Ma and Pa Kettle, Laurel and Hardy, and, my favourite, Lucille Ball. Then there is religious subject matter, which is always a favourite with the old priest from Paris, France. In this vein does he show us *The Robe* with Richard Burton, *The Miracle* with pretty Carroll Baker, and *Ben-Hur*. So long is this last that the principal orders an intermission during which we receive Kool-Aid and cookies. These are served by the ever-generous-of-spirit and quietly humble Sister Remy St. Joseph who, as usual, has made both treats herself. Rene slurps his Kool-Aid and devours his two oatmeal cookies in the space of three minutes.

28

If there is an absence of stores and gardens in far north Canada, then we have other means of providing our bodies with the nutrients needed for the rigours of life in a sub-Arctic climate. Nothing new there, as this has been the case with all peoples since time immemorial; even if a desert as parched as paper is their habitat, they find a way to thrive. The key to such inventiveness is that they know their pharmacies, their health food stores, their medicine cabinets— they're called "Nature." Who *didn't* know them, to name but one, was Jacques Cartier, "discoverer" of Canada. His star-crossed encounter, well documented, with a scourge called scurvy where skin turns yellow, teeth fall out, and the victim dies slowly, is proof incontestable. *He* was unfamiliar with *our* pharmacy.

Though it is more pleasure outing than act of necessity, one of our means of survival is what we call *meesta-soowin*. The word nonexistent in the English language, the closest I can get is "the scraping of trees." Though "tapping," as in "tapping maple syrup," might also work, for that's what *meesta-soowin* amounts to. The difference is that the trees we tap are birch, not maple. And we don't so much tap them—that is, stick a little tap into their trunks to drain their sap—as scrape them with the blades of knives.

Come early summer when Daniel, Rene and I have just arrived home from boarding school, the birch trees have already started secreting this wondrous humidity—blood from their veins, as has been said. So off we troop into the forest around us, either with everyone,

when the men are not out fishing, or just us children and women when
they are. Whatever the makeup of the travelling party, adults will
carry a twenty-two-gauge hunting rifle of the kind meant for game
like rabbits or ptarmigan, complete with knapsacks to contain quarry,
picnic supplies, and knives of a kind we use to *meesta-soo*.

Actually designed for the dressing of fish, what makes these knives
unique is that their tips are rounded, as opposed to pointed. Resembling the nose of Elmer Fudd, Bugs Bunny's worst enemy in the
comics, what that tip is meant for is the scraping of viscera, blood,
and mucus from the innermost recesses of a dressed fish's belly. As
such, it is omnipresent in fishing communities; most families have
several. Another point in this knife's favour for *meesta-soowin*? The
width of the blade, while making it impossible for children to stab
themselves with, makes it possible for those same children to lick it.
And, God knows, we lick those blades when we go out to *meesta-soo*.

Seventy percent of the trees in Canada's sub-Arctic, I would say,
are black spruce, fifteen percent jack pine, the remaining fifteen a
liberal mix of deciduous trees such as birch, poplar, and willow. And
then there is tamarack which, in any case, is rare enough to leave off
the list. Meaning to say that our fishing encampments are almost
always surrounded by spruce. Meaning to say that in order for us to
find stands of birch trees substantial enough in size and in number to
make the excursion to find birch sap worth the effort, we have to walk
respectable distances into the forest. Which is half the fun.

Trailed by Mom, Dad, Louise, and Daniel—Florence got married back in April when we were in school—Rene and Itchy and I are
bounding along on the spine of an esker kicking clouds of powder-
fine sand this way and that until we come to a stand of birch. And
when we do, as with every person in the travelling party, Rene and I
each walk to a specimen that looks promising and kneel at its base.
Reaching to the bottom of her knapsack, Mom, who happens to be
standing just behind us, pulls out two of these fish-gutting knives and
gives one to each of us. Aged nine, I drop to my knees as does Rene,
now six. I apply the rounded tip of the utensil to the tree's bark and
start slicing: a vertical line one foot in length, at face level, followed

by horizontal lines at each end of the first so that the design ends up looking like the letter "H" in upper case, lying on its side. Then I peel back the edges first with the knife and then with my fingers until bare wood is visible. Which is when I see that I have chosen my tree with acuity, for it drips with sap. The moisture glistens, runs down in rivulets; my mouth waters.

I scrape the exposed wood with the blade of my knife. When I lift the blade off, it has gathered a pulp, this mush of woody matter that sheds an aroma unlike any other, a sweet perfume. Taking care to hold the blade in such a way that it won't cut my tongue, I slide it across and slurp off the mush. Delicious. One tree over, Rene, too, is enjoying this treat. Then we go on to second trees, Rene and I. And thirds and fourths. All day long do we do this until our knees start hurting. We cast the bark off as food to be eaten by hungry soil. Or stuff it into our mother's little knapsack to use for kindling. As to the tree, no worry about it dying for, like snakes who grow new skin after shedding the old, they grow new bark and live to a thousand.

But that sap! Unlike maple syrup's rich brown colour, it is white and translucent. That's one thing. But more important, it contains more vitamins than come in pills from a drugstore. City kids may get Oh Henry! chocolate bars when a craving for sugar hits them. We get sap from birch trees.

The other "medicine" we get from trees is gum. Spruce trees, in particular, produce this substance. Like sweat, it seeps from their wood and through their bark where, once it has surfaced, it clots, forming a scab that is coated with this glue-like viscosity. As kids, we skip and walk and dance and hop, Rene and I, through the forest on whatever island we happen to be living on of any given summer when, out of the blue, lumps of gum attract our eyes. Stuck to the trunk of a good-sized spruce, they glisten with promise. Such outgrowths of the substance are, of course, ubiquitous. Normally the size of raisins, which is what they look like, this one that I have chosen today rivals a grape in size. *Weesaa-geechaak oomigi-ya*, we call them, "the Trickster's scabs."

We stop, reach, extract—it takes some effort but it works—pop them in our mouths, and chew. At first, they are coarse, like shards of bark which, of course, is where they come from. And their taste is bitter. Within minutes, however, they have softened to the texture of *pawpilly-cum*. It *is* gum, gum perhaps not sweet, for it holds no sugar, but that is, nonetheless, minty in flavour. Which is what makes it not only palatable but actually pleasant to suck on. It is good for colds, Mom tells us when we get home, and flus and arthritis and rheumatism. And flatulence.

"Flatulence?" I ask, perplexed.

"*Ya, ee-hee, p'weegi-toowin*," she answers.

The other "medicine" we get from Mother Nature's pharmacy is *weegees*, which is this hairy, gnarly, pungent, small root one finds on a plant known in English as "rat root." One finds rat root in swamps with its roots sunk deeply into the mulch. Pulled out then hung out to dry for a week to a month or even years, then broken into pieces one to two inches in length, traditional medicine people use it to treat heartburn, headaches, upset stomachs, and gout. When you need it, you put one piece in your mouth and chew. And within minutes, its cryptic juices will mix and mingle with your saliva. Which is what you swallow. The taste is bitter—as children, it makes us grimace—but it is good for the heart, the eyes, the veins, the blood . . .

Putting pebbles from a shoreline in one's mouth staves off thirst. Burnt bannock, or bread, as in toast burnt beyond edibility, cures constipation; the white man's Ex-Lax pales by comparison. And so goes Balazee Highway's encyclopedic knowledge of the pharmacy called Nature. She teaches us, we learn, we remember. For life.

29

That same summer, when I am nine, Louise is twenty-one. And drop-dead gorgeous, with the body of a model in an *ootoo-toosim-eeyaa-pi* ("tit-string," our word for "bra") advertisement in an Eaton's catalogue. Not yet married at what, for Cree women, is an advanced age, she holds off suitors, preferring to attend for the perfect man. She is picky, yes, but she can afford it. Or so she thinks . . .

One cool evening on yet another island on Reindeer Lake, she plays hostess to three young women from a nearby island. Friends since childhood, they are here for the night. Steps from the entrance to the tent she shares with me and Rene, all four young women are sitting, a rock, a stump, and a log their humble furniture. Neck-deep in a ritual unique to the north—roasting tripe of pike on an open fire—they are having fun. I can't remember where the others are—gone to Brochet twenty miles away for an overnight sojourn, something not unheard of, leaving me and Louise to mind the home fires—but I am drawn into the circle of womanhood as if by instinct. I don't question it. I am just happy.

As with wieners, we roast this tripe with stakes of willow we have carved to a point. The tripe, which, of course, is an intestine, is a tube which, depending on the age and size of the fish it comes from, can be one to two feet long. We use, however, only the fleshiest section of the organ, a length that amounts to perhaps ten inches. Each person present has a tube including me. We slice them open along their length then splay them out on a square piece of plywood laid out on the ground. Then we scrape out the detritus with a filleting knife, the one with the snub nose, wash and rinse it, then pierce one end with the point on the stake. In this manner we can dangle the object over the fire. At the beginning when it's raw, it glistens like glycerine and is white with hints of pink, blood still lingering from a life just taken. Quickly, however, it turns first tan then brown then sometimes black.

As, crouched like a hunter in front of the fire, I roast my tripe, I find myself pulled into a reverie induced by the flames. Loons taking flight, ten thousand caribou in northward migration, pine trees swaying, our ancestors dancing, I see and hear more inside the movement of that element than in any television set exhorting my wallet to buy Coca-Cola or Kraft Peanut Butter.

Their laughter like chimes in the cool night air, at the height of their beauty, these four young women are flames themselves, swaying and hissing and making marvellous cacophony. Only peripherally aware of their voices as ambient sound, I savour the fragrance of fish tripe roasting.

Men, life, love—Will they get married? Will they get pregnant? How many children will they have?—these are the subjects that fuel their talk. Their chatter, moreover, is marked by music. And not just any music but country music, recorded music, the question being, where does it come from when the virgin forests of northern Manitoba have no electricity? The answer? From a transistor radio the size of a hymn book dangling by a string from a horizontal pole on the uncovered skeleton of Mom's *agoo-wanis*, her smokehouse. Verna Hell, Aroozalee Highway (Uncle Eelee's eldest daughter of six), Thelma Flett—I don't remember which, but one of them owns this treasure. Where she got it is anyone's guess because transistor radios, like Apwee-tigwee Gunpowder's old black gramophone are, back then, a rare commodity in sub-Arctic Canada. The problem is that, no matter how big or how powerful the radio, there is no reception, not up there, not back then, at least not in daytime. Nighttime, however, is another story.

As I am to learn some ten years later, and insofar as I understand it, this reception apparently has to do with soundwaves and the movement of magnetic impulses as they rise and fall, acting in tandem with the position of the Earth, sun, moon, and planets. And that such "movement" intensifies at night when sun and Earth are too far apart for the tension between them to rule it, control it, affect it. Greek to me but, particularly with my limited English, that's how I understand it. I will also learn that this radio tower in Nashville, Tennessee, the uncontested world capital of country music, emits the most powerful airwaves on Earth, especially at night, when they are capable of infusing the air of entire continents.

So here we are in the boreal forest of sub-Arctic Canada suddenly getting programmes from Nashville. At night. What's more, the higher in the air you hold your radio, the better the reception. Which is why these girls have now hung theirs from the branch of an old spruce tree five feet from the fire. And have turned up the volume. And as we speak here of the late 1950s–early 1960s, singers such as Hank Williams, Hank Locklin, Hank Snow, Kitty Wells, the Carter Family, Patsy Cline, and a whole host of others rule those waves (stars such as Loretta Lynn and Tammy Wynette were as yet to make their mark). Kings and queens in our northern hearts, we worship them.

"*Keegay-seetawn*," wails Hank Williams, "*Kaamaa-maatoon*" (for this is what our Cree ears hear and our Cree tongues sing). It's Aroozalee's favourite; she melts when she hears it. "*Eemithoo-tamaaaaaaan!*" she wails like Hank, her full lips trembling ("I love it!" though in the context of sound only for, in Cree, each of the five senses has its own word for "love"), except that, in her case, it is more like howling. "*Maw meena*," she starts singing along with Hank, "*Kagee-nipaan* . . ." all off-key but she sings it anyway. As we Cree put it, "*eema-cheetaag-oosit*" ("she sounds dreadful").

"*Nigees-kwaan* . . ." The steel-like vocals of Patsy Cline pierce the boreal night air as with a needle, though one containing some elixir that gives you chills. "*Athis eegis-kee-thee-tamaan* . . ." Thelma Flett, who sings "*apisees*" ("a little" or "somewhat"), attempts a harmony. It wavers but passes. Barely. Next comes Ernest Tubb with his

"*Taa-pwee anima kye-titaan . . .*" For that one, the girls have to sit. Any other posture and they would faint, fall into the flames, and float off somewhere as "Ashes of Love" (another northern favourite). "*Maw niga-skee-taan taani-paa-aan . . .*" Ernest continues. All as they squat around the fire roasting their tripe to "Uncle Ernie's" voice. And roasting and roasting, turning the object this way and that so it will cook on all sides evenly.

At this point, Louise takes her tripe from the flames and, using the inside part of a length of firewood cut in half as her cutting board, scrapes off the singed and greasy surface with a fish-gutting knife. Then she cuts off two bite-size pieces, salts them, and gives me a piece, puts one in her mouth, and chews. As do I. The others follow suit, the music continuing to melt their hearts.

"*Niwee-sagee-theeteen niti,*" sings Ray Price, "*Nimaa-goo-taan kwayas . . .*" We are, of course, just starting to grapple with the English language but we understand enough to know that the lyrics to these songs are oh, so sad. "*Taatoo-geesi-gow eewee-naga-si-in,*" Ray Price's song continues weeping. Lovers are forever splitting up, hearts being broken, people feeling lonely, unwanted, unloved. These are sad people.

Until suddenly, upbeat music appears from nowhere. *Diddly, diddly, diddly,* goes a country fiddle all by itself until a band kicks in with an impossible-to-resist jigging rhythm. At which signal, the girls drop their tripe on whatever surface happens to be there, jump to their feet, and dive into a polka. "Hey, *Choe,*" sings Kitty Wells in her nasal mezzo-soprano, "*Awinak keegi-mootoo, keechi-moosa taa-p'wee-tha . . .*" Throwing each other around in quick small circles by means of arms entwined like hooks, they twirl and whirl around that fire, the fine dust flying. "*Apwee-tigwee kaanee-meetoo-naanow.*" At one point, Verna Hell grabs me and pulls me into the circle so that I, too, am now dancing a madcap polka. And laughing and laughing. Suddenly, a crackling noise cuts in reducing the song to bites and snatches. "Hey, *Choe, Kita-skisi-na,*" crackle, "*poosch-ka,*" crackle, "*kawa,*" crackle, "*eegas-skee-thee . . .*" Oh, no, the battery is dying.

It dies. Kitty Wells stops singing. We stop dancing. The sudden silence and stark immobility actually shocks us.

For *Moony-ass* culture, such a situation does not pose problems. Get a new battery from a drawer and go back to wailing. Or run to the corner store and buy a new one. But no, here, just under Manitoba's border with the Northwest Territories where ramble at will the moose and the caribou, this is the only battery we have. With the closest store a continent away, what are we to do? Jump in a taxi? Charter a bush plane? For one battery?

You know what we do? Growling with vexation, Verna Hell takes the object out of the radio, clunks it into a saucepan, fills the receptacle with water to its halfway point, and puts it on the fire. Yes, she boils that battery. So here we have these four beautiful young Cree women, and one girlish and very pretty Cree boy of nine, sitting in a circle around a lively campfire away up in the wilds of the near sub-Arctic, surely looking to those not in the know like we are conducting a ritual to honour the bears and the eagles. When all we are doing is boiling an Eveready single 9V battery (which was what transistor radios up in those parts back in those days functioned on). And as the saucepan simmers, the girls give me the job of poking its contents this way and that and stirring the water like one would a sauce. All as we keep cutting and chewing our tripe of pike. Until a half-hour later, Verna Hell scoops the battery out with a ladle, dries it on a dishcloth, and slides it back into the cherished little jewel of a radio. And the show is on again. Yes, dear friends and colleagues, boiling dead batteries for half an hour brings them back to life.

"*Maati peewee-chee-in*"—Hank Locklin has now taken over from Kitty Wells. Louise is quivering. If "Hey, *Choe*," is Dad's favourite, this is hers. And because it is, it is mine, too. She starts singing along with Hank, ". . . *Eesaa-gee-hitaan* . . ." We all join in, "close the tore to tantation, *maw napee-tig-waan* . . ." Someday, I will be able to play the piano like the pianist on that record, I tell myself. For now, however, these four young women and one Cree boy are howling at the moon like wolves in love.

And Louise, I know, will find her man. Soon. I am a Catholic. I will pray, and pray with fervour, to *Kichitaw Maaree*. (Unfortunately, the man she finds within good time will turn out abusive. Like so many women in *keeweet'nook*, she will be a battered wife, as sad as the people these country singers are singing of.)

30

Every creature on this Earth, of course, is as fascinating as the next, but there is something about the reptile known as "snake" that is doubly so. First is its skin, which is slimy and scaly, repellent to the touch. Second is the movement of its hose-like body, the way it slithers, writhes, coils, uncoils, and crawls on its belly. Third is its tongue which, thread-thin, comes to a fork that darts out at insects such as flies and mosquitoes though it eats, as well, slugs and earthworms, leeches, minnows, even small rodents. And fourth are its eyes which, with their yellowness and absence of eyelids, seem to inform you that it is perfectly capable of coming to get you in your darkest of dreams, coiling around your helpless body, and dragging you down to the depths of hell. The story in the Bible, of course, convinces—the creature is evil. It caused Man's downfall.

Sub-Arctic Manitoba, thank God, is snakeless; so much has been noted thus far in this narrative. Central Manitoba, however, is not. And central Manitoba, of course, is where the Guy Hill School is situated. Unhappily, the species of snake that are native to the region are limited not so much in their number as in their variety. Having nothing so glamorous, or as venomous, as rattlesnakes, water moccasins, or black mambas, and nothing as terrifying as the cobra, the python, or Brazil's spectacular anaconda, all of whom I've seen in books, magazines, films, and television, all central Manitoba can boast is the common, and rather lowly, garter snake.

A full-grown adult of this species in particular, at least in our area, is thirty inches long, give or take an inch, though forty is possible, just not very common, and this in the case of the very old only. And they are thin. At their middles, they measure no more than two inches in circumference, thinner than your average garden hose, even thinner at their tails, which taper to a point. Their skin, white on their bellies with a yellowish tint, glistens as with slime. Corrugated somewhat, their backs are black with an overtone of green, the latter slightly more visible when the creature undulates. And, like chalk markings, two white stripes run parallel along those backs from front end to back. They are not poisonous; in fact, they are harmless. The worst they can do is prick your hand with their thread-like red tongue and make you bleed, and that but briefly. The most you stand to lose is five drops of blood. They nest by the hundreds in dens that are hidden under boulders; the mothers give birth to as many as forty babies. Last, they are silent. They do not hiss, not even when threatened; they simply recoil and flick their tongue at you as if they intend to strike out at you. But don't. Unless you aggress them.

With my grossly imperfect English, I don't get all the facts but we are told that some university or universities down south are studying the venom of the garter snake. To find a cure for cancer or tuberculosis or measles? We don't know, but they need the liquid and are willing to pay. Five cents a snake. For pre-adolescents and adolescents of our economic background, that is a gold mine. In today's monetary value, such an amount would translate into a dollar per snake. And because this part of Manitoba is a breeding ground for the creature, it has been selected, by these universities, as the ideal place for their collection. In fact, something about the boulder-pocked terrain with its great wealth of grasses might even make the region the worldwide capital of the wriggling, skin-tingling *aya-weeya* (creature). And as with most creatures, spring is their spawning season. Something about their six-month period of winter hibernation, when their blood sinks into a state of suspended animation, gives their lives rampant re-invigoration when they re-awaken.

If the Guy Hill Indian Residential School is surrounded on three sides by a forest of the richest and thickest of greens both evergreen and conifer, its fourth is bordered by the ten-square-mile, turquoise-watered wonder that is Clearwater Lake. Whether fall, spring, or winter, we boys are allowed to spend Saturday afternoons, unsupervised, engaging in adventures in the forest outside the bounds of the steel mesh fence that encloses our playground. On one of those sun-splashed, silk-smooth afternoons in the last week of May the year I am ten, I am walking through this forest a mile from school. Studly Bobby Fitzgerald leads the way, followed by string-bean Nameegoos Kipawm. Both of Brochet, they are followed in turn by *Moony-ass*-looking Chally Canoe of Nelson House, the gangly and clumsy Gilbert Mitaas of South Indian Lake, then me. Five in total, burlap sacks thrown as casually as cardigans over our shoulders, we are out snake-hunting.

We wade our way through the stands of grasses, the leafy branches of birch and poplar embracing our shoulders, our waists, our legs, the sunshine, too, engaging in plots to slay us with pleasure. The conversation spare, we chirp like birds whose conversation, in turn, bathes us with music, the red-winged blackbirds, the wrens, the sparrows, the warblers. Suddenly, I see a garter snake slithering through the underbrush to my right. I apprise the others who stop on the spot and turn to look. The second the snake senses my unwelcome presence, it doubles its speed and runs for its life. Unhappily for it, such vaulting volition fails to arrest our movements to catch it, for all four of my friends have now joined in the general scramble. Shouting excitedly, we lose it; it has disappeared under . . . what? A rock? A stump? Then I see it, all eight inches of it, a teenaged snake, slithering to beat the band. I am leery of the exercise—I *don't* want to do this—but I dart forward to snatch it anyway, just to prove to the others that I am not a sissy. Dangling its writhing and black-scaled reptility above myself at chest level—repulsed to the ends of my being, my bare skin is screaming—I throw it in my sack and that's one snake. *Machig-wanaas*, as Dad would say ("dirt," i.e. "noth-ing"), I think, just to help me swallow my disgust.

We move on and, sooner than you know it, see two more. This time out, Bobby Fitzgerald and Chally Canoe are the happy recipi-ents of God's largesse. When we cross the gravel road that leads to The Pas, we see one more, rushing like mad to cross that road in time before we reach it. In such circumstances they are easier to catch, as they have no logs, rocks, or bushes to hide under, behind, or in. Twice we see unfortunate victims of passing cars, flattened to a paste in the middle of the road. Dead snakes, however, count for nothing; said universities want live ones only. But at this speed and in this manner, we may catch a dozen by day's end *if* we are lucky. Which is why our vaunted target is a snake pit. (At least that's what we call them; it is only years later that I will learn that scientists who study reptiles call them "dens".)

After trekking a good three miles through thick and thin with our burlap sacks containing three to six snakes each, zero in the case of Gilbert Mitaas, we come to a boulder of the kind that is known to harbour snake colonies which, apparently, is the name for the deni-zens of snake pits. Whatever the name, you know you have found one when you see snakes slithering out from under it a little too frequently and in too great numbers. We leap into action. Trying our best to keep our silence—for some reason, even though snakes are earless, we worry that they can hear us though, apparently, they have other means to sense our presence—we grab sticks, poles, whatever we can find to lever the boulder to the side. Even if the rock is no bigger than your average washtub, it is still quite the task. But we do it. And there they are, a thousand snakes—though the way they move, they might as well be a hundred thousand. Living spaghetti.

Not a minute to be wasted for they flee in twenty different direc-tions and in huge bunches, old, middle-aged, young, and very young—babies, in fact, not more than two inches long—we set to work. Into the wriggling mass of flesh, ligament, and bone do I reach with my right hand as my left holds the sack as open as possible—ungloved, my hand goes numb—grab them by the dozen and, with them writhing like maggots around my wrist and lower arm, peel them off and drop them into my sack. To fill our sacks just enough for us to be able to lift and carry them through two miles of bush our aim, one hundred snakes, when it comes to the question of weight, is no laughing matter. On top of which you can feel their collective wriggling against your back. Brrrr!

Back at the school, keeper Ronald Simpson, who scares the living daylights out of us with great ghost stories at "lights out," wears these heavy-duty leather construction gloves to count them. Taking them one by one from our sacks and raising them high for effect—a gesture he enjoys to the point of licking his colourless upper lip— he drops them into these barrels and gives us our payment. For 115 snakes, I make $5.75, enough for a house. For Itchy. And once he has filled fifty 50-gallon barrels with these slimy creatures, he puts them away with the help of a dolly and two Big Boys in this shed that stands solitary across the ditch from the playground. Remember, we are only five of one hundred boys who have amassed them that day— well, the Small Boys haven't participated, so make that sixty—so some six thousand snakes is what they amount to. And in those num- bers enclosed in one room, they have an odour that is unmistakable, like unwashed socks or dead mice in mousetraps. And there they sit waiting for this truck from The Pas to come and get them some two days later. Winnipeg, we speculate, is where they are going, to those universities who have ordered them. Still, if a cure for cancer is the goal those scientists had in mind, it is evident, today, that they didn't find it, not in those snakes, not in their venom.

Meanwhile, some of the more mischievous boys have surrepti- tiously kept one or two babies in their pockets and, later, in little boxes or jars in their lockers so that, in class on the Monday that follows, they throw the two-inch reptiles—and nothing can writhe like a two-week, two-inch garter snake—on the girls' desks. Or on their laps. To make them scream. Which they do. The day I speak of, the diabolic Samba Cheese Fitzgerald of Puck, Manitoba—the one who calls me "girl" or "*kimaa-maanow*" ("our mother")—is even foolish enough to sneak up behind Chichilia Kipawm of Brochet to slip one under her collar and down her back. Unfortunately, what he forgets is that, though Chichilia Kipawm, fourth daughter (of six) of Aroozalee Kipawm, the best home-brew maker in all Brochet, is fifteen years old and as hefty of weight as she is of girth, she is as quick of movement as Quick Draw McGraw, the cartoon cowboy. With a roar that sounds like a bull moose charging, she whips around and punches the slightly smaller, and certainly skinnier, twelve-year-old bully—*smack!*—in the nose. Blood goes flying. Applause rings out.

The moral of the story? For me? Sitting as I am two desks to the right of Chichilia Kipawm relishing the moment? If the snake in the Bible caused Mankind's downfall, then his distant descendant, this thumb-sized infant, caused Satan's, a devil-in-the-making named Samba Cheese Fitzgerald.

31

Having undergone a ritual for ten-year-olds called "confirmation," I am now a "soldier of Christ." Meaning to say that I can now go to confession and take Holy Communion . . .

I am kneeling on a pew in pitch-black darkness. The air smells of incense and mouldy cassock, not surprising as this is a confessional in the Guy Hill chapel, a small, dark room the size of a broom closet where one whispers to a priest about one's sins.

"Yes?" A voice, male, deep, old, whispers. For all I know, it is God Himself or, at the very least, a spirit, descended from heaven to commune with me. At this point in my life, I am so Catholic I believe such things can actually happen.

"Forgive me, Father, for I have sinned"—likewise whispering, I begin my confession in an English phonetically absorbed, for the prayers, thank God, are formulaic. Saturday evening and it is time for the act for, on the morrow, we take communion. Every weekend without fail does this happen. Communion, of course, is the physical act of receiving that coin-sized, coin-shaped piece of unleavened bread called the Host on the tongue and swallowing it. Though it looks and tastes like paper, we will have feasted on the body of Christ, thus earning brownie points with His Father, the King of Heaven. And to get the license to touch that Host—even if it's with our tongues only, for our hands are forbidden—you first have to cleanse your soul of all impurities which, of course, is what sins are. And only confession can do that. Or so we are told by Father Grew, our red-haired, red eye-browed catechism teacher.

The problem for me, as always, is my English. With its current state of development, I have a very hard time understanding such cryptic regulations. I might have learned them once, on lakes up north, but that was in Cree. "Sin," to me, for example, is *eepaastaa-oot.* "*Ni-paastaa-oon, ki-paastaa-oon, paastaa-oo*" ("I sin, you sin, he/she sins"). Lying is a sin as is stealing as is hurting a person either physically or just with an insult. Killing, too, is a sin, but of humans or dogs, or loons for that matter, I don't know yet.

Gradually, my pupils adjust to the absence of light; now I can make out shadows. Six inches before my face hangs a small square window made of latticework. I can even smell the lengths of wood that criss-cross each other as on a fishing net. Then, through that latticework, I begin to see the profile of a head that is human, its chin, its lips, its nose, its forehead. A man's? A woman's? I can't tell yet. Wonder of wonders, but it is on the other side of that window, making the confessional a sort of double-closet. As I continue with my opening prayer which, like the Hail Mary, is formulaic, the heavy-jowled, bulldoggy face of Father Picard bleeds into view. It is him whispering to me, not God, not the spirits. My heart deflates, but I rally. "It is one week since my last confession . . ." And away I go with my impurities. Impurity number one: "I stole."

"How many times?" whispers Father Picard.

"Twice," I whisper back. "Once was a cookie from the kitchen as I was walking by the counter where works Miss Darlene Sawchuk. And once was a snake from Gilbert Mitaas."

"A snake?!"

"Yes, a snake."

"Good God."

"I lied to my teacher about my homework."

"How many times?"

"Twice. I was lazy. I swore. I laughed at Nameegoos Kipawm when he peed in bed. I was proud [my way of saying I was arrogant]. I thought bad thoughts about Samba Cheese Fitzgerald; I wanted him to die." None of this, of course, shocks Father Picard, for I'm sure he's heard it all, and more, a thousand times; he has, after all, been a priest since World War One, according anyway to Father Grew. At the end, he gives me my penance. To cleanse my soul of all this sinning, I am to say ten Hail Marys and two Our Fathers. Then, with two waves of a priestly hand that traces a crucifix, he dismisses me.

Flushed and panting, I come stumbling out my door to the "closet." It was hot in there, and stuffy, making it difficult to breathe, so difficult that I had to leave out my killing a mouse and farting in class. Then I join the two dozen others, male and female, mostly older and mostly larger, who are kneeling in the pews some feet from the confessional which stands between two statues, one of *Kichitaw Maaree* and one of her husband, *Kichitaw* Joseph, its two doors facing forward, one for the priest, one for the sinner. The waiting confessors are jostling for position. Why? The closer they can get to the facility, the better they can hear the confession being made, for some people's whispers will rise on occasion or the priest will get impatient with someone and almost bellow. To do this, however, these eavesdroppers have to lean to their right and strain their ears, all while they're waiting their turn to tell the principal their sin-filled story.

"You did what?!" Father Picard attacks Opal Mobster at one point. Cowed, embarrassed to the hilt—for she tells me later—the long-limbed young woman from Nelson House, Manitoba, mumbles an answer.

"How many times?" the priest confronts her. All this time I'm reciting my penance in silence not far to the left of the two rows of eavesdroppers. So loudly does Father Picard say this last that my elbows jerk and my rosaries rattle.

The other exercise that is engaged in with shameless regularity, *vis-à-vis* confession, is that certain people with nefarious ambitions, the Big Boys especially, will time confessors and make bets as to whose confession will be the longest (for the square-jawed and hulking Man Fitzgerald of Puck, Manitoba, actually has a watch; where he got it, we don't know). And lo and behold, Bathsheba Kamaamagoos wins. That is to say, the prematurely buxom and full-fleshed seventeen-year-old from Island Falls, Saskatchewan, did the most sin-ning that week, beating out Geraldine Oogow (rhymes with "kapow") of Cross Lake, Manitoba, last Saturday's record-setter, by five min-utes. And making it evident that the old French priest has muchly enjoyed her—that is, Bathsheba Kamaa-magoos's perfumed company. (In fact, at one point, we hear him moan. Or think we do.)

"Five minutes?!" ejaculate in unison the bull-necked, large-chested Ferlin Wachask of Beaver Lake, Saskatchewan, and the olive-complexioned, movie-starrish Benjamin McMillan of South Indian Lake—whose mother, by the way, was a Mobster from Nelson House—as they are walking out the church and into the hallway.

"Five minutes," confirms Man Fitzgerald, tapping his watch with an index finger the size of a sausage, "*and* four seconds."

"Ho-leee!" exclaim Benjamin McMillan and Ferlin Wachask as one. Walking behind the studly trio, I hear and see these last four exchanges. Still, I've said my penance, my conscience is clean, and so I feel unmenaced by masculinity so incontestable.

32

I am flying through the sky in the arms of a birch tree. Or rather am I making a birch tree sway, for I have climbed it and am entangled in its branches some four feet from the ground to which it is rooted. From left side to right and back and forth I make it sway, the weight of my ten-year-old body propelling its movement. He and I partners in a game we call "Tarzan, King of the Jungle," I know the title well for I see the man in the movies on the odd Sunday evening.

It's early afternoon of the second-last Saturday in June, the sun is at its peak, and I'll be going home, to my parents, in just two weeks. Which last piece of knowledge constitutes half the pleasure of being held by a tree that is known for its suppleness, its grace in wind, and its fragrance. The experience exhilarates.

Having made the tree sway far enough away from its normal position, which, of course, is vertical, I am able to release my right hand so it can reach out to achieve hand contact with the trunk of the birch tree that dances next in the series of thousands that make up this forest. So now I am wrapped like a lover around the trunk of the second birch with both my arms and both my legs and making it sway the farthest it can. Now swaying close enough to a third, I make my leap. And again I sway. And sway and sway until I am ready yet again to make my leap. Thus do I make my airborne progress across this forest that surrounds so kindly the Guy Hill Indian Residential School.

Still, I am not alone in this journey escorted by shimmering leaf and whispering twig. I am with friends, all of whom are propelling themselves through the forest in like manner. In fact, "Tarzan, King of the Jungle" is a race like no other. Its trajectory? From the side of the forest that borders the road to The Pas to the side that borders the lake, a distance, at this point in the respective curves of road and lakeshore, of a mere half-mile, a distance that, of course, is nothing for walkers but is, for us tree-swingers, a challenge. Arduous and hazardous, we could fall easily, confounded by a branch, say, and thrown to the ground, risking, in the process, the breaking of an arm. Or contact with a rock that will cause brain damage. But my friends— Weezoo Kipawm, Bobby Fitzgerald, both of Brochet, Chally Canoe of Nelson House, Gilbert Mitaas of South Indian Lake, and Machaa-is Bacheese of Puck—are all, like me, but ten years of age so are as supple and elastic as the trees they swing from.

The Tarzan yodels that spring from our throats at regular intervals are our signals to each other as to who is leading in the race to the lake and might be crowned, at race's completion, "Tarzan, King of the Jungle." At one point, Chally Canoe yodels the signature yodel: "Yaw-eeyaw-eeyaw!" He is leading. I can't let him. At another point, Weezoo Kipawm yodels, "Yaw-eeyaw-eeyaw!" He is leading. I can't let him. Two others yodel at two different junctures. They are leading. I can't let them. Only the doltish Gilbert Mitaas never gets a chance to yodel for he never leads and, in fact, lags to the point where we sometimes lose sight of his angular *oosoogan* (spine).

Shrieking with glee, my face ghost-white (I am sure)—for this is one sport I am actually good at—I swing and sway and swing and sway, my line of vision a blur of green, the foliage of trees a thousand years of age and of wisdom. The entire forest is now embroiled in swirling movement, swallowing us, her six Cree children. A hawk in flight high above us must see an entire section of the great birch forest foaming and churning like a white-capped *pawi-stik* (rapids).

But you know what? That second-last Saturday in June that we play this game, *I* do the yodel at race's completion: "Yawwwww-eeyaw-eeyaw-eeyaw! I am Tarzan, Queen of the Jungle!"—that fourth-last word leaping from my mouth of its own volition. It shocks me;

I have no idea where it came from. But no matter for, in ten short days, I am going home with my little brother. To Mom and Dad and, of course, Itchy.

33

The summer I am ten, my eldest brother, Swanson, decides to get married, his bride, Suzette Gunpowder, this mixed-blood young woman who is handsome in a way that is decidedly masculine. I remember the day—August 2, 1962—as if it were yesterday. I remember because it is the only one of my siblings' weddings that I will ever see. For Vi's, I was not yet born, while for Florence's, I was away at boarding school. As for Louise and Daniel—and, of course, Rene—they, too, will get married within good time, just not yet.

That summer of Swanson's wedding, in any case, we are living on Boundary Island. A jewel of an island, it straddles the boundary between Manitoba and Saskatchewan which, of course, is why it bears that name. Some fifteen square miles in area, large for an island on Reindeer Lake, a good half of its surface was burnt to the ground by a forest fire some three decades prior, by natural causes, so far as is known, probably lightning. Whatever the cause, when one passes by that side of the island even to this day, one sees miles of denuded, ash-grey tree trunks with spindly branches. To our childs' eyes, they look like unboiled spaghetti, whether standing vertical, horizontal, at an angle, or simply lying prostrate. The upside of the story, however, is that that's the kind of land where flourishes to excess the wild raspberry.

But then there is the other half of the island which was saved from the flames—more than likely by, again, natural forces such as rain. Part of this unburnt section, in any case, is contained in this peninsula that is connected to the main part of the island by an isthmus, that is, a narrow strip of land. A half square mile in area, this "almost island" sits on a surface of granite that juts from the lake and slides back into it as smooth as a waterslide. It also points towards Saskatchewan, whose border, at that point, is barely a hundred yards away. And that peninsula is where we set up our fish camp that summer. And which is the setting for Swanson's pre-wedding party.

Alcoholism, thank God, doesn't run in our family though we, through time, have all had our moments, Swanson, Daniel, Rene, me. Even Dad, the wisest of all drinkers and the most responsible of men, once came *this* close to doing himself in at an all-night drinking party he chanced upon one summer evening on another island on Reindeer Lake. And Mom, too, I once saw dance a merry little jig after being roped, by Fire McMillan, the fiery wife of Maagisit McMillan, the Companeek clerk, into sharing a bottle of rye whisky with her, Aroozalee Kipawm, and my wicked Aunt Peechoochee. The night of the wedding of Fire McMillan's sixth daughter (of eight), Dad just happened to be away on some business or other; when the cat is away, the mice will play, as goes the saying. Indeed, the only time Mom ever fraternizes with her wicked sister-in-law is when Dad is absent. Why? Because Aunt Peechoochee left her husband for another man some two decades prior—the first woman in Brochet to *moostapi* ("sit barenaked," our expression for living common-law)—that's how Catholic is Joe Lapstan Highway. And that's how imperfect. Still, here's one party where all hell breaks loose in the Highway clan.

Now aged thirty this summer of 1962, Swanson is old for the culture *and* for the time to be getting married. If girls back then get married at sixteen or seventeen—as, for example, did Vi and Florence respectively, and Mom, for that matter—then boys get married at twenty. For boys, even twenty-four is late. The thing with Swanson, however, is that, when he was clearing land for the building of the railway from The Pas north to Lynn Lake, he was, indeed, twenty years old and ripe for marriage. Unfortunately, the girl he fell for—from Puck, the Cree First Nation halfway between The Pas and Lynn Lake and six miles off that railway line—died from some illness at age seventeen. Chichilia Bacheese by name, she left Swanson soul-dead for a decade. Or so they say.

Finally recovered from that dreadful loss, he has flown to Lynn Lake to pick up his bride, the aforementioned Suzette Gunpowder. But why Lynn Lake, which is one hour southeast of Brochet by bush plane, when Suzette Gunpowder lives in Wollaston Lake, Saskatchewan, which is one hour northwest? All I remember is that Suzette Gunpowder, all through her teens—and she is now eighteen—divided her time between Brochet, from whence comes her Cree/Metis father, and Wollaston Lake, from whence comes her mother. In fact, not only does intermarriage between the two communities transpire with a frequency that alarms certain purists, it is Wollaston Lake from which comes Brochet's entire Dene population. Suzette's maternal grandmother a Dene from Wollaston Lake who married a *Moony-ass* hermit trapper (though not Scandinavian), this makes Suzette one-quarter Dene, one-quarter *Moony-ass*, one-quarter Cree, and one-quarter Metis, a complex affair and one that is made even more complex by the fact of Suzette's mother's death upon her birth. Raised therefore by this Dene grandmother in Wollaston Lake, the happy result, for the orphaned girl, is fluency in both Cree and Dene.

The challenge Swanson faces in going to get her is that one can't fly directly from Brochet to Wollaston Lake because, put simply, no such plane route exists. And dogsleds are moot; this is not winter. Canoes? They are stymied by the web-work of waterways—too many portages. Hence does Swanson somehow arrive in Lynn Lake—from where, I don't remember—meets Suzette who has just flown into Lynn Lake from Wollaston Lake, and together they fly to our camp on Boundary Island on one of Dad's thrice-weekly fish cargo charters. Their day of arrival? The last day of July, 1962. Travelling by plane in *keeweet'nook* is, indeed, a complex challenge.

They bring liquor. But no candy. People who go to Lynn Lake *always* bring candy for their children. Rene, now seven, and I are crushed. We won't speak to Swanson. Fortunately, Suzette finds a bottle of pop in her luggage. We are appeased.

The party rages till sunrise. Even Rene and I are allowed to stay up till ten, something that *never* happens, as Balazee Highway is such a strict disciplinarian. As we share that summer a tent with Louise and Daniel off to the side of the one that houses our parents, we lie in our shared bed straddling the border between sleep and awakeness. And listening to the voices. And country music that bleeds from a transistor radio Swanson has bought. Or at least I do, for Rene is already wheezing out the sleep of childhood. Our shelter has walls, of course, that are of canvas, not thick enough to make them soundproof, so I hear the party next door as if it were happening right there beside my bed.

Florence is absent. Married that April at age seventeen, she is living with her husband, Oogeest (Cree for "August") Zipper, at the mouth of a river called the Sawbill halfway between Brochet and Kinoosao and right on that border that haunts us always. Twenty miles is too far away. They'll be at the wedding in Brochet in two days' time, or so Louise tells us. As for Vi and her husband, Manfred Gunpowder, they are living that summer at House Point, a sliver of mainland with a beautiful beach that juts out into the vastness of Reindeer Lake a stone's throw north of Boundary Island. Them, Dad can go and get. Which is why, at one point in the night, the revellers motor off to House Point to do just that. (Daniel at fourteen and Dad's Dene assistant, nineteen-year-old Paul Peter Beksaka, Lady Beksaka's elder brother, get left behind to mind me and Rene, or so I am assuming.) The distance to House Point may be ten miles only. For us back then, however, with our pathetic little motors, it might as well be one hundred.

So there they are in this tiny boat, a fisherman's canoe the back end of which is sawed off to accommodate a ten-horsepower outboard motor: Dad, Mom, Swanson, Suzette, Louise, and Louise's boyfriend, Norman Gunpowder, droning off into the distance, their voices gliding off the mirror-like water like terns in flight. At which point, I drift off to sleep.

That drone, the laughter, the chatter, all three sounds seep in like blood through the warp of silence that is my life here on this lake. In no time flat, or so it seems, the revellers are on their way back, only this time with Vi, Manfred, and their eldest, Mary Rose, thus now making for a party of nine. In a boat that seats six only. Then aged fifteen and thus my senior by five years, Mary Rose Gunpowder is still my niece and, even from afar, I recognize her voice whose Cree, to my ears, is a babbling brook. Brook or not, with all that weight propelled by a tin can one dares call a motor, the boat must be barely moving. As for life jackets, they remain unknown to north Cree culture. And these people are drinking, sharing between them, for all I know, two bottles of whisky. Or something just as toxic. And it is night, albeit one blessed by starlight. And no wind. And I fall asleep. And dream.

And in that dream, the motor is droning, droning, the voices chattering. Suddenly, amidst that laughter, nine people scream. In unison. The canoe has tipped over. And suddenly, the wedding party is walking underwater, the lake's sand bottom the road they tread. Their arms outstretched like those of zombies in films I've seen, their eyes are miniature floodlights. Weightless—for I am a ghost, an underwater sprite, a nymph—I float to the surface. But they don't. I scream a scream that is silenced by water. I try to fight my way back down to them but the absence of gravity prevents me.

Gifted beyond my years in subjects such as reading and writing, I once read in a book loaned to me by Sister Ann the story of a harpist named Orpheus whose wife has died, lost to the underworld. With his music, which is exquisite beyond human hearing, he lulls the King of Death, a god named Hades, into giving him license to bring his wife back to the land of the living upon spring's coming. On one condition, says the King of Death: Orpheus has to relinquish his hold on her—Eurydice is her name—at winter's arrival each year; that is, release her to the land of the dead. The ancient Greeks' explanation for the cycle of the seasons, the story impresses me; I will never forget it. Though not yet eleven I do conflate the myth of Orpheus, the harpist, with that of Persephone, who was forced to return to the underworld in the winter months for the crime of eating pomegranates. Still that night, inside my dream, I am Orpheus playing my harp in hopes of bringing my family back to the surface of Reindeer Lake, back to life.

I wake up. They are here; they made it; they didn't drown. It was only a dream. What's more, they are singing, which always means one thing: they are feeling good. Under cover of darkness, I sneak out to watch. At this point in that balmy, insect-free night, Norman Gunpowder and Swanson Highway are dragging out an uncut sheet of plywood—all six feet by eight feet of it—and laying it across the wood chip–carpeted ground in front of the main tent. This will be the dance floor. I can tell because Suzette is unpacking an accordion she has brought, which will turn out to be hers, and starting to tickle its keys and buttons and stretching its squeeze box this way and that, producing in this manner snatches of melody and chords that charm. Dad's accordion long gone to pay for a lead dog of sterling repute, he will provide the percussion with his feet in Kodiak construction boots. So there they have it—a two-piece orchestra for a dance unlike any other. Except, of course, for the *skweetaas* to come at the wedding itself in two days' time.

The next thing I remember is Louise and Verna Hell, her best friend at the time, making raspberry pies in the kitchen at our small log house on Brochet Hill, the fruit, of course, picked in bulk from Boundary Island. They are preparing the banquet that will go with the wedding and so have to make at least one hundred, says Louise. Which gives me and Rene plenty to do. Even the wild green grasses on the summit of the plateau that separates our house from the lake are swaying in a manner more animated than usual. They seem to be singing as we spend that entire morning running back and forth across that summit from our house to Companeek and back performing errands for the bakers, one of them the daughter of a Chief. Yes, Chief Albert Hell has replaced Chief Chi-Louie who died of old age some two years prior, making Albert Hell King of Brochet which makes, of course, Verna Hell a princess, she likes to say. (Verna's Cree mother, Chief Albert's first wife, died in childbirth when Verna was born, which is how Chief Albert Hell ended up with a second wife, this one a Dene woman named Maggie.)

"*Keeyaapich* paper plates?" ("More paper plates?") asks Maagisit McMillan from behind his counter, his big teeth exposed like those of the cat in *Alice in Wonderland*.

"*Ee-hee*," we answer, "*keeyaapich* paper plates." If Maagisit McMillan can mix up his languages, then so can I. He has grade four, I have grade four. So there.

But how foxy Louise looks each time she bends over in her form-fitting jeans to tend to the oven on that bulky stove. And how full-figured Verna Hell looks by comparison.

"*Lapwachin maa-a?*" asks Rene.

"That's your mom's department," answers Verna Hell as she takes out what must be pie number forty. "She's making it at Vi's. There's no room here." (*Lapwachin*, by the way, is our take on the idea of the wedding cake or fruit cake in general; more on that wondrous subject in a forthcoming chapter.)

Back then, of course, up in those parts, the wedding dress as most people know it—the white, the satin, the tulle, the veil—does not exist. The bride wears a dress that is new, one hopes, usually ordered from the Eaton's catalogue, and of no special colour. And a real-silk kerchief in brilliant colours for the head. And, oh yes, of course, low-heeled leather shoes also ordered from Eaton's in Winnipeg— "moccasins are for moose-hunting," says Verna Hell, "leather for weddings." She should know; she is a princess.

For the ceremony, Suzette wears a knee-length silk dress that she has commissioned from my godmother, Tarees Naasi-peeti-meek. Known for her skill at her stone-age manual Singer sewing machine, my godmother has outdone herself, for the dress, sapphire blue with tinges of purple, manages to be feminine and masculine at one and the same time, "just like Suzette," says Tarees Naasi-peeti-meek (whose inborn wisdom on matters two-spirit has always amazed me). Three half-inch-wide silk ribbons in the colours fire-engine red, sunburst yellow, and navy blue tied around her waist and hanging to her knees down each side complete an ensemble that makes Dene ladies, when they see her, sigh soft *koolsth-li*. As she walks hand in hand with the studly Swanson down the sandy footpath that delineates the summit of the hill, or low esker, before our house, the ribbons flutter in a breeze just come from the south. The church bell, meanwhile, peals out its festive announcement which means one thing: K's'chees-naanis—the bald one, the one who's been in Brochet since 1950 for there will soon be a new one—is at it again. Dressed in his cassock as opposed to his work clothes (which are those of a labourer), he is pulling the dangling rope at the church's main entrance, which, of course, is the force that makes the bell in the belfry ring out its signature *ding-dong*. Brochet residents, from Filament Mosquito in Minee-waati-meek (the Point) to Fire McMillan in Seepees-seek (Where the Little River Is), all prick up their ears and grab their rosaries.

If traditional wedding dresses for the women are a foregone conclusion, then tuxedos for the men are a bust. Swanson merely wears a black pair of dress pants, a white cotton shirt, dress shoes in leather, and a brown suede jacket just bought at Perpaluk's in Lynn Lake. As for a necktie, no Cree man in *keeweet'nook* has ever worn one so why, asks Suzette Gunpowder, should Swanson Highway?

The church service that morning has its moments. The room, for one thing, is packed to the rafters, so much so that latecomers like Half Ass Sam Well and Ann Kaakaa Kipawm, who are known for their shortness *and* their lateness, have to stand at the back and crane their necks. K's'chees-naanis plays his organ—that is his harmonium—Samba Cheese Weetigo leads the choir which, in essence, is the congregation. Father Cadeau's quavering baritone brays out the *Kyrie* and, of course, Jean-Pierre Yazzie clears the phlegm from his slimy esophagus and spits it, triple *fortissimo*, into his ambulant Libby's Deep Brown Beans tin-can spittoon. For years will it be said that it hit dead-on with its telltale *splat* the "do" of Swanson's "I do."

As wedding banquets are generally hosted by one set of parents of the bridal couple, so it is with us—Swanson's wedding banquet is held at our house. Brochet, in any case, has neither hotel nor community hall with a kitchen, at least not in the days of Chief Albert Hell.

And if hotels are non-existent, then so is the invitation, meaning that everyone, whether saint, criminal, or janitor, is invited. Which means that, because our house is so very small, we have to serve the meal as an endless series of sittings that last, in the end, the live-long day. Which doesn't mean that the languid aromas that come wafting from that kitchen like lengths of muslin are any less penetrating. In fact, if that breeze from the south that soothes our nostrils that wondrous morning were to grow to a wind, those aromas would have reached, I am sure, the suburbs of Winnipeg nine hundred miles to the south. So much food is laid out that day that five tables are needed to hold its weight even though, in reality, these tables are mere lengths of plywood: six-foot-long slats sawed in half lengthwise, balanced on sawhorses arranged in a horseshoe, and covered with oilskin tablecloths. All that is missing is lighting of the kind that illuminates *Kichitaw Maaree* statues in grottos, and that is because it is broad daylight.

Extraordinary courses rarely seen on one table at one time are served and swallowed—caribou *arababoo* in a rich, thick *mooskami*, *oopawma meena oospi-gahya eechee-patay-gaa-teeg'wow*, *ateega-meek eepa-gaasoot weechee-gaskoo-siya asichi*, *nameegoos*, *oogow*, *lapa-taag'wa* from gardens *maameek*, the vegetables (ditto), *oochak-seesa*, *beansak*, *jeerrrees kaagoo-cheeg'wow*, and *biskitsak*—caribou stew in rich, thick, gravy; hindquarters and ribs grilled over an open fire, whitefish boiled with onions, trout, pickerel, potatoes from gardens down south, macaroni, beans, canned stewed cherries, cookies. Plus the pies and bannock (baked with love by Louise and Verna Hell), the tea, the coffee, the milk, the juices, the pops, the sodas, the clear, blue water of Reindeer Lake, and, last, Mom's legendary, much-admired, black-pocked, juice-filled, succulent *mishti-lapwachin* (giant *lapwachin*), which is of a size that boggles the eye and which is not so much swallowed as sucked into oblivion as by osmosis.

People come, people go, people eat, people drink, people chuckle, chortle, giggle, cackle, guffaw, chatter, sigh, whisper, bray like moose, roar with laughter, make glowing speeches, sing silly songs, applaud, declare their loyalty to each other *and* to the nation (that is, Canada), make undying promises of the kind they make in romance

novels, shed tears then wipe them, sniffle, moan with pleasure, squeal
with delight, bang their chests and lance Tarzan yodels, rattle their
teacups, tinkle their glasses with teaspoons to demand discourses,
burp, slurp, hiss, rip, chew, masticate. Their cutlery clinks, pings, and
clatters, their dishes clang, ring, and rattle. Such a vast variety of sound
is produced in that room that sun-filled second day in the month of
August, all in the name of joy and happiness for the bridal couple,
that the couple just anointed with the sacrament of matrimony are
convinced to the cockles of their now-united heart that their marriage
will endure till the very last caribou on Earth has been killed, skinned,
and gutted. It gets to the point where, for me, at age ten years, all
Brochet has melted like wax to become one titanic mouth, one yawning abyss that knows no limit, to whom satisfaction is *terra incognita*
and which makes the *Weetigo*'s appetite for human flesh look tame
by comparison. As such, it opens and closes and opens and closes *ad
infinitum*, devouring to the last every blade of grass on the summit
of the hill that fronts our house, every leaf, every pebble, every ant,
every germ, every molecule. And time transforms to a great big *lapwachin* rolling and rolling through the great womb of space.

Dreamt or not, by the time it is over, the last crumb swallowed, the
last drop slurped, Louise and Verna Hell are so exhausted that they
collapse into chairs and come "this close" (they admit later) to going to
the dance "by proxy only." In fact, if it weren't for Ovide Gunpowder,
who appears at the door to convince them that doing things "by
foxy" does not "cut the mustard," suicide would paralyze the male
community of the village, for Verna Hell, in particular, is admired for
her jiggle. In fact, when she does the *taatoo-gipi-tamook*, she is known
to have garnered standing ovations at cemeteries both old and new in
Brochet, so, at least, has claimed Masky Jimmy Perkins.

34

At the time being chronicled, a brand-new building is under construction between the Dene quarter and the D O T. Apparently, it is intended as a meeting hall, with offices attached. As one big space for crowds to assemble, why not use it for more than bingos, someone has suggested, even if it is as yet to be finished? And with a floor made of plywood, Zebedee Zipper has reputedly contributed a sagely question: "Might it not be ideal for stomping and jigging? Of the kind one sees in *skweetaas*?" Yes, apparently, is the consensus. And so it is that my brother's wedding dance is held in a building that has no walls—just a roof, the beams to support it, and a floor made of plywood. Happily, however, the night is balmy, for the north, practically subtropical, the stars all out with a near-full moon to assist them in lighting what promises to be the best "hot panties" ever to be danced on Reindeer Lake.

Napoleon Zah, God bless him, comes with his fiddle (Pelican Narrows is way too far so forget Dad's father, who plays it better, or so they say). The husband of my mother's first half-sister (of three), the sylph-like and elegant Josephine Zah, he, too, like all Dene in old Brochet, has roots in Wollaston Lake, Saskatchewan. Which begs the question: How on Earth did he learn his craft? When Wollaston Lake, so far as is known, has no school of music? All that is certain is that Napoleon Zah has a talent for raising people's spirits to elevations vertiginous with the way he strokes and plucks his strings. Much in

demand at dances and weddings, it is only natural that he be hired for
Swanson's wedding dance.

Second-eldest son of Pitooria Wachask, the much-loved midwife,
and eldest of Alfred—for Pitooria had an older son before marrying
Alfred—Andrew Wachask accompanies Napoleon Zah on his country guitar; it is no secret that he knows three chords only but that's
all one needs in country music so he will do, say certain people who
would have preferred Joe Highway on his "titty-tickler." With his
killer Kodiak construction boots pounding like hammers on a one-
foot-by-one-foot, inch-high platform of pine two-by-fours nailed
cheek-by-jowl for the purpose, Norval Wachask, Andrew's obstreperous younger brother, serves as percussion. And a good thing, too,
say certain people, for when he drinks—which, thank God, is rarely,
alcohol being largely inaccessible to old Brochet—he is known for
inflicting concussions. As for the caller, Oogeest Zipper, my sister
Florence's recently acquired husband—they made it to Brochet just
in time for the ceremony—fills the role most fittingly for he has a
voice that is clear, articulate, and loud; one hears what he says when
he says it. And why. This is the orchestra, the band.

For those unfamiliar with the *skweetaas*, it is a dance that came
to the north by way of the Metis, whose bloodline runs thick in old
Brochet (at least Cree Brochet, for Dene Brochet is, of course, pure-
blood mostly). Though it came to us as the "square dance," the closest our Cree tongues could get to pronouncing the word, as previously
noted, was "*skweetaas*," which is actually two words combined:
iskwao, which means "woman," and *mitaas*, which means "pants."
Ergo, "women's underpants" or, in my writing, "hot panties."

"You wanna come to the hot panties with me tonight?" might ask
Ooskin-eegees Gunpowder of Watermelon Perkins, the girl he fan-
cies. Or, "They're holding a hot panties at Ann Kaakaa's next week,"
might say Oos'chi-gwaan McMillan to her sister, Cheechees (i.e. the
sisters "Head" and "Hand" McMillan, two daughters—of eight—of
the Companeek clerk, Maagisit McMillan, and his fiery wife, Fire).
"If I go," might answer Cheechees, "I am sure Peter Zipper will ask

me to dance which would be nice for, as you know, he *loves* 'hot panties,' especially mine."

One element that is essential among several in *skweetaas* is the caller. Without him, there is no dance, no movement, no point. The dancers will not know where to go, will not know what to do; they will just stand mutely around in their circles resembling statues (the four men and four women required for the dance, by the way, dance in a circle as opposed to a square; go figure). Which is where the caller comes in.

That is to say, the *teepwaa-chigao* (one who calls) calls out to the dancers what moves they should be making at any given point through the course of the dance. Sometimes the caller himself is one of those dancers; in my brother-in-law Oogeest Zipper's case, he can do both—dance *and* call—and so is permitted. Otherwise, the caller usually stands right next to the band. If there is electricity, he calls into a microphone. If there is none, which, of course, is the case in old Brochet, he calls out to the dancers over the music and all the attendant noise—people talking, children screaming, babies crying, dogs barking, floorboards pounding—which means that the caller *has* to have the voice of God. Which Oogeest Zipper does.

The music begins. As he always does, my uncle Napoleon Zah opens with an introduction, a kind of diving board that goes "diddle-ee, diddle-ee, diddle-ee" in sixteenth notes, on a double-stop, on a major sixth, without variation in pitch or in volume, and that lasts for at least ten seconds, as if he is relishing bringing the crowd to the point of insanity with anticipation. And true to his magic, an electric charge has just shot its way from one end of the room to the other. Maggie Hell, second wife to Chief Albert Hell, for one, can't help it—her toes start tapping. Indeed, the tall, gaunt woman with the beaver-like teeth as brown as bark stands with the seven other people in her dancing square like a wire vibrating—one more "diddle-ee" and she will explode and zoom through the ceiling. As with Maggie, her co-dancers' knees are bending and bobbing and bobbing and bending. Their hips pulsate, their rib cages sway. As for the rest of their bodies, they are ready at any second to plunge into gyrations of the kind one sees only in Bugs Bunny movies. Except they can't. Not, that is, until the caller has given the signal. Which he does.

"Bobs and Betties, bow to your partner," calls Oogeest Zipper above Napoleon Zah's fiddle. Maggie Hell bows to the dancer on her left who, as it happens, is the even taller and even more skeletal Happy Doll Gaazayoo. "Bobs and Betties now bow to the other," calls Oogeest Zipper. Maggie Hell bows to the dancer on her right who, as it develops, is man-of-honour Swanson Highway. "All join hands," calls Oogeest Zipper. Maggie Hell joins hands with Swanson Highway on her right and Happy Doll Gaazayoo on her left. "And circle to the right," calls Oogeest Zipper. The dancers start moving in one big circle, first to the right; from above, it would look like a wheel just starting to turn. "Spread right out like a caribou hide," goes Oogeest Zipper who, at this point, changes tack. "Circle to the left, go lickety-scoot." The wheel of dancers stops cold turkey and starts circling in the opposite direction. The women's skirts swish and men's pants shiver (back in those days, women wearing pants was deemed obscene).

"*A la main* left with the corner maid," goes Oogeest Zipper. Breaking the circle, Happy Doll Gaazayoo swivels to his right and reaches with his left hand for Maggie Hell's claw-like left. Chests careening this way and that, both feet stomping, Maggie Hell and Happy Doll slink past each other which gives Happy Doll the chance he needs for his knobby right hand to reach for that of woman-of-honour Suzette Gunpowder-just-turned-Highway.

"*Kimoosoom chimasoo, koogoom tapasao*," calls Oogeest Zipper and Suzette jigs off with Happy Doll Gaazayoo.

"Sidlee, sidlee, sidlee," Rene and I call along with our brother-in-law Oogeest Zipper from a corner of the room where people are jostling. (I don't remember the exact lineup of this first dance, but Half Ass Sam Well and Modest Loon are somewhere in there; Mom and Dad will join in shortly.) Chests throttling and heaving, feet kicking up a regular storm, Happy Doll and Suzette bounce past each other which gives the Dene Happy Doll the chance he needs to reach with his left hand for that of stick-thin, cockroach-like Ann Kaakaa.

For two entire seconds, Ann Kaakaa and Happy Doll jiggle with each other, the mouse-tiny woman laughing enough for three big people. With his right hand, Happy Doll moves on to reach for the right of Check Wheat He, a dusky Dene maiden not yet sixteen. Whipping her fulsome, swarthy figure past the man's bony right hip, Check Wheat He glides on. Thus does Happy Doll Gaazayoo arrive at the side of his dancing partner, Maggie Hell, who exposes, as she does when worked to a tizzy, her beaverish brown teeth as for a camera. "Swing your partner round and round," calls Oogeest Zipper. Happy Doll swings the scrawny Maggie Hell round and round with such pagan abandon that all one sees of Chief Albert Hell's Dene wife is a brownish blur.

"And promenade," Rene and I call with Oogeest and off we go, two small boys jigging hand in hand and arm in arm, right behind the bride and groom and all the other dancers who, as is usual with promenades, dance in pairs all the way around one great big circle, stomping and jigging and bouncing and jiggling and banging and jangling for this is now some fifteen dances later and dancers have changed at least five times. Rene and I try our best to dance like Suzette, who somehow manages to jiggle like a pudding and look quite stately at the same time. And laugh ourselves blue in the face. The movement is dizzying, the *rat-a-tat-tat* of Kodiak construction boots on a plywood floor infernal (Norval Wachask's are the least of it: to come to a *skweetaas* without such footwear is, for men, a mortal sin).

"*A la main* left with your left hand, bow to the partner, and there you stand." It has lasted for four hours. So far. Everyone dances at one point or other, even ninety-year-old Old Dice Chagaazay with her humpy spine, scarlet kerchief, caribou moccasins, and wrinkles so deep she looks like a prune. "Call your dog and grab your gun; let's keep dancin', have some fun." The room is now, to me, one endless, swirling tunnel of colour.

Obert and Apwee-tigwee Gunpowder, who now live behind us, arrive from their fish camp out on the lake some ten hours late—motor trouble, explains Obert Gunpowder, who looks like Gary Cooper, the American movie star—and so are dragged, as they pass by with their bags, paddles, and knots of children, into our house by our generous mother. Her purpose? That they take the last of the *lapwachin* which she has stashed away for their children, for she, for one, had not lost faith in their eventual arrival. Grabbing the dessert, which is wrapped in brown parcel-paper, and stuffing it into a jacket pocket, Apwee-tigwee Gunpowder flees like a wraith into the moonlit night followed on her heels by her handsome husband and at least eight children (of the thirteen they will have within ten years), for the older ones have scattered to the village like ants in flight. No matter the house, she is off to the dance and hell be damned.

"As you may know," says Obert Gunpowder by way of apology to Balazee Highway, "when it comes to the *skweetaas*, Apwee-tigwee Gunpowder cannot control her animal urges."

"Comb your hair and tie your shoe; promenade home like you always do," calls Oogeest Zipper back at the dance hall one half-hour after this meeting; his voice is getting raspy. Hand in hand and arm in arm, Obert and Apwee-tigwee Gunpowder come stomping by as part of the circle (and by this time, Mom and Dad, too, are dancing). "Dog in the corner gnawin' on a bone; meet your girl and promenade." As Rene and I crouch on the floor against one wall sleepily watching all this activity—it is now past midnight, but who's keeping an eye on the clock?—I see something pop out of Apwee-tigwee Gunpowder's coat pocket. It plops to the floor and bounces once, twice, and comes to a stop at my right foot. Unaware of this incident, the woman dances on. I look at the object. Wonder of wonders but it is a slice of *lapwachin* which, slipped free of its wrapping, looks like cake. "First you whistle and then you sing. All join hands and make one ring." Wilpaletch Kipawm comes stomping by in his Kodiak boots and, not seeing it, steps on the *lapwachin*, transforming the cake in one half-second back into a pudding. And with Rene sleeping already across my shoulder, I, too, fall asleep.

35

My grandfather, Joseph Highway, played the fiddle. His son, Joe Highway, played the accordion. And I, grandson to the former and son to the latter, play the piano. It is a natural progression, a God-given legacy.

I never knew my mothers' parents for both died young, her mother of some unspecified illness in her mid-thirties. My mother, then a girl of eighteen years and wife for two, was already a mother to the first of what would be, in time, twelve children. Her father, for his part, drowned in Mink Lake up north at age just sixty. She just forty that summer, I was born the December that followed, so I never met him, either. Still, neither grandparent was a musician.

Such was not the case with my paternal grandparents. Them I knew, though not much better. Because my dad had left his birthplace of Pelican Narrows, Saskatchewan, for the great sub-Arctic at age eighteen, and because technology up there back then was, in essence, non-existent, communication was minimal, so he hardly ever saw his parents again, meaning to say that *we* hardly ever saw them either. I remember seeing them once when I was five. Having paddled from Pelican Narrows the two hundred miles north to the northern extremity of Reindeer Lake, which is just inside Manitoba, we met them on this island that was, in effect, a gorgeous sandbar with a scattering of trees, a jewel of a place called Sandy Island. Having come to visit the eldest of their five surviving sons and his family, meaning us, we camped there for a week, a family reunion much needed and cherished. I remember Grandma—Josephine Highway-née-Ballantyne—looking an awful lot like her eldest daughter, my Aunt Peechoochee; just as beautiful, she was also just as fierce, just as wicked, or so legend has it. The second time I saw them—and last, as it turned out—was when I was twenty-two. They now in their nineties, I was up for a visit in Pelican Narrows with my brother Daniel, his now deceased wife, Myra, and their first child of two, then just an infant not yet walking. By that time, Granddad sadly no longer had his fiddle so I never heard him play, one of the very few regrets that haunt my life. And no one seems to know where that instrument went. All that is known is that, because Metis blood informed his veins, he had inherited "the voice." And not just any voice, but that of Metis old-time fiddling. When he played the jig known as "*Taatoo-gipi-tamook*," for instance, people aged a hundred years would jump to their feet and scream, is how legend has it.

As for my father, he walks in one day, back in the winter I turn six, with a gramophone. I leap to my feet. My hair stands on end, I gasp for air. An awfully large gramophone, I think, but I jump on the box which, at this point, looks like a suitcase. At my age, I can't manipulate the clasps so Dad, who is beaming, unclasps them for me. The suitcase opens. My heart plummets. If that's not a gramophone, then what on Earth is it? All I can tell, at least for now, is that it has, at one end, a keyboard of the kind that K's'chees-naanis plays on his organ at church on Sundays and, at the other end, rows of small black buttons that look like pills and shine like eyes. Keys and buttons in their rows flank this bright red casing whose sheen deflects light; the casing, in its turn, flanks this section that, when Dad unclasps this black strap of leather, turns out to be a corrugated box. And when Dad lifts the contraption to his chest and wraps these straps that appear from nowhere around his shoulders—and he, in the act of doing this, presses keys and buttons in haphazard fashion—it bleats and meows as the box expands and diminishes, expands and diminishes.

"*Kaasee-peegi-piteet kitoochigan*," he calls it ("the musical instrument that is stretched and stretched"). A "titty-tickler," I hear it called by Lawrence Loon, the Dene interpreter. An "accordion," I hear it called by Father Cadeau. Whatever its name, Dad got it from Moomoos Perkins in exchange for a dog who showed great promise as a leader—for Dad already had one, and two lead dogs for one man are unnecessary. But Moomoos Perkins was happy, for he'd just lost his "star" at a big game of poker.

Once Dad has learned how to play this box by pumping its bellows which, as it turns out, is what the corrugated section is, and pressing the keys and buttons this way and that, I won't let him stop. At first, he is terrible, but "persistence" has always been Joe Highway's middle name.

"*Keetawm, keetawm,*" I beg him ("Again, again"). For there he sits on a chair in our kitchen, manoeuvring the instrument with a skill that increases by the day. His rib cage swaying, his right foot stomping, his smile is infectious. "*Eegee-ginaw-peegan-thik kipaapaa,*" "*Maaskooch Kimoosoom Paasoo,*" "*Maagi-teethi-goom,*" and "*Kaachee-pata-pee-aan, oota mista-sineek,*" he plays them all to a rhythm that is jiggy ("Your Father Had a Long One," "Your Grandpa Has Dried Up for Sure," "Big Nostrils," and "As I Sit Perched on This Great Big Rock," a repertoire loved in old Brochet). When people cross the village to come and listen, they, too, stomp their feet and yell, "*Keetawm!*"

Still, that isn't enough. I have to learn to play the instrument myself. The problem is, Dad's accordion is way too large for a small-for-his-age mere lad of six. When he lays it down to rest for the day, I can't even budge it much less play it. Even if I press its keys or its buttons, no sound emerges for its "lung"—the corrugated box—isn't moving and there is nothing I can do about it. So I have to wait until I am big enough. Unfortunately, at one point before this happens, Dad is forced to barter his accordion for a lead dog just as Moomoos Perkins had before him. His current leader, Rich, is aging and ready to be put out to pasture, says Dad. Lead dogs are expensive, and Dad has no money. So he buys one with that accordion from Meat Toss Yazzie, the Dene hunter with a wife so tall it makes your neck bones creak when you look up at her face. That lead dog is Queen, the best we will have. But I am heartbroken. With no accordion in the house, that house is dark, that house is soul-less.

Fortunately, a Ukrainian woman fur trader named Mrs. Permafrost arrives in Brochet at around this time with, among other things, a jukebox. (Her name is actually Permachuk, but we call her "Permafrost" because, of course, we live on permafrost.) At least, "jukebox" is what she calls this pretty machine with lights that flash in the colours magenta, purple, pink, and blue and, behind its glass, a rack of saucer-sized records that change by means of an arm that whirs and clicks. The Ukrainian woman with skin so white it looks like baking powder, eyes that squint, and lips that simper like a fissure in a wall opens a store near Minee-waati-meek (the Point) near where live Filament Mosquito and her husband, Archie, and that's where she puts it. You put a dime inside this slot and away it goes. I am mesmerized. (A generator outside is its source of power.) There, Ice-keemee Minette with her country voice and her three-hour hourglass figure sits on the counter beside this object swinging her legs like "Hunty-Dunty" and wailing along to the songs that play and whose words, to me at that point in time, are a mystery. Besides, so rarely are we in Brochet that I get to see this jukebox four times only.

Some four years later, my eldest brother, Swanson, marries a woman named Suzette Gunpowder who not only plays an accordion like Dad, but owns one *and* sings. The difference is that, while Dad has a taste for jigging music, Suzette prefers gospel; she likes singing about Jeezoos.

Also, I am now ten, meaning to say that I am larger and stronger than I was at age six. It helps, of course, that Suzette's accordion is much more compact than Dad's. I can actually lift it. I can actually put it on my knees and wind its straps around my shoulders. Dad says that when I wear it, he can just see my forehead behind it, my eyes thus unable to see the keys on the right side of the squeeze box *or* the buttons on the left. But I can reach them. And I can play them, if by feel only. So after their wedding when she has moved in with Swanson—and us—on Boundary Island, I borrow my new sister-in-law's accordion when she will let me, which is often.

So here I am at age ten years, strapped to this instrument three sizes too big, waddling off into the forest of spruce behind our camp. A quarter of a mile and I find myself in a meadow. A flat rock to sit on and I am ready. To play. I don't care what. I reach for those keys and those buttons and make whatever sound I am capable of making. *Squeek, squack, bleat. Squeek, squack, bleat.* The squirrels scurry off as do the chipmunks as do the rabbits. I even scare the ants. But that doesn't stop me. I practice and practice and practice and practice, every day, two hours at a stretch, sometimes three. And, note by note, chord by chord, day by day—a snatch of tune here, an interval there, a chord, a rhythm—I start making something that could pass for music. If I start at the beginning of August—that is, right after my brother's wedding—then by month's end, I am playing a tune I learned at boarding school. Except that, having grade four already and being ambitious, I "write" my own lyrics as well (that is, inside my head). And lo and behold, the squirrels return, as do the chipmunks as do the rabbits. So good is my music that, before I know it, they have even formed a kick line (in my child's eyes) and are doing the cancan, a dance I saw in a cowboy movie at school the year before. And as they dance, the animals squeal with piercing delight and join me in singing my song (which is actually "Pop Goes the Weasel" but with a difference): "Round and round the circle, the rabbit wore a *weeskits* [vest]; when the buttons went diddly-doo, off came the *weeskits*." And how we laugh, how we chatter, me and those animals.

And then there is the piano. At the Guy Hill Indian Residential School, my eleven-year-old, pre-pubescent boy soprano stands out in choir. I have a voice. Combine this element with the innate musicality that I have inherited from my progenitors and "you are talking talent," says Sister St. Clare to Sister St. Aramaa (for I overhear them one day) after choir practice.

On top of this, the choir director keeps catching me looking at Matilda Mitaas, our accompanist, with envy—in fact, I'm not even singing, I'm too busy watching her piano—so she puts me under the charge of this same Sister St. Aramaa. Now we're talking turkey, for

Sister St. Aramaa, who, by the way, looks like a turkey, takes me on—finally!—as a student. "I will be able to play like Melinda Kamaa-magoos," I say to Rene with untold excitement in the yard that day as we are making a fort in the snow by the seesaw.

The first thing the sixty-ish nun teaches me is to read music—the precise position on the keyboard, for example, of the middle C and the five-note scale that climbs from there to D to E to F to G and back down to C. That takes five fingers precisely; the hand itself does not even have to change position. From there, she teaches me the difference between whole notes, half notes, and quarter notes. She teaches me the difference between a major key and a minor key. From there, I go on to play by reading the score (such as it is, a piece for the right hand only that is written in the key of C-major—all white keys, no black—and travels in quarter and half notes). The piece is called "Loudly Brayed the Donkey." I hear it to this day. Later, she teaches me the meaning of musical terms that are all in Italian, terms like *allegro, allegro con brio, allegretto, andante cantabile, andante sostenuto, largo, presto, presto con fuoco, poco a poco,* and so many others, words that will help me immeasurably with my learning of the Italian language decades later. By the end of that year, I have progressed to sonatinas by Italian composers such as Muzio Clementi and Anton Diabelli. And it's only a matter of time before I move on to Bach, Mozart, Chopin, and a whole world of wonders that will change my life irrevocably.

Most children who are "forced" to take piano lessons by their parents hate the experience; not only do they refuse to practice, they learn to hate their teacher. Me? I love it. Wild moose couldn't pull me away from that keyboard. I am smitten. I am obsessed. As with Suzette Highway's accordion, I practice and practice and practice and practice. I sneak into the "lie-berry" where the piano sits off-limits to plebeians—only its students can touch it—and where Sister St. Aramaa gives her lessons; I practice until my fingers hurt. The result? By the end of the year, I do what it takes your normal student five years to accomplish—I reach grade five in the piano syllabus of Toronto's Royal Conservatory of Music.

Within three years, the little old nun with the face like a road map will enter my name in the Kiwanis Music Festival which takes place every late February in The Pas and I will capture first prize. I will beat out all those privileged middle-class white kids in what I learn, only years later, is a racist town, and win a trophy and a scholarship. My picture will appear in the local paper. Under the image of this pretty, brown-skinned Cree boy with a mop of black hair, a white cotton shirt, a baby-blue cardigan, and his trophy cradled in one arm will read the headline, "Brochet Lad Wins Piano Trophy." As an adult, I will take those lessons, turn them on their head, and transform them into a million-dollar business. More important, I will play my way around the world—Rome, London, Berlin, New York, Tokyo, Rio de Janeiro, Brochet—giving joy and beauty to so many people that I have long ago lost count. And I will play benefit concerts to help raise money for those who need it. I will give and give and give to my community. I will give until it hurts. And the person at the top of a very long list of those to whom I owe my thanks for this gift from heaven will be this squat, dumpy, much-maligned, wrinkled old nun named Sister St. Aramaa.

36

It is now April of 1963 and Easter exams are on the horizon. For some reason, the school stopped taking students from Churchill after Freddy Begay's first year so Freddy has long been a memory. Apparently—and this I will learn only years later—the community he returned to, Churchill, Manitoba, is living through a nightmare that will last three decades. Airlifted by force from their home community of Tadoule ("Tadoo-lee") Lake some one hundred miles northeast of Brochet and some hundred west of Churchill, they are plunked on a surface of treeless rock on the shore of Hudson's Bay. Housed in shacks made of plywood that, unshielded from a wind that comes from the Arctic and thus are impossible to heat, they lose their livelihood, drink themselves into oblivion at the cost of the lives of half the original population of three hundred people, one of the most tragic chapters in recent Canadian history.

Meanwhile here at the Guy Hill Indian Residential School, I have advanced in grades and numbers—and, of course, in size and age, which is eleven—to arrive at grade five and the rank of Boy Number Sixty. I now sleep in the Medium Boys' dormitory beside Robbie Hatchet who comes, like me, from Brochet. At least on the same floor as Rene in his Small Boys' dormitory down the hallway, I still go to see him in the middle of the night whenever I can.

Lights out for both Small and Medium Boys is eight-thirty. After prayers, which we say on our knees with our elbows on our beds, the Medium Boys' keeper bids us "good night," we answer in kind, he turns off the lights and is gone, off to his room that is wedged like a sausage between the two dormitories. They keep changing, these keepers, from year to year; the most they stay is three years and always three in number, they take shifts. Normally it's three laymen, but this year, it's two laymen—that is, non-brothers—and a brother named Felix Lemoine. Forty years old, or so he tells us, though to us, he looks seventy, he comes from a village called Elie, just west of Winnipeg, where his father once raised cattle. As French-Canadian as Sister St. Aramaa, my piano teacher, he wears horn-rimmed glasses and smells of peppermints.

All is now quiet, so quiet that you can hear the drops of water from a faulty tap in the washroom some dozen yards down the hallway from my bed. Like the thirty other boys aged ten to thirteen, I am wrapped in white sheets, a wool blanket, and thick cotton bedspread, ready for a long night of sleep. And dream. Except that I harbour a secret. A textbook lies hidden under my pillow, inside the pillowcase. Taking books out of classrooms is forbidden—evening study periods make the activity redundant, or so it is said, the problem being that evening study period, for me, is not enough. I love learning. I love studying. Which means that I am risking my sterling reputation as a son of Joe Highway by breaking a rule. I could be punished. I could be beaten with a belt on my bare bum, like Ernest Kipawm of Brochet was last week for beating Lady Beksaka bloody. So the book has to be hidden.

I wait for the wheezing, the sign as always that children are sleeping. Ten minutes pass, perhaps fifteen, I don't know, but I finally hear it, that telltale sound. Good. I raise my head. Like a loon just surfaced from Reindeer Lake, I turn it this way, I turn it that way. Yes, they are out. Thus assured, I slide my book from under my pillow and, under my sheet, slip it under the shirt of my sky-blue-and-white-striped flannel pajamas where I hold it tightly against my chest. I slide out of bed and pad in the darkness on my bare feet down the aisle between two rows of beds, down another, out the room, down the length of the corridor, and into the washroom, the one with the toilets, the one room on the floor where the lights are kept on all night long.

I enter a cubicle, lock the door behind me, drop my pajama bottoms, and sit on the toilet. To be convincing, I must look the part. I bend over and peek under the cubicle partitions to the right and left to assure myself that I am alone, that no one is doing his "lower activities," as Father Cadeau of old Brochet used to put it, in the three other cubicles. No one is. And only then do I feel safe.

Still, one can't sit there singing "Dixie," as Ten Hut would put it. Mr. Dubois, the former keeper, Norman Dubois's father and the school's nightwatchman, roams the building in its length and breadth the whole night through on noiseless feet, looking with his flashlight for "untoward activity"—theft, vandalism, even a fire that, as with Guy Hill's predecessor in Sturgeon Landing, might burn down the place. But I have a plan to confound his vigilance.

I pause once more. Turning my torso toward the washroom's entrance, I hold one hand to an ear like a megaphone. I hear nothing, not even that one tap dripping. No footsteps, whispers, not even sighing. Finally, I slip the book from under my pajama top. There in my hands the world's greatest treasure: my grade five English grammar book. I put it on my lap. I open to the chapter we studied that day with Mrs. Babchuk. I start memorizing what she calls "conjugations": *I am, you are, he is, we are, you are, they are.*

Why not all "are's"? I ask of no one. What are the "am" and the "is" doing in the middle of it all?" The debate goes on: Why can't I say, "I are, you are, he are, we are, they are, you are?" It makes no sense. I'll have to talk to Mrs. Babchuk about it tomorrow. Then there's this: *I sing, you sing, he sings, we sing, you sing, they sing.* Why can't the third-person singular be just like the others, as in, *I sing, you sing, he sing, we sing, you sing, they sing,* as in the verb's past tense which goes *I sang, you sang, he sang, we sang, you sang, they sang?* Then there's *I fight, you fight, he fights, we fight, you fight, they fight.* Why can't it be *I fights, you fights, he fights, we fights, you fights, they fights,* as in its past tense where the pattern is uniform, as in, *I fought, you fought, he fought, we fought, you fought, they fought?* And what's that "gh" doing in the middle when we were taught, two days prior, that "bite" was pronounced the same as "fight" and yet has no "gh," and "dot" is pronounced the same as "fought" and yet also has no "gh"? Shouldn't "bite" be spelled "bight" and "dot," "dought"? How on Earth can anyone ever learn this confounding language?

Suddenly, I hear the shuffling of feet wearing slippers. I bend over to look under the beige-painted separating wall of the cubicle. From there, I can see that the door to the room is opening and the beam from a flashlight is sliding across the linoleum floor. I stop breathing. It's the skeletal, cadaverous, vulture-nosed Mr. Dubois, the resident vampire of Guy Hill School, as Ferlin Wachask of Beaver Lake, Saskatchewan, once called him. If he catches me here reading my book, I will be spanked, I will be beaten. He beams his light under the doors of all four cubicles. Too late; he has seen my feet and lower legs. I plunge into action. As kind Nurse Kratzen calls such activity, I "strain at stool." And *p'weegitoo* (fart). Not too loud, not too soft, just one of those smooth purry ones—yes, I purr at Mr. Dubois. And he is convinced. The beam from his flashlight tracing circles large, small, and medium across the floor and ceiling, he shuffles back out, closes the door, and is gone. Thank God, I can go on with my work.

One hour later, I am pluralizing nouns. There's "goose," the plural for which, according to what we were taught last week, should be "gooses." But it's not: it's "geese." Then if that's the case, why is the plural of "moose" not "meese," but "moose"? And the plural of "noose" not "neese" or "noose," but "nooses"? Then there's "mouse" and "mice" and "house" and "hice" and . . . no, it's not "hice," it's . . . I fall asleep right there on the toilet, God knows for how long. Probably ten minutes, but it might have been an hour. Whichever it is, no one has caught me. I close my book, pull myself together, and make my way back to my bed.

"What are you doing here?" whispers Robbie Hatchet, in Cree.

"What are *you* doing here?" I whisper back, also in Cree. "This is my bed."

"No it's not. It's mine." He tries to push me out. I try to push him out. And the tug-of-war continues until I realize he's right and, barely awake, climb out of his bed and into mine which is just one bed over.

How many times I sleepwalk that hallway—and I'm the only who ever studies in the middle of the night sitting on that toilet—I never count but it is often.

At the Guy Hill Indian Residential School, marks for exams are always announced three or four days after the teachers have marked them. Father Picard rolls like a tank into each classroom and reads them, out loud, from one subject to the next to the next, thus arriving at the overall average. We all have to stand, each in turn, when our names are called. Those who've done well puff out with pride; the three second-highest achievers in my class cluster around 84 percent as an average—Melinda Kamaa-magoos, the young piano player, Arabella Beksaka, both of Brochet, and Wilfred Gunpowder of Island Falls, Saskatchewan. Those who have not done well cringe with embarrassment, with rank humiliation; the lowest, in fact, has plunged to 33. Percent. Poor Roseanne Bacheese of Puck. Because Father Picard reads from the lowest average to the highest, my name comes last. I stand. He reads through the subjects and their corresponding marks. When he arrives at English grammar, he reads *100*. Percent. The room gasps audibly. My average? 95.

"*Cheest, Paapaa?*" says this voice inside me. "*Keetha kichi kaagee-toota-maan.*" ("See, Dad? I did it. For you.")

37

I am flying through the snow in my dad's dogsled. He the driver, I the passenger, I am five years old and sitting on the floor of the birch-wood vehicle. My back to the headboard, my legs stretched out before me, my be-mitted hands cling to the siding of stiff, white canvas. We are crossing Nueltin Lake from west side to east, our destination the small log cabin where waits my mother. Today, she bides her time with her youngest child, two-year-old Rene. Five long gone up to heaven, three others are at school and two, now grown, are on their own. That school so distant—Dad says it is over four hundred miles south of here—the question that haunts me is: Will I ever see Daniel again? And Florence and Louise? Is the school they are at the one I will go to as well some day? The snowfall accumulates. The wind picks up. And now we are driving through an all-out blizzard.

The white-out paralyzes. I am in a trance. And in that state, an old face emerges. Suddenly, time has no structure. Whatever that time is, a worm-thin tongue shoots out from the face, red, glistening. The face is of a snake, it dawns on me, a garter snake with its eyes dis-tended, unblinking. The snake, I realize, is coming for revenge for my abduction of her progeny that one day last spring. Coming towards me, it writhes and writhes. My blood curdles.

But then the image of the reptile melts into the face of a white man of forty, though he looks tired, old, more like seventy. And sad. His skin is so white it could be enamel, except that it is wrinkled. The face gets closer. Clean-shaven, waxy, its eyebrows black with hints of grey, its breath is minty, a sweet perfume that hits me softly, it is that close. And it wears glasses. In fact, I can see my face reflected in their lenses. Who is this man? Where am I? Light fades, darkness takes over. I peer into its murk and it dawns on me.

I am in my bed in the Medium Boys' dormitory on the second floor of the Guy Hill Indian Residential School on Clearwater Lake here in central Manitoba, and these windows that I see are a part of the line that forms one wall from west side to east of this chamber with thirty *naapees-sak* (boys) sleeping between them. As with the others, crisp white sheets and earth-brown blankets enfold me. But under those covers and under my pajama bottoms and on my skin, something is moving. A snake? A hand? If so, what kind of hand? Whose? And what's it doing there? Whoever it belongs to in this now-fractured, disconnected series of images, the hand, cold and impersonal, reaches my penis, coils its fingers around it, then squeezes. Then writhes and writhes to a rhythm that is regular, like warm blood pumping. The hand uncoils into a wrist—I can feel it wriggling across my belly—then a lower arm then an elbow then an upper arm then a shoulder, the latter two encased in a shirt of fine white cotton with pin-thin pink stripes, then a neck then a chin then a face. The face—and the chin and the neck and the arm and the hand and the fingers—are all of a piece, it dawns on me. The man these limbs belong to is on my bed sitting and crouching over me. And, lo and behold, they belong to none other than Brother Felix Lemoine, the keeper that year of the Medium Boys' dormitory.

I am eleven. I am a child. I feel nothing. A late bloomer always, my sexual awareness hasn't yet emerged. I don't know that what the man is doing to me is wrong. I assume that all *Moony-ass* men do this to their children; that this, in effect, is a rite of passage. Adult words escape me; this act has no language. The man moves on. And now he is sitting on the bed of Gilbert Mitaas of South Indian Lake, Manitoba. Crouched over in silence, Brother Lemoine manoeuvres his right hand under the sheets. And once he is finished, he goes on to the bed of Machaa-is Bacheese of Puck, Manitoba, then Nameegoos Kipawm of Brochet. Four per night the man does on average. He "does" each boy at least ten times throughout the school year. With the turnover of students in the six years he is there, Brother Felix Lemoine ends up stealing the bodies of one hundred boys ten times each, at the very least.

This all confuses us. We don't understand what is happening. Something about an institution and the power structure that governs its behaviour silences us. We say nothing. We tell no one. Not our parents, not our siblings, we don't even talk about it amongst ourselves. For me, this whole experience is so beyond human experience, beyond human language, that I don't even think about the fact that this might be happening as well to Rene. To me, it's just touching; no physical aggression is involved; that's all I know, all I understand.

The results are horrific. The men these boys grow into have nightmares. For life. They are sexually dysfunctional. They don't know how to love. They don't know how to relate to other people. They have dysfunctional marriages marked by violence. They make dysfunctional parents. Their lives are destroyed. And they think about it and think about it and think about it. Sometimes to make the thinking stop, they kill themselves. And the fallout goes on to affect the next generation and the next and the next. The field is littered with dead male bodies. From what I understand, that is their experience. And one day, I hope they write about it because I can't. And to those who can't, I have tried my best to write this story of survival for you.

In the Catholic Church, Brothers are young men who, in their youth, evince a desire to enter the priesthood and serve their God, but don't make it. Not intelligent enough? Not talented? Only they know. Whichever it is, they end up working as servants to priests in their parishes. In old Brochet, rotund and bald K's'chees-naanis cleans Father Cadeau's residence. He is janitor, cook, dishwasher, gardener, snow-shoveller, organist at Mass, bell-ringer, you name it. Most fundamental, Brothers swear themselves to a lifetime of celibacy. For them, that is to say, there is no sex. That is a Brother. (For nuns, it is much the same—even though many come from impoverished French-Canadian farming communities where families have twenty, twenty-five children, because the Catholic Church ordained it, they, too, are deemed sexless.) And for those who can't get positions in parishes, they work at residential schools like this Brother Lemoine does. Except that, as in every line of work, not all Brothers are virtuous. Brother St. Arnaud and Brother Menard were saints and we loved them dearly, as they did us. Brother Felix Lemoine was not. He always had a package of peppermints on him. And was forever sucking on one.

But why? Why waste my time thinking about something that happened sixty years ago? When there are so many people out there to fall in love with *and* be loved by? When there are so many people out there to thank for the love they've given me, my parents not least? When there is so much laughter, so much joy, to be engaged in, so much music to dance to? When the very act of breathing, for me, is reason a-plenty for permanent astonishment?

38

Having crossed northern Manitoba a thousand times by dogsled, canoe, bush plane, and foot, Dad knows it well. Which is why he picks Robinson Lake for his fishing enterprise in the summer of 1963. Located one hundred and fifty miles northeast of Reindeer Lake but perhaps one-twentieth its size, it is still quite large as lakes up here go. And if it's possible, it is even more stunning. Still, the best part of it is that, apart from us and sundry Dene, there are no people. We, in other words, have this lake and the thirty-some others that surround it all to ourselves. King Joe Highway of *keeweet'nook*, we, his sons, his princes.

Unfortunately, this summer, he has run short of men. Of the four canoes he normally works with, one will be manned by my brother Daniel and Norman Gunpowder, my sister Louise's new husband (they got married the December previous with us not there); the second by Swanson and Oogeest Zipper, my sister Florence's husband; the third by cousin John Joe Kipawm and my Aunt Dorothy's husband, Philip Gunpowder (short and bouncy, Aunt Dorothy is the youngest of Mom's three half-sisters). And the fourth? Stymied at first, Dad thinks briefly. Then solves the problem.

"You," he says, pointing at me, "and me." Which is how, at age eleven, I become a fully accredited, professional, commercial fisherman.

We rise at three—*a.m.* Six days a week. That's when, up in those parts, in early July, the first glint of daylight makes its appearance. Ablutions, breakfast—the gas tanks we've filled the evening before—the three-mile-long drive to the first net and, by four, we are working.

Dressed in frog-green rubber coveralls that come to my collarbone and hang off my shoulders by means of straps, knee-high Wellingtons covering my lower extremities, and semi-water-resistant white canvas gloves—the uniform of fishermen in northern Manitoba—I am sitting on a crate turned upside down at the middle of our vessel, this crimson canoe with a ten-horsepower outboard motor attached to its stern; but I am not idle. I am gutting fish after fish after fish that Dad keeps throwing into a second crate that sits at my feet, this one turned right side up. He throws them from the bow where he stands, bent over the gunwale, hauling in a net that hangs underwater for a good half-mile. Dressed like me, he stops at intervals to disentangle a fish from the webbing on the net with a hook. Of his own making, the handle of the implement is of birch from which pokes a nail he has hammered to a curve. The fish he then throws slime-covered, thrashing, and wriggling into said crate, from where I take them one after the other and after the other to dress them, my work table, propped on an aluminum wash-tub, a square piece of plywood with a square hole sawn into the centre. The hole is for the offal—the gills, the entrails, the scales, the blood. The fish I've just dressed, meanwhile, I rinse in the lake which, from where I sit, is within reach, and throw into a third crate. And a fourth and a fifth, their numbers amassing as the long day advances.

As for the net, after freeing it of fish entanglement, Dad squeezes it into a rope-like length to wring out the water so that he can wind it, lead weights and floaters included, into yet another crate that sits at his feet. All as he continues reeling that part of the net still in the water into the boat, extracting a fish, throwing it into my crate, drop-ping the net into his crate, reeling the net in, extracting, throwing, dropping . . . Free of motorized propulsion, the only sound our crimson canoe makes at this juncture is its sides being lapped at by waves so small they barely exist. In reaction, Dad and I rock almost imper-ceptibly. The offal we will feed at day's end to the sled dogs, away out on their islet two miles from camp where, on summer respite from their winter labour, they wander untied.

When we finish with the net—or, rather, three nets tied end to end so that they make a kind of "super net"—I reclaim my seat at the stern in front of the motor, take out the oars that sit lengthwise along both gunwales, and start rowing backwards. Which gives Dad the movement he needs to reel the net back into the water on that spot if the catch has been generous. And if it hasn't, I drive us to another a mile or two in whichever direction our instincts take us. Once arrived at this second spot, I stop my motor and, one more time, take out the oars and start rowing backwards. Accordingly, Dad reels the net into the water at our new location a yard at a time. Once finished, we move on to the next net, a mile or so to north or south or east or west.

Unfortunately, the ride is smooth and warm only on days when the weather is agreeable. Because when we are fishing for trout, which live in deep waters, and there is a wind, there is no shelter from it— read: no islands—the experience can be not only frightening but life-threatening. Try gutting five hundred fish the live-long day while you are rocking to waves the height of tents. And rocking and rocking and that Arctic wind—and God help you if it starts raining—lashes at your unprotected face as with pin-pricks and your body is chilled to the bone, well wrapped as it is even if it is summer. And your hands are freezing from sub-Arctic waters even through work gloves which are waterproof only in part. And this for ten hours non-stop.

Then there is pickerel. Yellow-bellied, black-backed, its dorsal fin lined with points as sharp as needles, it lives in shallow waters close to swamps where blackflies and mosquitoes breed in vast numbers, at least in early summer, and forests shield those insects from wind so that they can't be blown away. Which gives them the freedom to feast on your face. And you can't swat them away or scratch. Because, even if they're gloved, your hands are covered with fish slime. Hell on Earth has no better description.

Fortunately, a) the blackflies are gone by mid-July, b) the greater chunk of our time is spent on open waters fishing for trout and white-fish, and, c) August, in particular, is known for its mildness.

If the raising of the net and its harvest of fish takes half an hour and its re-setting about ten minutes, then it takes us forty minutes per "super net," of which there are twenty. All of which translates into twelve to fourteen hours of work per day. Meaning to say that—and here's the upside to the story—if it takes us from three in the morning to six in the evening six days a week for the two months of summer, then it means that I get to spend more time with this magnificent man, my dad, Joe Highway, *in one month*, than most boys, *Moony-ass* or otherwise, get to spend with theirs. *In one lifetime.*

For commercial fishermen, trout and pickerel tie for first place as money-makers, whitefish second, pike third. As for the suckers, mariah (a sort of catfish with whiskers, a fish I've seen in pictures), and grayling (which resembles a large sardine), they don't sell. Rarely caught in any case, mostly because of their small populations, mariah and grayling are usually thrown back into the water alive and breathing. Suckers, on the other hand, are more common. If every fifth fish we catch, in deep water, is a trout, in shallow water, a pickerel, and every sixth fish in either depth a whitefish, all three cherished, then every seventh fish we catch, also, like whitefish, in water deep or shallow, is a sucker. A pest more than anything, the sucker is a fish that we feed to the dogs or, if we eat it at all, constitutes the lower end of our diet; like Klik or baloney, it is the poor man's steak, to be eaten only when times are hard. And only when made into *namee-steek* (smoked fish).

It, for one thing, is toothless. All it has to prove its fishness, beside its fins, are rubbery lips on a rubbery face that make it look like a cartoon character. While the pike is sleek and can, at its largest, be four feet long and move like a bullet, the sucker has a dumpy little body that toodles along. At their longest, they reach ten inches. Compared to the pike, he is a midget, the runt of the family.

It is Saturday evening, the end of a long and arduous work week. We are exhausted. But tomorrow, thank God, is Sunday, our day off. I can, for one thing, play with Rene, who misses me (he tells me at night, as we still share a bed). When we pull up in our boats, Rene and Mom come down to the dock to help us pack our day's catch in ice. (At least, Mom does; Rene just plays.) The fish house and ice house stand five feet apart just up from the dock. Both log cabins of Dad's construction, the first is where we keep the fish packed in crushed ice in aluminum tubs until the Norseman comes to get them on Monday. In the second, we store the ice in blocks under piles of muskeg before, using picks, we chop it into small pieces and pour it over the fish to preserve them. The size of trunks (of the luggage variety) before they are chopped and poured on the fish, these blocks of ice were sawn from the lake by Dad and Swanson back in the spring, extracted with industrial-sized pincers, then dragged here by dogsled. Meant to last us the summer and therefore numbering twenty or thirty, these blocks of ice have taken their toll—they are huge, they are heavy, and they have been gathered, what's more, at the height of bug season.

Now dressed with her floral-patterned granny smock stuffed into a pair of rubber pants and boots of the kind worn by male fishermen, Mom scandalizes pink the women from the two Dene families who live with us that summer and who, having never seen a woman dressed like a man, have come down to gawk.

"*Koolth-sli*," opines Seagull's Little Poop with a saliva-engorged esophagus, her snow-white hair practically rising an inch with shock. Does Mom care? No. She chisels in a crate a large chunk of ice, chopping it to shards and hand-sized slivers, then shovelling them onto layer after layer of fish that has been dressed by me all day that day. All man's work. Now being packed in crates by Daniel—and Dad and Swanson and the crew in its entirety—they will soon be ready for storage and shipping by Norseman.

When all is done, Daniel and I, and sometimes Rene, who enjoys evening cruises on glass-smooth waters with his two older brothers, will drive to the islet two miles away where live the sled dogs to feed them their supper, the offal. And sometimes the heads of suckers that have been put aside for making *namee-steek*. Our homework accomplished, we glide home in a light infused with pink. And as we do Rene and I sing our loon cries to the droning of the motor being driven by Daniel, the loons in the distance answering in kind.

A pot is boiling. We can hear it bubble. Just outside the main tent on Mom's cooking fire does it sit, sputtering. And bubbling and steaming. Something is cooking, but what? Twenty sucker heads that Mom has washed with care, having salvaged them from the crate containing the fish guts and blood. As we fall asleep in the boys' tent some ten feet away, Daniel, Rene, and I hear our parents in their tent, slurping and sucking and slurping and sucking. The absence of dialogue their ambient music, they are relishing every second of their Saturday-night date, every single drop of their evening snack: sucker heads boiled with salt and pepper and fresh-sliced onions. They slurp and suck one bone after the other after the other. In one hour, they slurp their way through the entire structure that comprises the head of *nameepith*, the clown-like sucker.

None much bigger than twenty-five-cent coins, the bones drip with wetness, with fish oil, with lovely humidity. Some shaped like boomerangs, some like ovals, some like triangles, and some like circles, Joe and Balazee Highway suck the bone called the frontal, the bone called the turbinal, the bone called the periorbital ring, the infraorbital ring, the maxillary, premaxillary, mandible, dentary bone, postympanic, suprascapular, operculum, tubercle, preopercle, interopercle, branchiostegal ray, olfactory bulb, pharynx, snout, upper jaw, gill cover, gill arch, cheek—which is scrumptious to the point of bringing tears to the eater—cartilaginous endocranium, palate, even a fragment of spinal cord, a spherical lens . . . they suck them all. And are deeply, deeply in love . . .

39

"The Christmas concert, the Christmas concert, please don't cancel the Christmas concert," I sing in silence as I make my way with ginger care down the hallway with a tray full of glass: thirty thermometers. Working alone when times are normal, the gentle Nurse Kratzen can't manage it this time. She needs help. Desperately. Why? The times, most decidedly, are far from normal. In a word, one hundred and seventy of the two hundred students registered at the Guy Hill Indian Residential School—and thirty of the staff, who number fifty—are sick, bedridden, out like lights. A "floo epidemic," Nurse Kratzen calls it which is why, as sole health-giver here in residence, she herself is barely alive from working sixteen hours a day. Even in her uniform of starched white hat with its two black stripes over the forehead and white dress, white shoes, and white sheer stockings, she looks bedraggled. So, as one of the fifteen boys and fifteen girls spared as yet from this dreadful virus, I, aged twelve, have been corralled like the others into service as all-round helper, as waiter, dishwasher, cook, orderly, nurse, doctor, whatever it takes to keep life going at Guy Hill School. Which is why I am carrying this tray with thirty thermometers just disinfected in boiling water from Nurse Hannah Kratzen's infirmary on the third floor down the corridor past the Big Boys' dormitory to the top of the stairs that lead down to the Small and Medium Boys' dormitories where lie stricken some fifty young patients with temperatures rising to 105 degrees, says Nurse Kratzen. My mission? To make it down those two flights of stairs. There, at the bottom, Brother

Lemoine, the only keeper left available, will receive my bounty and administer it. And a challenging act of balance it is—one wrong step and, like Humpty Dumpty, I fall down those stairs with thirty thermometers destroyed completely. "The Christmas concert, the Christmas concert, please don't cancel the Christmas concert," I sing in silence with my teeth gritted, just to help me keep my focus.

I love the Christmas concert. It is easily the highlight of my year every year here at this school. This year, I get to play "Sonatina in G" by Muzio Clementi on the piano in front of two hundred people. Grace of my teacher Sister St. Aramaa and her "lie-berry," to which she has now given me free rein, I have been practicing. And practicing and practicing.

The fact that it takes both my hands to hold this tray makes my progress that much more perilous—I won't be able to hold the stairway railing if I should stumble. The steps are the colour of Arctic terns' eggs, grey-green stone with small black speckles. And polished to a sheen by the Norwegian janitor, Mr. Rasmussen, husband of the seamstress, Mrs. Rasmussen, they look slippery.

No one knows where this virus has come from. From the wind, the water in the taps, a wayward animal, a visiting parent? The answer is moot. All that is certain is that it started with Bobcat Mitaas, his elder brother, Gilbert, tells me in whispers. Older than me by two months so is now thirteen, Gilbert Mitaas of South Indian Lake, Manitoba, younger brother of Matilda Mitaas, the Cree piano player, sleeps this year in the bed next to mine in the Medium Boys' dormitory. We, therefore, are privy to secrets in that island of time between lights out and "doe-doe," as our keeper, Erik Laporte, who is also sick, calls sleep. It has been three days, in fact, since Gilbert Mitaas tells me that his little brother, Bobcat, who sleeps six beds from my brother, Rene, in the Small Boys' dormitory, has caught some bug. His forehead is hot, says Gilbert Mitaas, he is sweating profusely, his bones are aching, his nose running a constant flow of liquid mucus, and he can't stop coughing. Excused from school, he lies bedridden. A serious "floo," has said Nurse Kratzen, one that borders on something she calls "ammonia." Neither Gilbert Mitaas nor I have any idea what either is, especially ammonia, but they sound serious. All we know is that, if it worsens, Bobcat Mitaas will be taken to the hospital in The Pas or maybe in Winnipeg. Beds, however, are not available, not in The Pas, not in Winnipeg, as neither are doctors, nurses, or sisters, says Nurse Kratzen. The epidemic is universal, she says, the whole world has it. Except the remarkable, unbeatable, indefatigable Nurse Hannah Kratzen. And her young assistant, Tomson Highway.

Shortly after Bobcat Mitaas falls sick, it is discovered that Machaa-is Bacheese of Puck, Manitoba, too, falls victim and is bed-ridden—though this time not in the Small Boys' dormitory, but a mere four beds from mine in the Medium Boys'. Same condition as Bobcat Mitaas, we learn from our keeper, Brother Lemoine. Then from my cousin, Virginia Highway of Beaver Lake, Saskatchewan, comes news, shared in our class of grade six students, that Chichilia Kipawm of Brochet has also taken ill. Exact same ailment as Bobcat Mitaas, says my cousin. Word gets around. Chichilia Kipawm is followed by Catherine Kitoochigan of The Pas, Cordelia Kamaa-magoos of Island Falls, Adelaide Flett of Nelson House, Maureen Gunpowder of Pelican Narrows, Charlotte Zipper of The Pas, and too many others. And that's just the girls' side of the school, where the numbers keep climbing from one day to the next and to the next, says my cousin, Virginia Highway.

On the boys' side of these alarming statistics, Bobcat Mitaas and Machaa-is Bacheese are followed quickly by Caayoots Beksaka and Lady Beksaka, both of Brochet, Vernon Zipper of The Pas, Simeon Kamaa-magoos of Brochet, William Peeskwa and Jericho Quickly of South Indian Lake, Albie Owl of Granville Lake, Marty Mistat of Nelson House, Philbert Nigik of Pelican Narrows, and Rene Highway of Brochet, and so it goes. Like a cloud of flies just hit by a spray of insect repellent, boys and girls from grades one to eight keel over one after the other after the other (Guy Hill now teaches to the grade eight level). As the classrooms empty out as do the yards and the play-rooms, the dormitories fill. Even the staff is not immune; teachers such as Sister Ann and Miss Crispy, keepers such as Norman Dubois,

Butch Bouchard, and Sister Oo-hoo (recently arrived, we call her "Owl" because of her spectacles which are owlish; I never did learn her actual name); the laundress, Mrs. Dubois, her husband, the Dracula-like nightwatchman, Mr. Dubois, the cook, Darlene Sawchuk, the engineer, Mr. Van Dyke, his wife, Irene—all fall victim to the dreadful scourge. And as the numbers climb, those few students left healthy just keep working harder and longer thus rendering them—that is, us—as bedraggled as poor Nurse Kratzen.

Today, I am a nurse. I check temperatures, I dispense medicine, I soak squares of absorbent cotton in boiling water and apply them as compresses, all, of course, under the direction of the blue-veined and increasingly pale-of-complexion *Chaariman* nurse. I am one busy beaver but I choose to enjoy it. Grace of Joe and Balazee Highway's trenchant philosophies on life and love, I like helping, I like being useful to others. Rene, for example, is parched and thirsty so I serve him water in his delirium; his temperature reads 104; I stroke his forehead and pray for him. Not rocket science, I know, but it makes me feel like "Doctor" Highway. Then I scoot down the hallway to the Medium Boys' dormitory which is my real fiefdom today. Like the Small Boys' dormitory, it, too, is almost full of "dying patients." There I serve glasses of orange juice from a trolley wheeled in by Sister Tiny, the last nun living, I am sure of it. Then I scoot back over to the Small Boys' dormitory—I scoot back and forth between the two sleeping quarters a lot these days—where I serve lunch, including to Rene, from pots the size of cauldrons—chicken noodle soup with roast beef sandwiches and milk and apples. Vitamins, says kind Nurse Kratzen, all good medicine. Such shifts in placement depend on the workload and who has taken sick and who has not. Needless to say, this workforce keeps diminishing in size, so that the few left standing are fading away from lack of sleep.

In hopes that everyone will heal in time for the concert, tall and wiry Mr. Babchuk is halfway through constructing the floor of the stage for the annual pre-Christmas event when he, too, gets hit by the virus. He has no choice; he must stop working. So much I learn from Chally Canoe of Nelson House. Just as I am reaching the fourth-last step of the second flight of stairs that it takes to arrive on the second floor with my tray of thermometers—almost there, almost there, I sing in silence—I cross paths with him, my best friend at Guy Hill, as he is running up the stairs from the empty playroom with two packages of white towels tied with string.

"The Christmas concert has just been cancelled?" I ask him, afraid of the answer.

"The Christmas concert has just been cancelled," confirms Chally Canoe and zooms up the stairway.

So upset am I by this news—I feel like crying; no piano-playing, no "Sonatina in G"—that I slip on a step and spill my tray. Thirty thermometers go flying, hit stone floor, and shatter; the resulting explosion a flash of light, it looks like sparks from Mr. Babchuk's circular saw cutting lumber. As the hundred shards of glass go tinkling down the steps like chimes in wind, the mercury released wriggles away this way and that in inch-long rivulets, like infant snakes. I am horrified.

It is all a blur. Gentle Nurse Kratzen speaks her mind. Explaining tersely that she will now have to do with a grossly reduced supply of thermometers to take the temperatures of one hundred and seventy sick children in six dormitories—for she, as well, is responsible for the girls—she chastises me but doesn't abuse me. Which is when I finally succumb.

All I see is white. White, white, and yet more white. Inch by inch, a dogsled advancing bleeds intermittent but inevitable into my blurred line of vision. The lone man standing at the rear is travelling alone. Upright at its stern, his hands to the headboard, he exhorts his dogs to extreme effort for the elements are plotting against them, the north wind starving, the swirling snow determined to blind them. The man, Joe Highway, is passing through a blizzard that knows no limit, that has no heart. Then, like water devouring a man who is drowning, the snowstorm erases his shadow, his fog-like image. The blizzard dissipates. It melts into a surface that is white and solid, the question being: The surface of what? Of Earth? Of heaven? I am incapable of discerning any reality beyond my nose. Still, I realize slowly that this is a ceiling. And not just any ceiling but that inside the Medium Boys' dormitory here at the Guy Hill Indian Residential School where I am in love, and serious love, with two hundred children and adolescents. Which is when I remember: I am sick. I am very, very sick. I am in bed sweating a river, my bones are aching, my throat sore, my nasal passages blocked completely. And now I remember, if only vaguely, that the stern but gentle Nurse Hannah Kratzen has told me this morning that my temperature is 105. Yes, I have a fever, an intense, pounding, constricting fever. In fact, I am dying. And King of the North, Joe Lapstan Highway, has come to get me in his dogsled and take me to heaven. I close my eyes and fall back asleep.

The plague concludes. No one dies. All recover two weeks before Christmas, way too late to start rehearsing for the Christmas concert.

40

They're warming up the drums in the Dene neighbourhood. About time, too, I tell myself, for Happy Doll Gaazayoo owes my father. If it's a game of *pageesee*, as opposed to a round dance, that they are warming up those drums for—and I've heard it's *pageesee*—then Happy Doll Gaazayoo, the best *pageesee* player in all *keeweet'nook*, will surely play. And if he does, then he will win. And pay my father.

I pause in my chopping of our daily stock of firewood in the fading light of a late-August evening to consider all of this. Happy Doll is desperate. The propeller on his Evinrude seven-horsepower outboard motor, which he uses for his fishing—as with everyone, his bread and butter—ran into a rock on Reindeer Lake which, of course, is normal in a body of water that is known for its shallowness. Having practically destroyed it, Happy Doll has decided that the tired old "tin can" is not worth fixing so has purchased one from Nicotine Yazzie: a second-hand Johnson ten-horsepower at the cost of five hundred dollars, two hundred of which Happy Doll had to borrow. From Dad.

"Much more efficient," has declared Masky Jimmy Perkins of the only motor on the market in all Brochet at this point in time. Meaning to explain that Happy Doll Gaazayoo hasn't had a choice in the matter. Unhappily for him, his drumming quite aside, Nicotine Yazzie is known for his tightness, with money, with bullets, with guns, with caribou *weeyaas* (meat). And with motors. Tonight, for example, the notorious Dene *sasaagis* (tightwad), as some wags call him, is tuning up his drum for a game of *pageesee* after demanding, and getting, this exorbitant amount from Happy Doll Gaazayoo. Fortunately, if Nicotine Yazzie is known for his tightness, then Happy Doll Gaazayoo is known for his gambling, which is why he *pageesees* obsessively. He'll even go all the way to Wollaston Lake to do it. Meaning to say that, tonight, Happy Doll will *pageesee*, Happy Doll will win, Dad will get his money back, and I will get the accordion he's been promising me since Swanson's wedding to an accordion player whom I plan to best by age thirteen which will be this coming winter. Should I go and watch? Do sled dogs fly?

Having finished chopping and then piling the wood beside our house, I run down the trail that snakes its way past Bernard Yazzie's clay-caked log cabin past the new cemetery and on to the neighbourhood where reside the Dene. Arriving in a cloud of swirling dust, I run up to a fire in front of the tent where lives Old Dice Chagaazay, Nicotine Yazzie's gnarled old aunt who looks like a *choggy-lat* (chocolate bar) she is that swarthy, especially at that hour. Why that fire? Because Nicotine Yazzie is crouching behind it heating his hand drum. The circumference of a pail for the hauling of water, the instrument could pass for a moon if hung from the sky. Or a cake-pan three inches thick. Held by a cross-string of sinews on its underside, the surface is a length of untanned hide of caribou stretched across a slat of birchwood bent circular by long-term soaking in lye-mixed water, its two ends nailed to each other so that it forms a perfect circle. Which is the surface the drummer applies his drumstick to to make sound agreeable to ears that know. The warmer this skin is, the tighter it is, and therefore the higher the sound it produces.

Which is why Nicotine Yazzie is crouched like a bear over those flames. He wants high notes. High notes show his soaring falsetto to best advantage, explains his Aunt Old Dice Chagaazay, and this kind of chanting demands falsetto; the higher it is, the better. As he tickles the surface of his drum with a tremolo he taps out with his drumstick, he swivels it around, face-down and slowly, over the flames by four mere inches so that all parts of that surface are tickled and heated; the tickling, apparently, ensures that tightening. The result?

As this skin tightens, you actually hear the sound it makes rising in pitch. Until the instrument's owner deems that pitch ready to accompany the gambling game called *pageesee*. All as one by one, two by two, and in singles, boys and girls appear from the shadows to take in the spectacle. Aged eight and upward, Caayoots Beksaka, Nameegoos Kipawm, the gap-toothed but fetching Hilda McMillan, seventh daughter (of eight) of Maagisit McMillan, the Companeek clerk; Check Wheat He, the dusky Dene maiden, now eighteen; twelve-year-old, achingly pretty Melinda Kamaa-magoos—the best piano player in all Brochet and thus my hero—and her sister, Velma, these are just six of many. Like me, they stand there watching what are now three drummers, for Bad Robber Yazzie and Lawrence Loon, two other drummers of repute, have just joined Nicotine. With the flames of the fire dancing in the glass of their star-struck eyes, the drummers look unearthly, unbound by gravity. Meanwhile, in front of another tent some ten feet further and closer to the inlet we call Seepees-seek, players are amassing at another campfire. The residence belonging to the diminutive but luminous-spirited Half Ass Sam Well, he has agreed, it is evident, to play host tonight to the favourite game of the Dene.

The *pièce de résistance* of that sub-Arctic nation's cultural activity, *pageesee* is an odd and highly entertaining, indeed spectacular, hybrid of dance and game. As such, it puts into the shade all other events, social or otherwise, engaged in annually here in Brochet. Only the *skweetaas* comes near to competing. The trick with the dance part of the game, however, is that only the upper three-quarters of players' bodies actually move. The lower quarter—that is, the legs from the knee down—doesn't. It can't. It can't because players have to kneel from one end of the game to the other in order to play. Still, if dance is by-product, and by-product only, of this animated social ritual, then gambling is its purpose, its hair-raising, spine-tingling, and sometimes heart-rending *raison-d'être*—one can win money in amounts unheard of, at least in Brochet. Or lose it. As such, it has four prerequisites: it is played by men only, at nighttime, outdoors, and, so far as I know, in summer only.

True to form, Happy Doll Gaazayoo is already kneeling on the ground when I arrive at Half Ass Sam Well's. His eyes like spirals on a cartoon drawing, his eyebrows twitching with rank impatience, his bony knees touch the edge of the blanket that lies spread out on the sand to be used as table for the act of gambling. Modest Loon, Meat Toss Yazzie, and, of course, Half Ass Sam Well join him to form the first team of four. On the other side of the blanket, meanwhile, materializes the second: the lynx-like cousins, Henry Beksaka and Beejee-aazay, Samba Cheese Meesay-tee, and Napoleon Zah, my uncle by marriage, the great fiddle player. Two rows of four men each, that is to say, now kneel facing each other across that blanket like starving huskies. Before they leap at each other's throats, however, the aforementioned trio of drummers emerge into the light of the second campfire—the one where the game will be played—and drop to their knees at one end of "the table." Their drums in one hand, their drumsticks in the other, they are ready to make one unholy racket. Just then, my brother Swanson's friend, the clownish jigger Adoo-naazay, pops from nowhere like a jumping bean and plops himself at the end of the blanket across from the drummers. He, it seems, will be scorekeeper, for at his knees jut from the ground twenty-four stakes of sharpened-to-a-point branches of willow. Leaning towards him at a forty-five degree angle, these will be his scoreboard, an important job, for one stake is worth five dollars. Once all participants are on their mark, the orchestra of three starts banging its drums. And chanting and wailing in haunting falsettos a pentatonic melody in six-eight time that, note by note and beat by beat, climbs to the stars. Now out in their trillions in a cloudless sky, they, too, will serve as onlookers, rabid, famished, in this game that Happy Doll Gaazayoo is so good at that he will surely destroy, hook, line, and sinker, his foolhardy competitors, I stand there praying.

Their lower legs held motionless by the act of kneeling, all eight players, three drummers, and one scorekeeper start moving like pistons from the knees upward. Their thighs contract, release, contract. Their groins do likewise as do their torsos, their shoulders, their necks, their heads. As for their arms, they wave at liberty this way and that, summoning spirits, ancestral energies, animal complicity such as that with bears and wolves—I wonder which, as I stand there watching. With one hand open and one hand closed, all players conceal a thumb-sized object—a pebble, a key, an inch-long stub of caribou antler, even a crucifix detached from its rosary—to be thrown from one hand to the other and back. Or hidden behind one's back as the entire body (save, of course, for the lower legs) moves to the rhythm. The point? Each player is to guess in which hand is hidden, at given points in time, the opponent's object.

Samba Cheese Meesay-tee, for instance, hides a bullet in his left hand then throws it two feet in the air, only to catch it with his right, which deft extremity he then snaps shut and slides in one half-second behind his back, thereby changing its place of concealment. All as his torso pulsates and throbs to the rhythm of Nicotine's drum and, of course, Bad Robber Yazzie's and Lawrence Loon's. On the blanket's other side, meanwhile, kneels the artist with the jaw that looks like a lantern, he, Beejee-aazay, also, like Samba Cheese Meesay-tee, engaging in movement of wild invention and holding his arms out and up to embrace the elements. Their hands clasped shut, they dare his opponent directly across—Happy Doll Gaazayoo, as his bad luck would have it—to guess which hand conceals his talisman, the claw of a ptarmigan. Raising his arms and throbbing to the rhythm like all there present, Happy Doll Gaazayoo snaps his hands down, claps them like a whip, and points with his right index finger to Beejee-aazay's left. Whooping ecstatically, Beejee-aazay snaps his left hand open, thus revealing to his foe that it holds nothing, that his guess is wrong. Happy Doll curses and, much to his ire, loses a point. In response to that fact, scorekeeper Adoo-naazay pulls one stake of willow from the ground and stabs it aggressively into the ground on the negative side, that is, to his left.

The game goes on. The whoops and hollers ring out undisciplined, the piston-like throbbing goes on uninterrupted—players go, players come—an audience amasses (including Rene, whom I see peeping from under the elbow of Ann Kaakaa, the worst housekeeper in all Brochet, which is why her name). Happy Doll wins, Happy Doll loses. He wins, he loses. As his score keeps oscillating and writhing and churning and tossing and churning again, I find it increasingly difficult to go on watching—what on Earth is happening? He usually wins—so I flee into the shadows to the great knot of kids that has started dancing a great wide circle around Old Dice Chagaazay's still-raging campfire. Unable to resist, Rene is among them. Remember, Brochet has no electricity at this point in time so all light is natural: candles, kerosene lamps, campfires, moon, stars. The leaping flames throwing our shadows on the tents behind and around us, we look like caribou with our antlers afloat in silver-tinged starlight. Stampeding ever northward, our frenzied stomping devours the drum beat, the pounding drum beat devours our stomping. All Brochet becomes enmeshed in the all-embracing grip of a frantic intensity, a monstrous insanity. And in that roar descanted by men's voices wailing in falsetto, I pray. I pray to the caribou, I pray to the north wind, I pray to starlight, to Earth, to God up in heaven that Happy Doll Gaazayoo's well-known good fortune will come back raging and he will again be victorious at the game called *pageesee*. And I will get my accordion.

Unfortunately, Mom comes calling with her signature trumpet-like blast. Always a mother who trains her children in the ways of discipline, she tells us it is late. Rene and I must come home to bed. The game will go on till daybreak anyway, she says.

"And Happy Doll will win?" I ask her wistfully as we are walking home past the D O T.

"Happy Doll will win," says Rene.

Once at home and under the covers, my left arm wrapped around my adored little brother, I drift off to slumber with Dene drums resonating in the distance like men's hearts throbbing in artful unison.

Next morning, I hear the news from my Uncle Napoleon Zah, who comes by for coffee. Not good. Happy Doll's fortune came back to him and he kept winning. Then lost at the end. To Henry Beksaka's team. Meaning no accordion for Tomson Highway.

41

"Token, please," says Samba Cheese Fitzgerald of Puck, Manitoba. Like a street panhandler, he is holding his hand out. To me, it looks like a weapon. With the palm facing up and the way he is scowling? A knife.

"*Neeee*, what did I say?" I ask, surprised. Chewing on a gob of *pawpilly-cum* I have just bought at Father Picard's little store in this closet next door to his office, I am savouring the thought of where it comes from—three five-dollar bills post-mailed by Dad, one for Rene, one for Daniel, and one for me.

"You said 'it tastes good' in Cree," says Samba Cheese Fitzgerald.

"I did? I said '*weegit-soo*'?" Speaking one's native language is, of course, like breathing. I am hardly conscious of the fact that I have just used the word a second time, if second time it is.

"See? You said it again. Now you owe me two." In a flash, I make my mind up—I will argue the point to the end of time. Samba Cheese Fitzgerald—Bully Number One at Guy Hill School—is not to be toyed with. But I will.

"I did not."

"Did so."

"Did not."

"Did so."

"Did not."

"I'm gonna tell Mr. Laporte."

"Tell him what?"

"That you spoke Cree twice and didn't give me two tokens."

"I don't have any left."

"Liar."

"I've been caught speaking Cree ten times this week so they're all gone."

"*Awas, michisk. Kigi-thaaskin.*" ("Bullshit, asshole. You're lying.")

"Token, please," I shoot back, holding my hand out; my turn to look like a beggar. And I fully expect that he will give me one; it, after all, is the law, the name of the game. No such luck. Instead, Samba Cheese Fitzgerald, he of the mean, thin eyes and lipless mouth, punches me. On the nose. Hard. He is taller than me by at least three inches and is heavier. In fact, he is muscular, an athlete-in-the-making; I, quite scrawny, a nerd-in-the-making. My nose bleeds. I staunch it with a hand and cry outright. At which point, Mr. Laporte, the Big Boys' keeper that year, appears from nowhere. As one who has graduated, at age almost-thirteen, to "Big Boy" status, even though you would never know it by the way I am bawling, I am now in his fiefdom, his circle of care. He quells our fight.

A pudgy little man in his early twenties from Gilbert Plains, a farming village some two hundred miles north of Winnipeg, Erik Laporte is kind for the most part though can be prickly when rubbed the wrong way which, when you think of it, is par for the course. I mean, what person unkind or kind would rain someone who insults him with affection? But that fall day—we are confined to the playroom because it is raining—he is kind to me. When apprised of the situation in my still-fractured English, he takes both sides, sort of. He makes me give Samba Cheese Fitzgerald a token—not two but one—and makes him give me one, thus balancing our accounts. (I had lied to Samba Cheese; I had one token left, one I was saving for a day like this one.) At which point, the unpleasant little tussle peters off to a memory, if a sour one. And Mr. Laporte sends me to the washroom to stop my bleeding.

Where all this comes from is that the strict but ever-efficient Sister Ann has taken exception to the fact that we are not learning English. We can't. If for most people, learning another person's language is impossible—ask an anglophone who's tried learning French, for years, and still can't speak it—then we're no different. We can't, for example, understand why "weight" and "wait" sound exactly the same when they look completely different. And mean something completely different. And why is the "ou" in the words "through," "though," "thought," "rough," and "thou" pronounced in five different ways—and which is which? And why is the "gh" in "bough" not pronounced, while it is in "rough"—and that as an "f"? How on Earth can you get an "f" from a "g" and an "h"? And this is not including the physical act of pronunciation; the three last consonants of a word like "mouths," for example, give our tongues cramps. It drives us crazy.

According to Sister Ann, the problem has become so acute that it is endangering our other courses; we will never learn our history, arithmetic, social studies, or other subjects if we don't learn to speak and write in perfect English. We will fail. Father Picard has recently retired because of his age and his younger replacement, the hairy-nostrilled and bald Father Laval, who hails not from Paris but from Winnipeg, heeds Sister Ann's impassioned protestations; he gives her his blessing. So that now she is free to invent a system that will combat the problem. That system? Tokens. Hence my tiff with Samba Cheese Fitzgerald.

On the first day of October, Mr. Manning, my grade seven teacher, gives me ten tokens. Rectangles of pink construction paper, they resemble postage stamps, only thicker. Everyone in our class gets them; Onyx Mobster (whose sisters are Opal and Pearl) is particularly excited; then again, the adorable tall, brown girl with the gangly frame from Nelson House, Manitoba, gets excited at the slightest provocation. Rene gets blue ones as do all his classmates, the grade five students. Daniel gets red ones as do all his classmates, the grade nine students (for Guy Hill now teaches up to grade nine which is why he is still here). By the end of the distribution of such largesse, every student in the school has each ten tokens, each grade with a different colour. Comparing our colours, Rene and I disagree as to which is better, his or mine. He says his is better because blue is "manly" while pink is "girly." I disagree. Colour, I say, has nothing to do with being a woman. Whichever gender is better, we are told to go out there and collect as many of these tokens as we can by the end of October. Why end of October? The student in each grade who has amassed the largest number of tokens by that time, and by the end of each month that school year, will get a prize. And how you collect them is to stop speaking Cree (or Dene) and start speaking English only. That is to say, every time you catch someone speaking Cree (or Dene), you ask them to hand over one of their tokens. And the race is on. The long-term objective? Within two years, everyone will be speaking, and writing, in perfect English. And thus succeed in all their subjects.

The problem being: How do you stop speaking Cree when you can hardly speak English; when learning another person's language is the hardest, and most humbling, thing one can ever do in one's lifetime? Example: *Qu'est-ce que c'est ça sur les marches devant la maison a côté, c'est-à-dire, la maison des Madame Dussouillez? Une feuille? Une souris?* Unilingual Anglos have been practicing that phrase for twenty-five years and still can't speak French. Well, welcome to the good ship Lollipop.

We try our best. "I tink it's lurnch time." "I like it the spigittis" ("I like spaghetti"). "Operator one, operator two, operator three" (when making a phone call to the hospital in The Pas where an uncle lies dying, Gilbert Hell of Brochet is overheard saying this in the visitors' parlour where a telephone serves such emergencies). "You commit crime." "She smell she skunks." "What happened? *Kitoogaapin*" ("Your eyes are open"). "*Neee*, look at taat, *eemataat*" ("Look at that"; as for the "*eemataat*," you don't want to know). "You want some the *soony-ass* [change], you cute little *Moony-ass*?" Meaning to say, with the last three examples, we get the two languages hopelessly entangled—though less frequently as time goes on, it must be admitted. And because Cree has no gender, the boys call everyone including the girls "he" while the girls do the same with "she." Five whole years will it take us to get that right.

And the epithet "token, please" rings out like gunfire. We hear it in the day, we hear it in the night, we hear it coming from the mouths of boys and girls Big, Small, and Medium; after a while, we hear it coming from the walls: *Token, please; token, please; token, please* . . .

Herman Bigfoot of Pelican Narrows, Saskatchewan, has a reputation for being slow. Fortunately, unlike Samba Cheese Fitzgerald, he is otherwise the same size and age as me and Nameegoos Kipawm of Brochet: "fortunately" because Nameegoos Kipawm and I will need such protection in what happens next . . .

The fence that encloses the boys' yard is bordered on one side by a ditch that starts at the back entrance of our gymnasium and reaches halfway to the lake, so is some fifty yards long. For excess rainfall? For drainage of spring thaw? We don't know and never do find out; substandard English will do that to one. One thing the ditch does do is separate the fence of the boys' yard from this field where grow wild grasses and, in spring, crocuses and dandelions (though there is also a shed that serves no visible purpose except for the storage of snakes just captured, so far as is known). Otherwise, the field sits unused, a no man's land where nothing ever happens and which is off-limits to us boys, even on those Saturdays when we are allowed to play in the forest that otherwise surrounds our enclosed compound. Aside from its length, this redundant gully is three feet wide and three feet deep, thus qualifying it as a "big tits." Like it or not, that's how the term "big ditch" comes out in Cree.

"Where's Tomson?" a boy will ask.

"Oh, he's over by the big tits playing marbles with Chally Canoe," a second boy will say.

So one day towards the middle of October, Nameegoos Kipawm, third son of Brochet's best home-brew maker, Aroozalee Kipawm, and I are hanging out at the swings near this fence, and therefore near this gully. Kicking loose gravel at leisure before it gets iced over, savouring the air of a northern October, and comparing the number of tokens we have—we each have twenty—we bet each other as to who will win the prize at month's end; for our grade, they say it is a comic book that features Tarzan, King of the Jungle.

"I will win," says Nameegoos Kipawm matter-of-factly.

"*Awas, maagi-choochoos*," I say.

"Token, please," says a voice behind us. We turn our heads. It is Herman Bigfoot of Pelican Narrows, Saskatchewan. He has walked up without our knowing it.

"*Neee*," I retort, "what did I say?" He points at the ditch behind us.

"You said, 'Go away, Maggie Big Ditch.'"

"*Neeee*," sneer Nameegoos Kipawm and I in unison and burst out laughing.

What has just happened is one of those Trickster-inspired, head-on collisions of languages. You see, in Cree, *choochoos* means "nipple" or "breast" or, more colloquially, "tit." And *maagi*, of course, is one of our two ways of saying "big," so that what *maagi-choochoos* ends up meaning is "big nipple" or "big tit," and can be pluralized in the same breath just like "fish" and "moose" can in English. That, combined with my Cree writer's license to invent the spelling of what is a previously unwritten language only adds to the fun; changing "*maagi*" to "Maggie," which is how the word is pronounced, is but one instance.

Which is how Herman Bigfoot, in his not-too-rapid, easily confused cerebellum—and very feeble English—has somehow ended up using the concept of "big" in two languages one after the other—as in "big-big Ditch"—which is why it comes out as "Maggie Big Ditch" but hits our ears as "Maggie Big Tits." The result? A nickname is born. From that day onward, Herman Bigfoot is no longer. He is—you guessed it—Maggie Big Ditch. Which doesn't mean that I have to give him a token. Nameegoos Kipawm and I are two, he is one, so we have strength in numbers and Maggie Big Ditch knows

it. Like a dog just cuffed, he slinks off not one token richer. And
Nameegoos Kipawm and I remain tied for first place, so far, in the
monthly collection of tokens for our level, grade seven.

Being almost all French-Canadian, the nuns, priests, and Brothers
speak French amongst themselves almost exclusively. And if we have
difficulty understanding English, then imagine our relationship to
French. Whatever it is, one of the phrases we hear most frequently
among them is the question "*Qu'est-ce que c'est?*" which I will finally
learn, at high school in Winnipeg, means "What is it?" What hits our
ears, however, is, "*kaskasi*" which, in Cree, means "your fingernail."
Kaskasi, naskasi, ooskaseeya. "Your fingernail, my fingernail, his/her
fingernail." Thus do we joke amongst ourselves that, if the nuns are
speaking Cree, then shouldn't one of us go up to Sister Oo-hoo, to
name but one, and say, "Token, please," when we catch her saying
"*kaskasi*"? Not only does Bertha Mistat of Nelson House, Manitoba,
in particular, enjoy torturing the younger girls with that linguistic
crossing of wires, she enjoys victimizing the occasional boy as well.
As in this case.

Some two weeks later, school is out for the day and it is therefore
dark in the hallway on both sides of which stand rows of classrooms
when I find myself walking to the "lie-berry" to practice, in secret,
my beloved piano. Suddenly, I hear a voice behind me.

"*Kaskasi,*" it says. It is older. And female. I stop, turn around, see
the person only in silhouette. All I can tell, for now, is that it is a
woman. Not a girl but a woman.

"Token, please," I say. It is the last day of October, and so determined am I to get one last token to win that Tarzan comic book,
not for me but for Rene, that I am willing to risk hell, Hitler, and
high water.

"*Kitaaseek anima* 'token, please,'" the owner of the voice fires
back. ("You'll find 'token, please' inside your pants," our way of
saying "Go fuck yourself.") My eyes acclimatizing themselves to the
absence of light, I recognize the terrifyingly masculine, tall, large-
boned, and thick-lipped Bertha Mistat of Nelson House, Manitoba.

Two years older, she towers over me like George Peter Buckskin of Pelican Narrows, Saskatchewan, used to.

"I was speaking French, not Cree," she says in note-perfect English and, her "maggie big tits" threatening me with premeditated asphyxiation, corners me. And hisses, again in English, "*You* give me a token, you fucking know-it-all precious little princess." So stunned am I by being thus attacked that, before I know it, she has taken not just one but *ten* tokens from my outstretched hand, the ten, that is— *half* my stores!—that have somehow appeared on my quaking extremity of their own volition. And with not one twitch of gratitude or recognition, she sweeps by imperiously and fades like a stench down the very long corridor. No one—*no one*—ever gets a token from the large, brutish, and prematurely buxom Bertha Mistat of Nelson House, Manitoba. Which is how Nameegoos Kipawm of Brochet, Manitoba, ends up winning the Tarzan comic book at month's end. By ten tokens.

Needless to say, the ingenious system of language training hatched by the demanding but ever-industrious and ivory-complexioned Sister Ann turns out a bust. Or does it? Such early and Jesuit-rigid discipline of that muscle in the brain that absorbs sound, only two components of which are language and music, will, over the years, give mine the elasticity and muscularity it needs to absorb other languages much more easily than if I hadn't had such early training. In this way, for instance, am I, at Guy Hill this year in particular, merely adding English to my already acquired repertoire of Cree, Dene, Latin, and music, so that, later in life, I will speak six languages. And counting . . .

Joe Highway's lesson in life and love: from disaster make something spectacular.

42

Pow! I see stars. Then pitch-black. I don't know what's happened but when I come to some two minutes later—or is it five? Ten? A hundred?—I learn that I have been punched, hard, on my right temple. I have flown six feet, or so I'm told, have crumpled to the floor and blacked out briefly. And where that punch has come from is this . . .

I am walking down the hallway on the third floor of the Guy Hill Indian Residential School in bare feet and pajamas. On the way from the washroom where the sinks are located, I have just brushed my teeth and washed my face. Now I am going to my bed in the Big Boys' dormitory. Our keeper there at that point in time is Native, the first and only we have ever had. Or will ever have. I see him coming. Walking in the opposite direction with his usual swagger and short man's complex, he stops in front of me, thus blocking my passage. I say nothing. He says nothing. A solid young man of perhaps twenty-five, he may be short but he is built like a fire hydrant. Not an ounce of fat on his frame. Though aged thirteen, I'm small for my age, have heard it said that I could pass for eleven. And am built like a flower, a waif. (A late bloomer, my height will shoot to its present five foot eleven when I'm sixteen.) My face five inches from his, I can see the flames inside his eyes. They burn with hate. They burn with fire. I am facing the devil.

"Turn your head," he says point-blank. "Look to the right." I do.

Pow! the punch comes out of nowhere. So powerful is the impact of the monster's hit it could have given me permanent brain damage. Or knocked an eyeball from its socket.

Fortunately, I, too, am powerful in my own way—especially my skull, which is preternaturally thick. A boy with less would have been killed outright. Where do I get that power? From my heritage. When you're born in a snowbank in the dead of winter in forty-below weather in far north Canada and survive the experience, it will take a transport truck to kill you. Five of us didn't have that strength and so died as children. Me? Touch wood but I've never had a headache, not even after that punch. I've never had a stomach ache, never had a broken bone—and I've had spectacular accidents—never had a back problem, I get the flu once every three years, all the aches and pains known by most people I have never known.

The perpetrator of this act of aggression is a Saulteaux Indian (pronounced "Soto," as in "photo"); from a First Nation in northeastern Manitoba near its border with Ontario called God's Lake, his name is Stanley Blackbird. He thinks I'm a sissy, that I walk with a mince, that I talk like a girl, that I am a girl. In modern parlance, Stanley Blackbird is a homophobe, and I am a two-spirit. Like Charles Darwin's animals, plants, and even minerals and ancient Greece's god/goddess, Hermaphrodite—son/daughter of gods Hermes and Aphrodite—I was born a hybrid of both male and female. Like all beings animal, vegetable, and mineral—yes, Virginia, there are two-spirit cows, two-spirit bulls, two-spirit fish, two-spirit trees, and two-spirit rocks; the universe seethes with gender; two-spiritness is a biological normality—my male self was spliced with my female at the moment of conception, perhaps even prior; my body is both genders as is my heart as is my spirit (though I should specify that I do have male genitals and male genitals only and greatly enjoy them!). As are all people's, either to a greater or a lesser extent, depending on who they are. In a Catholic school, no such idea exists. In a Catholic school, there exist but two genders. You are either 100 percent male or 100 percent female and anyone who tries to cross that line of division gets killed. By homophobes. To a homophobe's thinking, it is healthier for a man to rape a woman or beat his wife to death—or kill a "faggot"—than to love or be loved by another man. Some five decades later, for example, will Lady Beksaka die in a brutal beating at the hands of homophobes; three of them will gang up on her in a downtown Winnipeg hotel room and tear her to shreds just like one of Dad's dogs, Boblin by name, will be treated next summer by her rivals in her sled dog lineup, her entrails strewn across the sand on a blissful beach on a blissful island.

Not me. If that punch has accomplished anything, it has given me the power to dedicate my life to the dismantling of that hateful, destructive, two-gender structure that arrived on our continent in 1492 and replacing it with another, one with three genders—or four or six—one where a woman is no longer the rib-bone of her husband but the husband is the rib-bone of his wife. That insult, that is to say, will, from that moment onward, go the other way. That idea was born somewhere deep inside me at that precise moment. With this "gift" from Stanley Blackbird, I am bound and determined to help make that change.

Joe Highway's lesson in life and love: from disaster make something spectacular. From manure most painful, most disgusting, springs vegetation most magnificent.

The impact on my head is one thing. But the impact on my spirit is another. First Samba Cheese Fitzgerald of Puck, then Bertha Mistat of Nelson House, and now this. In bed that night when I can't sleep from the throbbing of my skull—not pain but throbbing, and I refuse to cry even if I know that that man tried to kill me—I am hit by one flashing moment, stark white and blinding, where I hate every single fucking Indian on the face of the planet with every single ounce of my being. Joe Highway's children, that is to say, are *not* perfect children.

Pow!

43

On this bright morning in late July that same year, I am babysitting my niece, Molly, Swanson's first daughter (and first child) at our camp on an island on Mariah Lake, the lake and island where I was born thirteen years prior. Now two years of age, she has two dolls, one male, one female. A sort of Ken and Barbie before their time, they each have a wardrobe. At the moment, I am buttoning the back of Barbie's dress on Ken, much to Molly's amusement. Pretending the doll is me, I am thoroughly enjoying the exercise in cross-dressing when I hear a bell. It's Seagull's Little Poop's. The kind used by teachers to call their students to class, she got it from a grandniece for her ninetieth birthday, so legend has it, and where the grandniece got it was in the ashes of the fire that incinerated the Sturgeon Landing Indian Residential School, Guy Hill's predecessor. True or not, the old Dene woman with the shamanistic bent to her persona is ringing the instrument with an enthusiasm and energy most impressive for a woman of her advanced age. The clarion call, of course, means one thing and one thing only: Mass. Or at least, prayers.

If the Cree up north are known for their loyalty to the Catholic religion, then the Dene should be made saints. They believe in Jeezoos to the point where, as Masky Jimmy Perkins once gamely claimed, their dogs go to confession on a basis semi-regular and can bark the first two lines of the *Kichitaw Maaree*. They—that is, the Dene, not the dogs—pray and sing hymns with a frequency, enthusiasm, and intensity that makes us Cree look like *machi-mantoo-wak* by comparison (another way of saying "devils"). If Mom and Dad's last act of every day is to kneel at their bedside, he in his long johns, she in her slip, and say one decade of the rosary with lips that move but make no sound, then the Dene, I am sure, recite all five decades of that rosary at their bedside every night *and* say High Mass.

It is Sunday, and with the nearest priest in Brochet one hundred miles to the south, "Who else, pray tell," asks Seagull's Little Poop of Balazee Highway, "is there to take over his job?" As the oldest person in all *keeweet'nook*, she, and she only, is the obvious candidate, she says. So here she is replacing Father Cadeau in leading a service. It may not be a Mass, for the Holy Eucharist—the body of Christ in the form of the Host—cannot be touched by a woman; but at least she can lead whatever congregation that she can rope in to recite the rosary and sing, what's more, a selection of hymns.

And lo and behold, within ten minutes of that bell's ringing, everyone resident at this remote little settlement in sub-Arctic Canada will be at her tent on their knees with their rosaries clanging and the pages of their hymn books fluttering in the breeze like the wings of a tiger swallowtail.

Our camp's population this summer—small as it is, it is still bilingual, in Cree and Dene—is about thirty people: our family; that of my eldest brother, Swanson, his wife, Suzette, a toddler, and an infant; that of our cousin, Lucy St. Anne (Mom's drowned brother Alphonse's daughter), her Dene husband, Manuel, a toddler, and an infant; and at least three Dene families, to one of which the widowed and childless Seagull's Little Poop is an honorary grandmother of sorts. And then there is Lady Beksaka, my two-spirit colleague from residential school who haunts the environs with her lynx-like movements. Being good Roman Catholics, we all drop everything we are doing and jump to the summons. I hang my doll, which is actually Molly's, on the branch of a spruce tree and take its owner up the slope to Swanson's tent some ten feet off before I continue to our main tent.

Though we try our best to *waweesee* (dress up), we don't have much in the way of fashion, not even with the Eaton's mail-order catalogue at our disposal. Used mostly for toilet paper anyway, half its pages are missing or torn down the middle. Still, we do our best. At least our shirts are laundered, says Mom philosophically as she grabs her little *Kichitaw Maaree*–shaped plastic vial of holy water from her sewing kit and slips it smoothly into the pocket of her purple cotton windbreaker. Then she dons her multi-hued faux-silk head kerchief and off we go in single file up the well-worn footpath to the tent where lives my mom's friend and ally, Seagull's Little Poop.

We get to her tent. This morning, because of the heat, she has pinned the sides and the front walls of her dwelling to standing poles so that it looks like a giant version of Sally Field's headdress in the TV series *The Flying Nun* (which we saw every Friday evening at Guy Hill School). As to Seagull's Little Poop herself, she squats like a bear in the middle at the back, facing the entrance. Her hair is so white and frizzy it could have served as beard to Zebedee Zipper when he played *Saanchi Giloss* that one fabled Christmas Dad speaks of with such affection (for we, of course, were at school), her neck so withered it looks like a turtle's, her "southern hemisphere" widening to a girth that would challenge certain pieces of furniture if the tents we live in were to have them which, happily for her, they don't.

Now, because northerners do all their cooking either on campfires in front of the tent or on woodstoves inside that tent, both kinds of fires fuelled by wood, all front yards at fish camps up north—and all houses for that matter, Brochet's included—are always covered with a two-inch-thick layer of wood chips and shavings, debris from wood just split and chopped. Seagull's Little Poop's tent is no exception. Add to this element the fact that my mother has always insisted on having a bitch as her personal house dog and you have yourself the makings of a very good story. Always small, black, and a mutt, this dog follows us everywhere we go, even to Companeek to buy *kinoosees-sak* ("little fish"—that is, sardines in cans). The long-deceased Itchy's successor, "Doggy" is only the most recent in a long line of such cherished animals. So it is that Doggy comes with us to "Mass" that Sunday.

Aside from airing out its stuffy interior, the wide-open flaps of the old woman's tent address themselves to a second purpose—to accommodate overflow. If Seagull's Little Poop's humble abode has room for six people at the best of times, with such an expansion of space out into the open, another two dozen can spill out onto the carpet of wood chips that lie scattered in front of the dwelling.

The size and shape of Mr. Christie's crumbly soup crackers for the most part, these wood chips number as many as a thousand, I venture to guess, that morning at Seagull's Little Poop's, which doesn't add an inch to their comfort level—kneeling on the bastards, *sans* knee pads or cushion, for any length of time can prove quite painful, not to mention leave imprints on your *kipoochim* that look like waffles (that is, if you sit on them as opposed to kneeling). But there we are, kneeling at the rear of this ragtag assembly, Mom, Rene, and I, as the last three people to arrive, squished in together behind the hefty Mist Ass-Lick Beksaka and her niece/nephew, the sinuous and sylph-like Lady Beksaka. As for Doggy, she stretches out behind us with the intention of having herself a good long nap, something she does with extreme skill. For her, the wood chips are moot. Dogs, they're like that.

Seagull's Little Poop begins the proceedings. Droning bee-like, she recites, solo, the *Credo*, then launches with vim and with vigour into her first *Nootaawinaan* (Our Father). She recites the first verse. The congregation responds with the second. Next, she bursts into full-throated song—the first verse of a hymn that barely makes it as hymn, her vocal cords are that old, that worn. "*Kiti-maagi-heeminaan*" is a favourite of hers, Mom has told me. Written in the key of A-minor (according to Mom's hymn book, which I am sharing with her), Seagull's Little Poop starts it in C-minor, two keys higher than was intended by its composer. By the time she gets to the last line of the first verse and the congregation is ready to join her with the second, she has somehow climbed to the key of E-minor, four keys higher. The congregation tries valiantly to accommodate the unseemly modulation but, alas, the new key is too much for Stare Loon. Admired in music circles for her creamy contralto, she can't sing soprano and it shows in the way her voice starts squeaking; her face beet-red, she can barely breathe. Fortunately for her, the hymn comes to an end.

"'Have mercy on us' is right," lisps Lady Beksaka, who speaks both Cree and Dene (for that's what "*Kiti-maagi-heemi-naan*" means) and we roundly agree with robust grunts expelled in unison. The congregation white-faced with relief, it can't wait for the *Kichitaw Maaree*s to begin so they don't have to sing.

Seagull's Little Poop drones out the first verse of the first Hail Mary, the verse that calls our dear Jeezoos a fruit—our one thing in common, I've always thought; the congregation responds with the humble admission that we are sinners hook, line, and sinker. Thirty Native people reciting prayers in a monotone, we sound like cows with udders in serious need of milking. There are ten of these *Kichitaw Maaree*s, so the intermittent mooing continues for a stretch, Mom in the thick of it with lips contorting and rosaries a-jangle. But the faith is real; these people are connecting with a higher power; it gives me a chill. In fact, Lady Beksaka starts looking like a statue of *Kichitaw Maaree*.

All of a sudden, I feel a poke on my left arm. I look to the perpetrator. It is Rene. He is pointing his lips in the classic Cree manner at something he wants me to look at. I turn my head in that direction. And, wonder of wonders, there stands Doggy having the time of her life. With not just a visitor but an admirer. And not just an admirer but a lover.

It turns out that there are two other mutts in the village such as it is, one of whom is this old brown thing who is so useless that he has no name. All he does is lope lazily around in search of scraps. No one owns him at the same time as everyone does. And no one really cares; in fact, he serves conveniently as a compost receptacle—fish tails, duck bones, scraps of Klik, that kind of thing—which is why we tolerate his mangy presence. Unfortunately, this morning, he has followed Doggy to the service and evidently has lost no time in "getting down to bra straps," as Masky Jimmy Perkins so gamely calls the act of *maseewee* (fucking). All as Seagull's Little Poop goes on with her praying.

"Dogs have no style," a friend once said when describing their approach to the act of *maseewee*—there *is* no approach. No longer lazy or loping, the male just climbs on the female and starts pumping away. Nothing wrong there; the birds and the bees—and humans— have been doing it since time immemorial. The problem is that there just happens to be a church service in progress right there before the entwined lovebirds. So close, in fact, are they to the back row of faithful that they might as well be "doing it" right in front of the braying and wailing Seagull's Little Poop.

By this time, the congregation is well into the second decade of the rosary. Attuned to the prayer, Mom's lips are moving like lightning, her spit flying, her rosaries on the verge of exploding into flame. When she sees Rene and me trying to suppress our gut-busting laughter at God knows what, her eyes flare up. In so many grimaces, she signals us to "stop it" while her lips keep moving uninterrupted. All as Rene and I continue suppressing our hysteria to no great success. Until she sees it—her beloved Doggy getting "the treatment." Then her lips *really* move. Way too Catholic to stop her prayer in mid-sentence and get up, walk over, kick Doggy, pull her out from under her lover, and drag her home by the tail, what choice does she have? The best Mom can do is throw wood chips at her. And scowl her fiercest scowl in hopes Doggy will get the message.

"Hail Mary full of grace . . ." first wood chip, fuck, fuck, fuck, "the Lord is with thee," second wood chip, fuck, fuck, fuck. "Blessed art thou amongst women . . ." third wood chip, fuck, fuck, fuck, "and blessed is the fruit . . ." fourth wood chip, fuck, fuck, fuck, "of thy womb, Jeezoos" (all said, of course, in a mix of Cree and Dene). No result. Doggy and the mutt just keep on working the wheels of love, Doggy, by this time, with her pink tongue drooling, her eyes rolling heavenward, her thin legs trembling with wanton passion. The second decade over, Seagull's Little Poop has started singing the next hymn. Fuck, fuck, fuck. As only she faces her yard, her congregation all with their backs to the action, only she can see it, except, of course, for me, Rene, and Mom away off at the back. Fuck, fuck, fuck. Like Mom, however, the resident priestess of all the Indians in the world can do nothing. She can't; she is busy connecting God with them. She blinks her rheumy eyes, rolls them once, lifts one massive buttock, blows one blast of a fart that rocks the very eskers to their foundation, and soldiers on. "*Keespin kisaagee-hee-inaan . . .*" ("If you love us . . .") she wails. Fuck, fuck, fuck. Even if she were to answer to the impulse of leaping to her feet and marching over to kick the offenders, her age won't let her as won't her girth. Fuck, fuck, fuck. By this time, Doggy is whimpering. With pain? With pleasure? We don't know, we don't care, Rene and I. Fuck, fuck, fuck. Their key changes climbing, the congregation crescendos, Mom right there with them note for note. All as she keeps throwing wood chips and every grimace in her immense library of grimaces at her dog.

Kita-tawee Doggy *kaapaask-sigee-pathit.* ("All of a sudden, Doggy goes off like a gun"—Cree for he/she has an orgasm.) At which point, Rene and I can hold it no longer. We burst out laughing. And laugh and laugh and laugh and laugh until tears drown us. Never have you seen a congregation so shocked, so scandalized. Which still doesn't stop it from continuing to modulate ever upward, grace of the tone-deaf Seagull's Little Poop. Stare Loon now practically a coloratura soprano, she is singing so high that only Doggy, I am sure, can hear her, especially after having expended the last of her love juices (that is, Doggy's, not Stare Loon's). "*Keespin . . .*" but the male dog hasn't so, fuck, fuck, fuck, he continues, "*kisaagee-hee-inaan . . .*" fuck, fuck, fuck . . .

We get sent home.

44

"*Ninee-mee-itoon*," sings a woman on a record in the boys' gymnasium as I shuffle to her voice and the band that backs it, "*anima*-Tennessee Walsh . . ." The sound is silky; it makes me shiver. (Cree still unwilling to leave me, the words transform themselves into the language inside my head.)

"The waltz," one of our two dance instructors declares: "the simplest dance." Using me and my partner as model interpreters—which we, most decidedly, are not—she explains this fact to a crowd of teenagers who number sixty.

"*Niwee-chee-waagan kaagee-waap-maat* . . ." The woman's recorded voice continues, as does our teacher's.

"For all it is is *one* two three, *two* two three, *three* two three, left foot forward . . ." And she sways like a willow behind me as she guides my arms in the act of holding my dancing partner, the lanky and lipless Cordelia Kamaa-magoos of Island Falls, Saskatchewan. "Your right hand gently around her waist, your left hand holding her lovely right. Girls, hold your rib cage nice and high." In fact, so high does the glum-faced Cordelia hold her rib cage she has trouble breathing. Fortunately, her waist is thin so she looks quite fetching which is good because, in the classroom where she sits one desk from mine, she stabs me with her pencil regular as clockwork to "test my temper," as she puts it. All around us, sixty-two teenagers male and female, Cree and Dene, swirl in couples this way and that across this *ersatz* Indian ballroom.

Every Thursday evening through the course of the winter, at least this year, two dance instructors, a husband-and-wife team in their middle years, drive the twenty-five miles from The Pas north to our school to give dance classes to the Big Girls and Big Boys. Yet another night when the girls are allowed in the boys' gymnasium, it is always an event to anticipate, for the older boys, in particular. For not only do they get to listen to country music, they get to see the girls they like and touch them, perhaps even squeeze them.

"*Igwa meegwaach*," continues the song, "*Eenee-mee-itoo-chik . . .*"

Since I first got here eight years ago, the school has not only extended its syllabus in increments, from grades seven to eight to nine, it has also widened its catchment area; students from reserves like Cross Lake and God's Lake in the northeastern part of the province are now here with us. Still, because of the remoteness of most of our communities, students, in some cases, don't start school until age ten, resulting in the fact that Guy Hill has students in grade nine who are eighteen—people, in other words, whose bodies have matured to adulthood. That is to say, these bodies evince sensations and shed liquids that they did not when they were children; sweat and tears are the least of it. The problem is that their access to members of the opposite sex for which said fluids are the natural conduit is limited. Still, here's how some of the more adventurous practitioners of "the dance of love" fulfill their urges.

In the three dormitories where sleep boys Big, Small, and Medium, "lights out" for the Small and Medium boys is half-past eight. For the Big Boys, it's ten. Our beds, of course, are still arranged according to age and number. At age fourteen, I have been promoted to the rank of Boy Fifteen in the Big Boys' dorm. Meaning to say that I sleep in a bed in the middle of the room away from the older boys and so remain uninvited to nocturnal events they sometimes engage in. Besides, I am "not a boy," blares Samba Cheese Fitzgerald to all and sundry every chance he gets, so why should I be invited? According to him, I should go down to the Medium Boys' dormitory where Brother Lemoine is probably busy *eenoo-chipi-chigeet* (rooting around).

But the Big Boys at the far end of the room where are located beds numbers one to ten are very interested. In girls. But why would I be?

So, once lights are out, they wait for the sound of young men wheezing. And I, too, am about to fall asleep when something hits my elbow—Ferlin Wachask of Beaver Lake, Saskatchewan, as it turns out, is crawling past me on the floor on all fours so it is his shoulder that has hit me. Seeing I'm awake, he shushes me. Still, he is not alone in his subterfuge. Chuck Fitzgerald and Simeon Kamaa-magoos, both of Brochet, Benjamin McMillan of South Indian Lake, Manitoba, and Kipoots McDonald of Pelican Narrows, Saskatchewan, are doing like-wise, creeping on the floor like prowling cats toward the room's main entrance and out. Unwillingly, I drift off to sleep. The rest I hear later from braggart inveterate Ferlin Wachask.

Once out the door, the five boys leap to a standing position and, in their flannel pajamas and with feet bare, skulk down the hallway to the top of the stairs, down two flights, down a much longer hallway, leaping now and then into alcoves to avoid being seen—all in dark-ness—and into the dorm where sleep the Big Girls. Once inside, they drop to their knees and start "their hunt." At which point, Chichilia Kipawm of Brochet, Manitoba, who is sleeping in that room among thirty others, takes over as narrator . . .

But first, back in the boys' playroom, the dance instructor—I don't remember his name or that of his wife—wears a cowboy shirt in two shades of blue, of silk, with bright pearl buttons and a bolo tie. Laun-dered Levi's ironed to a state of nerdy perfection, cowboy boots, and a ten-gallon hat complete the image—Roy Rogers, the American sing-ing cowboy. The only thing missing is his white-maned horse, Trigger.

Fortunately, his wife is with him and wouldn't you know it but she looks like Dale Evans, the wife of Roy Rogers on the TV show. White cowboy boots and a cowboy shirt, though hers is red with white silk tassels that fall from her chest, complementing her husband's. In place of jeans, however, she wears a skirt that swirls and flounces. And she is hatless. As pretty as a doll with her bright red lipstick and wax-like complexion, what piques our youthful curiosity is her hairdo—its popcorn pouffe moves not one smidgen no matter which way or how fast she moves. If a bomb were to explode a foot from the woman, not one hair on that monstrous construction would budge.

The class started at eight; we are now into the second half-hour. Sitting on the floor like a great big chest, the speaker sits erect, the record player ready on a table brought in from the boys' refectory for the purpose, the records placed in a stack beside it.

"Three steps this way, three steps that way," cries Roy Rogers in his raspy tenor, for now we are into the dance called the polka and the music, voiceless, is mostly accordion. The song? The "Beer Barrel Polka," a lively number, much faster than that for the waltz. Overseeing as he does all movement in the room, Roy Rogers waves his arms this way and that: "One, two, three and two, two, three; one, two, three and two, two three . . ." His wife, meanwhile, flutters around us, gently touching our shoulders here, our rib cages there, guiding them this way and that for the steps, indeed, are one matter but the movement of the body, according to her, is another, even the head. Especially the head.

Chichilia Kipawm, who, at this moment, is dancing with the odious Samba Cheese Fitzgerald, will much later recount that when the Big Boys enter the Big Girls' dorm late "*that night*," they do so crawling in darkness. In their patterned pajamas with white background, they look like sheep, says the hefty daughter of Aroozalee Kipawm, Brochet's legendary home-brew maker. Making not a sound, they reach the beds they have in mind, slide into them, and "go for the jugular." This remarkable event is followed on its heels by a rustling of bedsheets. With lust-filled grunts, the five Cree studs fight with the spirit of Brother Lemoine—they slap his hand away from their rock-hard *chimasoo* (erections), if metaphorically, then charge their way to pleasures unheard of in the annals of education Aboriginal. The girls, in turn, respond with ardent, loon-like ululations and much gyration, says Chichilia Kipawm.

"I won't go into the details," she adds. Being large of buttock and large of breast and of a height imposing, she herself remained untargeted by such intentions but she had ears and she had eyes. "All

I am going to say," she says to me one drunken night at the Thompson Inn in Thompson, Manitoba, some thirty years later, "is that they were dancing. And not the polka."

"Chin up, chin up," trills Dale Evans, "look proud and regal. You are kings. You are queens. Loosen your waist; don't tense it up. In this dance"—the "shuffle," as she calls it—"one has to sway like a reed in a river, not clunk about like a block of cement." Still, in the midst of my struggle with my clumsy feet, which my partner, Cordelia Kamaa-magoos, abhors and will wreak her revenge for in class next day with her stab-happy pencil, I catch a peek, over her shoulder, of Kelvin Mitaas of South Indian Lake, Manitoba, holding the winsome and large-haired Annabelle Ateek of Puck, Manitoba, awfully close. His lips on her neck—I am sure—he looks like a vampire in the act of sucking human blood. His cavey nostrils flaring with passion, he twirls her around and glides in the other direction. Now that his partner faces me, I can see that Annabelle Ateek is in heaven. Her eyes are closed, her lips parted slightly, her neck betraying the stamp of love bright red in colour; even her hair seems to be higher than usual. Distracted, I step on Cordelia's foot, she stumbles, I apologize, but she glares daggers—I can already feel the pencil pierce my arm. During which tussle, Kelvin Mitaas and Annabelle Ateek glide from view. Evidently, Mr. Mitaas is determined to prove, if only to her, that he has not lost his masculinity to his rapist, Brother Felix Lemoine.

Back in the Big Girls' dormitory that one night of which speaks with such conviction this Chichilia Kipawm, every single light in the room snaps on. Suddenly, all is as bright as a railway station. How Sister Oo-hoo has detected the invaders no one knows, but she has; her owl-like spectacles have done their job. Five girls scream as five boys jump out of sheets and dive under beds. When Chichilia Kipawm looks under hers, there is Chuck Fitzgerald lying curved like a fetus trying his best to be invisible. Still, it is too late; the glowering, flame-cheeked Sister Oo-hoo commands them to come out of their hiding places and march straight back to their own sleeping quarters.

"*Mawch isa apoochiga awinak eegee-pask-sigee-pathit*," says Chichilia Kipawm matter-of-factly at the Thompson Inn as she orders ten more beers. "*Oosaam eegee-papaa-sipi-chigeechik*." (So much for this dance of love. Nobody even had the time to go off like a gun. They were too rushed.)

The foxtrot, the jig, the bunny hop, the watusi, the tango, the samba, the rhumba, the cha-cha-cha, the Charleston, the two-step, the *sk-weetaas* which, of course, the *Moony-ass* call the "square dance," we learn them all. Through the course of that winter, we master so many steps that we could form a chorus line in a Las Vegas show (which we've seen, here at this school, in a movie called *Viva Las Vegas*). And through every one of them, the Big Boys paw, in some form or other, the Big Girls and the Big Girls paw, in some form or other, the Big Boys. All while Brother Felix Lemoine stands off to the side taking this scene in. I'd like to say he was licking his lips but he wasn't. He just looked sad, unloved completely. No dance of love for him. Ever.

Another dance of love . . . The nuns have created a grotto in a meadow enclosed by the forest, a ten-minute walk behind the girls' yard. In the centre of that grotto stands a life-sized statue of *Kichitaw Maaree*. Perched on a pedestal, she stands draped in her usual veil—"*della Robbia* blue," as Father Grew calls its colour—her rosaries dangling from entwined hands, and gazes at space with eyes as expressionless as the stone they are. The ground all around her, meanwhile, is strewn with pebbles which bald and humble Brother Menard, who has succeeded the retired Brother St. Arnaud as general handyman as opposed to a "keeper," has soaked in white paint, dried, then spread with a rake. The point is for nuns and girls—the site, for some reason, is off-limits to boys—to kneel on those pebbles at their leisure and pray to the Virgin. The only thing is, it doesn't always work out quite that way. As certain girls recount the old yarn, Bertha Mistat arrives late at supper one evening all flushed and panting, her hairdo askew. At first, Sister Oo-hoo, the chubby little nun with the owlish spectacles, is peeved. Until she sees the Cree girl's knees which, of course, are exposed, for all girls wear dresses. With the telltale imprint, on those knees, of the pebbles in the grotto, bumpy and welted with flecks of paint as white as flour, it is obvious that Bertha Mistat of Nelson House, Manitoba, has been praying to *Kichitaw Maaree*. Sister Oo-hoo puffs out with pride.

The truth, however, is that certain of the more adventurous, older, and concupiscent boys have also gone to the grotto via a trail that leads through the forest that separates the boys' yard from the girls' by a good half-mile. Except that praying had nothing to do with it. In fact, they haven't even knelt. They have just stood there with their backs to the statue, their legs held open, as for a shootout in a John Wayne movie, and their zippers . . . well, let's just say they enjoyed, with verve, the dance of love, Brother Lemoine be hanged.

"Plame it on the possa mova," sings a singer named Something-or-other to drums that excite, "with its wondrous zing . . ." "Now we are into a dance called the bossa nova," explains Dale Evans to us all, "from South America, where the temperature is hot." For this one, we have to shake our entire bodies as if we are having epileptic fits. Man Fitzgerald of Puck, Manitoba, a strapping young man of eighteen years, greatly enjoys it. A frequent visitor to the grotto to "pray to the Virgin," he is good at shaking and rocking and reeling. And squeezing and kissing and stroking and poking. And, what's more, doesn't have to feel a twinge of guilt.

"And you know why?" he crows to the masses. "Because I can always 'plame it on the possa mova,'" and he pauses for effect, his English still, of course, far from perfect, "'that she was so good at,'" and he rolls his eyes to the heavens. And by "she" he means . . . well, let's just say that the "service provider" shall remain anonymous. And let's just say that it was, most expressly, not Brother Felix Lemoine, keeping in mind that all these boys, now older and wiser, were residents, too, some five years back, of the Medium Boys' dormitory.

Still, the dance I remember best is the one the instructors call the quadrille; and it is always the one that ends the evening.

"One step forward, two steps back," trills Roy Rogers. And we do just that. Much slower than the polka, much too civilized, this, decidedly, is not a *skweetaas*. In fact, it is more like a country gavotte. Or a minuet, terms I have learned at my weekly piano lesson. If a *skweetaas* takes eight dancers per circle and we number sixty-four, then that's eight circles. For this dance, however, we form one big circle: thirty-two girls, thirty-two boys (Daniel is absent for, now eighteen, he is in high school in Winnipeg). Cordelia Kamaa-magoos, Melinda Kamaa-magoos (the greatest piano player who ever lived, in my opinion), her sister Velma, her brother Simeon, Gloria Moostoos, Norma Saagweesoo, Man Fitzgerald, Ferlin Wachask, the sisters Opal, Onyx, and Pearl Mobster, Choggy-lat Kipawm, Arthur Bigfoot, Machaa-is Bacheese, Gregory Crumple, Caayoots Beksaka, Lady Beksaka, Arabella Beksaka, William Peeskwa, Michael Mitaas, Rufus Skylark, Tomson Highway, we are there, dancing the quadrille with silent dignity, a circle of unity, a circle of honour. And the words of the song, called "White Silver Sands," go:

Ita nipi kaasee-peeg'waak
Ita thee-g'wow kaa-asteek
Igoota kagee-ocheemak . . .

Most people post-1960 are lucky if they have one sibling, two at most. Here, at the Guy Hill Indian Residential School, I have been given two hundred siblings. So with this dance, I give thanks from the bottom of my heart for all they have given me all these years—companionship, laughter and, yes, love in all its richness. I love them to death, I love them to pieces. Even the crude and cruel Samba Cheese Fitzgerald and Bertha Mistat have a place in the circle. In the prime of youth, to my mind's eye, all these young people are flowers in full bloom at springtime swaying in a garden that knows no pain, no guilt, and no unhappiness.

When the music stops, Brother Lemoine flicks out his tongue, licks his upper lip, writhes through the roses, the tulips, and the delphiniums, then slithers out the door that leads upstairs, down two hallways, and into the chapel where waits for him his God of Love.

45

"The time has come to pick *naadlaaray*," says Dad. To me, the word means muskeg. And not just patches, but miles and miles of the squelchy, waterlogged, orange-coloured substance, a deep quagmire in which you sink past your ankles if not to your knees so that it is work, pure slave labour, to walk through. I don't like muskeg which, regretfully, is where grows in abundance this *naadlaaray*. And wouldn't you know it but the wondrous berry also just happens to ripen at the height of mosquito season. Thousands descend on those with blood—dogs and humans are the least of it—and suck to the point where their bellies bloat literally with the liquid and they have difficulty becoming airborne.

So far north does this wild Arctic berry, this *naadlaaray*, grow that most *Moony-ass* have never even heard of it much less seen it much less tasted its succulent extraction. The reason, of course, is that only in the most inaccessible extremities of Arctic and sub-Arctic regions does it flourish. Alaska is one such territory, or so I've read in a magazine in Father Cadeau's visitors' parlour. Greenland is another, Siberia another, sub-Arctic Norway, Sweden, and Finland yet others, and, of course, far north Canada. "The circumpolar axis," the picture-filled magazine calls such lands as a group, this Arctic union that serves as sentry to global climatic balance, as states the article. Here in Canada, only the Dene and the Inuit, whose home-land, of course, is the Northwest Territories, thus have access to this splendid fruit (though northern Newfoundlanders will argue the point that their land, too, has this berry though under a different name, albeit in English: "bake apple"). Whatever the argument, we splinter group of Cree who broke from the motherland and migrated so far north that we are now practically Dene ourselves are privileged—we, too, grow up knowing this *naadlaaray*.

According to Dad, we first came across it when he, as a young man of twenty, hazarded upon Old Dice Chagaazay, herself then just forty, emerging from the forest on an island on Lake Machi-mantoo carrying a pail filled to overflowing with some scarlet harvest which turned out to be this *naadlaaray*. Which is why the word is Dene, not Cree, though we promptly absorbed it into our language, just one instance of an "l" given us by the Dene (as opposed to the French, with their *lapwachin*). So we thank Joe Highway for having pulled up roots in mid-north Saskatchewan where grows no *naadlaaray*—where it is so non-existent it doesn't even have a name in Cree—to re-plant them in soil where grows this ambrosia in such riotous abundance that the Dene writhe with pleasure when the subject arises. And even if it grows in terrible terrain at a time that is terrible—muskeg, mosquitoes, muskeg, mosquitoes—the berry is delicious, well worth the effort that it takes to find and pick it.

Now what is too frequently assumed by those not in the know is that far north Canada is a seething hive of blood-sucking insects from one end of the summer to the other. Not true. Only in June and early July is this the case and then only at dusk and dawn. Though there are exceptions depending on the landscape—swamp or beach, for example, make one big difference—this is the pattern. If, quite to the contrary, you should happen to come up in high mid-August, you will be surprised to find yourself cavorting with two or three of the cute little buggers (for they are cute, like microscopic Cessnas) but that's it. And thus will find yourself scratching your *kipoochim* with extreme rareness.

Trailing Dad, Mom looks like a shaft of vapour floating through the forest. Her feet free of gravity, or so they give the impression of being, she is that graceful in this, her natural environment. Unfortunately, such is not the case with her youngest sons (Daniel, eighteen,

Florence, twenty-two, and Louise, twenty-six, now flown the coop, it is just me, Mom, Dad, and Rene). Our black Wellingtons with their thick red lips squelch and squish and thwack and fart with each step we engage in. *Ping, ping, ping,* meanwhile, goes the metal of our empty tin lard-pails—receptacles for berries to be picked—against brush as they swing from our hands like bells in churches, a welcome counterpoint to the *thwack, thwack, thwack* of squelching muck. Given the mosquitoes—for this is early July—our heads are covered with netting for, in muskeg, the rule that governs their twice-daily forays, namely dusk and dawn, applies no longer. That is to say, they may not be present in numbers near as great as those at dusk, say, but they are there—that's where they are born, in swamps soaked with stagnant water—making life difficult for all and sundry. Rene moans out his misery.

"*P'mootay-in,*" he pleads with me. ("Carry me.")

"I can't," I say, "you're too heavy." He persists. I repeat. He persists. By this time, we are lagging behind Mom and Dad by twenty-some yards. Mom stops and turns to shout out her encouragement. Her arms reaching out and her height on par with the tiny spruce trees around her, she looks like one. In feigned despair, Rene falls forward. I squelch over. Reaching him, I squat, turn my back to him, let him climb on. I know he's playing, exaggerating inability, but I love him to a fault so I play his game—I carry him piggy-back. And, yes, he is heavy; when he was four, I was able, but he now eleven and me fourteen, I am no longer. Still, I try. Each extraction of each foot from the sludge a monstrous suck, I grunt and trudge and groan and trudge. His flannel-covered arms around my neck, his body against mine, his breath grazing the nape of my neck like a wayward feather, I swoon with love. But if the spirit is willing, as Father Grew claims Jeezoos once said to "his men," the body isn't—I trip on a root and tumble forward. Rene goes flying, right over my head, and lands in the muck. And now we are wet, socks, jeans, shirts, denim jackets, everything. What are we to do? We sit there and laugh. And laugh and laugh. And when we look up, there they are, a million, a hundred

million, *five* hundred million *naadlaaray*. Northern Manitoba has
turned blood-red with berry fertility.

Naadlaaray is structured like a raspberry, but that's where ends
any and all similarity. First, the former is easily twice the size of the
latter. Second, the latter is soft and squishy, the former hard and
crunchy. Pinhead-sized kernels that cluster together as hard as kernels
of corn cling to cob and each other. As to colour, it shines bright scarlet at the top then bleeds into orange in the middle then yellow at the
bottom, where it sprouts from a sub-stem, making for a tri-coloured
berry neatly cupped by a four-leafed cushion which is straw-like in
texture and corn-husk beige. And which is what anchors it to the sub-
stem. Four sub-stems to a plant, say, each sub-stem will hold two or
three berries anchored by two or three leaves that look like mint. And
the central stem from which sprout all four sub-stems is what roots
the plant to the muskeg. Their average height? Three to five inches.

When grown to maturity, the flesh of the berry is as crispy as
apples. Which is when we pick it, for it keeps better then without
refrigeration which, of course, is unheard of in the north. Other
regions of the world, or so I understand from Father Cadeau's magazine, let them ripen to the point where they turn bright orange,
translucent, and mushy, which is when they are at their sweetest. Up
here in *keeweet'nook*, if one dares wait beyond this point, they fall
from the plant and rot in the muskeg. Or are gone to the blackbirds
who, by the way, are our guests at this banquet table. Or we are theirs.
Whichever it is, we Cree never let the ripening process go that far as
neither do the Dene.

Ping, ping, ping go our pails, though this time with berries hitting
merrily their round tin bottoms. As they grow low and tight to the
ground, we must squat and crouch like bears. Thus hunched and
working, Rene and I sneak every third berry into our mouths; we
can't wait to get home and eat the entire pailful. And as we make our
squelchy way picking *naadlaaray* across this meadow which, for all
intents and purposes, is a field, the mosquitoes have a holiday on our
exposed hands. Still, we try to ignore them. All while the level of the

berries in our pails keeps rising. We've arrived at noon. By two, we are finished. Thus encumbered—in fact, we are euphoric—the family treks back to its waiting canoe a mile or so away with its harvest in tow and motors the five miles back to camp. And for the next three days, Mom makes delicious orange-coloured *naadlaaray* jam and *naadlaaray* pies.

And that's just *naadlaaray*. Then there are the wild raspberries which, thank God, grow on landscape much less conducive to physical discomfort. In fact, not only is Brochet one big field of wild green grasses, it is also one big field of wild raspberries. When times are normal, it takes ten minutes to walk from our house to the store. At raspberry time, which is July, it takes two hours; you stop that often to *moominee*—that is, to pick them and eat them right from the stem (another verb exists for picking them to consume later: *moysoo*). Even walking to the church from Seepees-seek can take four hours, says Pitooria Wachask; the berry is that omnipresent. *Itnee-meena, weesagee-mina, askee-mina, peethigoo-mina, mitheechee-mina, pilaps-chowee-mina, oocheep'waani-imina*, we have them all and in vast numbers. *Keeweet'nook* in its endless entirety, a virtual orchard.

Seagull's Little Poop has ants in her pants. She appears at our tent to inform Mom as such. Diapers are needed, she says to her friend—not for her, she stops to qualify and catch her breath, but for the babies in the camp, of whom there are three: Swanson's, cousin Lucy St. Anne's, and Aunt Dorothy Gunpowder's, Mom's youngest half-sister of three. The mother of five (so far) with a husband ten times her age (according to estimates; Philip Gunpowder *looks* that old), Aunt Dorothy has decided to come up to Thunder Lake, one hundred and fifty miles northeast of Brochet, to live out the summer with us.

Up here, you can't run to a pharmacy when you run out of Pampers; you make them yourself. So, heeding the cry of her ancient old buddy, this Seagull's Little Poop, Mom sends her youngest sons to "round up the troops." And within ten minutes, Rene and I have amassed ten women: Mom, Seagull's Little Poop, Cousin Lucy, Swanson's wife (the accordionist Suzette), bouncy Aunt Dorothy, and five others, among them Lady Beksaka, who is actually a man but counts as a woman; two years older than me and thus much taller, she has long ago accepted her aristocratic title. In fact, the discussion as to whether or not she should be included in the plan proves contentious. Fortunately, Seagull's Little Poop silences nay-sayers with a wave of a claw and a saliva-foam-thick "*koolsth-li*"—Lady Beksaka, she announces to the group, may look like a rope with her sinuous androgyny, but she is strong, capable of carrying immense bulk and gunnery (for all her failings on the masculine front, Lady Beksaka, it must be said, is a cracker-jack hunter of game such as rabbit).

Fortunately, children—at age fourteen, I am still a child to Seagull's Little Poop—are allowed in the assembly, so Rene and I get to tag along. And off we troop in single file into the forest behind the encampment bearing sheets and blankets and folded squares of canvas the size of those blankets, the hardy material turned grey by smoke. These will be the means by which we will carry our booty back to camp. Come to a "find," we unfurl the canvas and sheets and blankets and lay them out on the ground which, of course, is muskeg, but only half-wet to the root. Not only is it now August and therefore drier and no longer pestilent with mosquitoes, this part of the forest is sparse; a forest fire some two decades prior has ensured that.

Twenty-five feet our relative distance from each other, all twelve people get down to work. Working side by side, Rene and I, like the women, bend over to pull handfuls of muskeg from the ground and hang them either on a branch or the summit of whatever tree or skeleton thereof happens to be standing closest to us. And we work our way through the forest in this manner for at least one hour, as do the women—each in her own direction, her own route. For her part, Lady Beksaka is keeping up, handful of muskeg by handful of muskeg, but it's true, I pause to stand there and think, she does look ropey. But I feel for her—deep under that feminine and wistful smile, she must nurse hurt for being looked at as not quite human.

Whatever the pain of Joseph Beksaka (her real name), the purpose of this part of the process is to store muskeg for visits later that summer, allow it to dry until it is ready to use as diapers. Once we have judged that we have enough stored away to last us the rest of the summer, we turn to our blankets and squares of canvas and pile them high with more clumps of muskeg. These we gather up as a package, tie in a knot, and bear home as great big swag bags, absorbent padding to be tied with squares of white flannel to babies' bottoms.

For the moment, however, when I, at the tail end of the conga line of swag-bag-bearing women, pause in my steps to throw a thank-you prayer at the forest I've just left behind me, what meets my eyes are new-growth spruce and skeletons of spruce well-spaced one from the other, all draped—some from branches, some from summits—with clumps of muskeg. The daylight fading and now rife with shadows, the forest is a place that is haunted by women, I think, women wearing hats with stoles on forearms—these trees—an elegant impression, a trenchant image, one that will stay in my mind's eye for years and years.

Seagull's Little Poop has ants in her pants. Again. This time it's for carpets. The old ones are threadbare, she says to my mother, gone to the dogs. So, thanks to the woman who is now past ninety, we clear out our old ones—that is, dead spruce branches strewn across the floors of our tents reduced to what, in effect, is kindling—"fire hazards," as states my mother. On her orders, Rene and I gather up our family's carpet of dry branches and needles and pile them high by the campfire pit outside our tent; they will, indeed, make good kindling, I say to Rene. Then, carrying their sheets, blankets, and squares of canvas, two dozen women, including, of course, the contentious Lady Beksaka, troop off into the forest in single file. And again, Rene and I are privy to the caravan and all its secrets.

Reaching that part of the forest that we judge to be richest in spruce branches, Rene and I snap them off one after the other after the other and pile them onto our blankets and squares of canvas. Once they are ready to be bunched up and tied shut with a knot, we march home, ants in a line of swag-bag bearers. And, bingo, a fresh, new carpet of spruce boughs, its fragrance effulgent, welcomes visitors to the Highway hearth.

46

Of the two churches that stand in Brochet, only one remains as such. The other decommissioned though still standing, the new one replaced it the year I was born. At which point, the new one was sanctified by the bishop of The Pas, who arrived on a barge escorted by a flotilla of flag-draped canoes. An event legendary for its pomp and grandeur, he looked like a Pharoah, says Lawrence Loon, the Dene interpreter, who was eight at the time and who knows these things, for we certainly don't. To me, a Pharaoh is someone who comes from "phar away"—which is what this bishop had to do in order to get here for, having no choice in the matter, he had to come by water which meant that the portages alone, of which there are ten between The Pas and Brochet, almost killed him.

As for the old church, it was put out to pasture. The back room, which was once the sacristy—where, that is, the priest and his altar boys would don their "costumes"—is now a storehouse for rummage sales. As for the front room, which is much larger because, as transept, it held the pews for the faithful, it is now a sometime bingo hall and cinema—when, that is, K's'chees-naanis can get a film (which is not very often). Where he gets them, we don't know and he never tells us. This new K's'chees-naanis, that is to say—for there was the bald one before him, "gone up to heaven," as says Father Cadeau—has hair but is not very voluble, to the point, in fact, where Masky Jimmy Perkins doubts sincerely that he even has a tongue. Pale of complexion, he wears thick glasses, is short and scrawny—a miniature man, says Meat Toss Yazzie—and wears a dog-like expression that tells you nothing. He will, however, need every single one of his forty-five years to defend himself from drunken attackers who, as you'll soon see, are on their way.

This old church smells musty—but then so do some cinemas, in The Pas, for example, where crabs (of the insect variety) have been known to attach themselves to moviegoers and make them miserable. Built in the 1860s, when the first missionaries arrived on the lake looking for Indians to convert to Catholicism before the dreadful Protestants nabbed them, it looks its age, dilapidated, worn at the seams, like a barn on the verge of crumbling and falling. To us when we were children, it was haunted; we were scared to walk by it at night. Built of pine boards sheathed in tiles of black, gummed tarpaper, its most striking feature is its roof, which is of tin off which bounces sunlight so that it glints like a mirror refracting light, thus rendering it visible for miles. In fact, when you round this one island when coming in from Koowap, Boundary Island, House Point, or Thigh Daddy, it is the first thing you see. From five miles away, it is a landmark.

This one summer evening I am about to describe, the new K's'chees-naanis is about to show a film on the back wall of what was once the sanctuary—where, that is, once stood the altar. All in black and white, which is normal for the time, the films he shows are war films, Westerns, or of cops and robbers, slapstick comedies such as those that feature Laurel and Hardy, Charlie Chaplin, and, my most recent favourite, the Three Stooges. As it happens, we are "in town" that evening. And we go. What else, after all, is there for one to do in a place such as this of a late summer evening in high mid-August?

K's'chees-naanis the Second (as I sometimes call him) is showing a Second World War film whose title I can't remember. Fighter jets exploding in mid-air, bombs blowing up entire villages, flames all over, that's all I remember. The Elders, in particular, aren't used to seeing such violence. In fact, for some of them, this is the first movie that they have ever seen. It doesn't help, of course, that they don't understand a word of the language. At one point, when a fighter jet comes swooping down on the camera, and ostensibly the ground, there to buzz some building and strafe it with bullets, Jemima Perkins, seventy-something wife of Moomoos Perkins and sitting beside me and Rene, screams, "*Nimantoom, katawa-oogoonow!*" ("Oh, sweet Jesus, it's gonna hit us!") Thinking it is coming for her, she grabs my hand and dives behind the seat in front of her though, if a younger age had allowed her such movement, she would have dived *under* it, taking me with her and probably dislocating my shoulder. When people see (and hear) the old Cree woman in full-fledged panic, a veritable tsunami of *koolsth-li*s and *neeeeeeeeeee*s sweeps through the dark. When, suddenly, the door at the entrance to the cinema bursts open.

"Ho!" K's'chees-naanis ejaculates from where he sits, on this perch above the door with this cute little table on whose steel top sits the movie projector, the machine he is currently busy operating. And so he should—ejaculate, that is to say, and ejaculate loudly—for, just then, four young men come roaring in like moose stampeding. Led by Victor Fitzgerald, Alec and Geraldine Fitzgerald's fourth son of ten (they also have four girls, if you can imagine), the others are Norval Wachask, Pitooria Wachask, the midwife's third son of four; Leonard Gunpowder, Apwee-tigwee Gunpowder's fifth son of ten and the most evil among them; and Dafell Gunpowder, my wicked Aunt Peechoochee's fourth son of six: the four rabble-rousers of old Brochet, the curse of the village. And it is as evident as day that they have been drinking untold amounts of some *peechi-poowin* (poison). One large bottle of Crown Royal rye whisky, the usual suspect, is the cause generally accepted of such lunacy for who can't smell it, sniffs Black Lady Hatchet who, it is true, is known for nostrils that can smell odours un-smelled by others. Ann Kaakaa Kipawm, for her part, proffers the notion that that bottle has been snuck into the village via Norseman bush plane by the notoriously obstreperous Norval Wachask then shared in the bush—in one hour—with these other three muscular and robust young thugs of twenty-some summers.

"Drunk as skunks they were when they came in that door," says Samba Cheese Weetigo at the Companeek store some two days later, for he is the one who found the telltale bottle behind Alec Fitzgerald's green-roofed house on the bucolic south bank of Seepees-seek.

Having come to look for someone on some pretext or other—whether to settle some old score or simply create general havoc, if for the simple reason that general havocs are their great talent, is a moot point—there they stand at the entrance to the cinema, such as it is, reeling as if their bones are made of rubber, shouting imprecations that are, in the end, unintelligible. And unprintable. All we hear, we think, is something to do with the Dene because these brawlers, in particular, are forever picking on the poor hapless creatures.

"Alright you fucking Chipewyans," yells Leonard Gunpowder (in Cree, of course), "get your asses out of here or I'll beat the shit out of every one of you." It is fortunate that he hasn't brought a gun, or there would be a free-for-all with lethal results—dead bodies strewn from one wall to the other, I can see it in my mind's eye. As it is, there are already enough gunshots—including, most especially, that from machine guns—and explosions filling the room, grace of the movie. And enough yelling and screaming, from women, from children, even men, to fill three cinemas. All have jumped from their chairs—and there are at least one hundred of both, chairs and people, the chairs unattached to the floor (for this, of course, is a makeshift movie house)—and are recoiling in clumps, some with backs against the wall and with eyes big as bannocks, others crushing through the door that leads to the room at the back—that is, to the former sacristy.

Sitting perched like a chickadee on his little wooden platform not one foot above this mayhem, K's'chees-naanis the Second stops the projector. The result? Only a general cacophony produced by live human voices remains as sound. The change in sonic texture from electric to real is actually shocking.

"*Wathaweek!*" ("Get out!") yells K's'chees-naanis (for he, too, has learned some Cree—not very well, but enough to communicate with Indians when times are tense). "*Wathaweek seemaak!* ("Get out right now!") He points his finger and glares something awful at Victor Fitzgerald who, standing his ground, glares right back.

"*Kitaaseek anima 'wathaweek'!*" ("It's in your pants, this 'get out' of yours!"—Cree for "go fuck yourself!") retorts Victor Fitzgerald, most disrespectfully, it must be said, his voice deep and snorty like his father, Alec Fitzgerald's. And then lunges for the little cleric's leg. The little cleric pulls it away in the nick of time. In all the years that he's been here, which is five, I have never seen the man open his legs and I express my astonishment accordingly.

"*Neeee!*" says Rene who stands next to me, loud enough to be heard by those around us. "*Eetoo-gipa-thoo-oot!*" ("He's snapping his legs open.")

"You shouldn't be doing this, you guys," K's'chees-naanis pleads, in Cree. "Go home. Go home and pray to *Kichitaw Maaree*."

"*Kaagitoo, michisk*" ("Shut up, asshole"), retorts Victor Fitzgerald, and lunges once more for the man's right leg. This time, he manages to catch the bottom corner of his pant leg. Which is all that is needed for a tug-of-war of epic proportions to spring to the fore. The hulking monster, Victor Fitzgerald, pulls at the pants. The petite K's'chees-naanis pulls right back. The aggressor loses his grip but makes another grab, this time getting a handful of the garment in question. He pulls. Brother pulls. Shrieking something unprintable, Victor pulls again. Wailing something unmentionable, Brother pulls back. By his fifth attempt, Victor's hold on the pant leg is so vicious, so determined that K's'chees-naanis's worn grey dress *mitaas* (pants) begin a descent that is most perilous. In fact, we see his long johns which are pink (and laundered). With one hand, he clings to the garment by the waist with the desperation of a man on the verge of drowning, with the other to the projector which, most happily for him, is nailed to the table which, in turn, is nailed to the floor of the platform. If they hadn't been, Victor Fitzgerald would have been successful in pulling all three of man, projector, and table down to the floor there to destroy them.

By this time, Rene and I, together with four of my cronies, all, like me, fourteen years old, are killing ourselves laughing looking at this. Nameegoos Kipawm, third son of Aroozalee Kipawm, Weezoo Kipawm, third son of my Laughing Aunt Margaret Kipawm, George Fitzgerald, fifth son of Alec and Geraldine Fitzgerald, and my nephew, Aataar (Arthur) Gunpowder, second son of my eldest sister, Viola, and me with Rene, all of us are standing there against one wall doubled over shedding tears of hysteria, one step from paralysis. In between great gasps for air, we just manage to yell encouragement at K's'chees-naanis to the effect (in Cree, of course) of, "you can do it, Brother, you can do it," and "hang in there! Don't let the bastard get you!"

At which point we hear the breaking of glass coming from the back room. Someone back there has broken one or two or perhaps even all of the tall gothic windows that line both walls of the former sacristy. The main room now empty, the rough wooden chairs and benches scattered willy-nilly, on their backs, on their sides, piled one on top of the other, it looks like the aftermath of a bar fight in a John Wayne movie. Pushing furniture aside, Rene and I scramble to the back with our four companions.

And what greets our eyes is even more dramatic, even more exciting. The Dene who, of course, have all been watching the movie but have fled to the sacristy, are lining up at three broken windows, which is the source of the shattering we just heard. Chairs have been placed upright at each. Which is what the Dene are climbing in order to leap out the windows. They look like sheep jumping over a fence one after the other after the other. At one window, Caayoots Beksaka, third son of Henry Beksaka, and Keesk'wee Chaanee, he of the large, pendulous lower regions, of which more later, are standing on either side of one chair at one window helping the old ladies over the ledge (and, hopefully, someone else is catching them on the outside, for these windows are as high as stepladders). The tall-as-a-tower Kinaws-koo Sophie Yazzie, the large-bottomed Mist Ass-Lick Beksaka, Chooch-Sag-way Marie Antoinette Inik Win Aaree Rogers, the wrinkled-as-a-scrotum Old Dice Chagaazay, even white-haired and bent-over-double Seagull's Little Poop with her great big bum, all go flying out the window and into the darkness, wraiths on broomsticks (to my mind's eye) cackling and flying to the fiery moon. And the screaming and yelling both inside and outside the building sounds like cats cater-wauling and martyrs burning on stakes in fields.

And that is movie night in Toontown.

47

My forehead flowing with crepe-paper streamers in every colour of the rainbow, equally spectacular helium-filled balloons attached to my neck by parcel string and floating above me like cartoon dialogue, I am marching down a quarter-mile section of the road that leads to The Pas, a cloud of sand billowing around me. The spring air pounding with piped-in music that blares from speakers mounted on Brother Menard's black half-ton truck, the vehicle, too, is decked out as for a circus, for it leads the procession of which I am a part and one part only. The kind of music intended to be marched to in stately parades (as we've seen in movies), its drums go *paagoopee, peegoopee, p'weegitoo*, its trumpets blare, and its cymbals clash. Before me marches Kipoots McDonald of Pelican Narrows, Saskatchewan, who, like me, is a riot of balloons and crepe-paper streamers. If he looks ridiculous, then I must, too, but I don't care; I am having too much fun looking like a showgirl from a Las Vegas movie. Beside me marches my best friend Chally, of Nelson House, Manitoba, who, too, is a cavalcade of colour. Still, Chally Canoe, Kipoots McDonald, and I are far from the only students to be prancing about in this manner so arresting, for over two hundred of us—a number that includes the white staff's children—are involved in the march. The only exception to the pattern is that the white staff's children all have bicycles, making for two teenage Van Dykes, two teenage Dubois, and two pre-teen Babchuks who are travelling on wheels in place of marching. With the steel-mesh fences that enclose the boys' and girls'

yards both wild with colour, grace of more balloons and crepe-paper
streamers, then why not the bicycles, someone has asked, so much
is evident. So it is that a half-dozen of what look like psychedelic
chariots go rolling down the road in front of, beside, and behind us.
Intertwined with lengths of crepe-paper streamers, the spokes of
their wheels, in particular, mesmerize with their kaleidoscopic spinning while the pom-poms on their handlebars flutter, bristle, and
flap in the breeze of this warm spring morning in the last week of
May, 1967. In four long lines, two for the girls, two for the boys—
along with, of course, the bicycle phalanx—we all turn at the corner
a quarter of a mile down the gravel road and retrace our steps—not
very far, it's true, for a march, but enough to qualify it as the best one
seen at the Guy Hill School since the Bishop of The Pas came last
September to inspect his flock and anoint two statues.

The morning air alive with excitement, its intensity is augmented
by a fragrance unique to the season—grass being cut. The smell of
going home, I have always thought. After one long winter of leaving
it buried in three feet of snow, Brother Menard has been at it again,
mowing the lawn that lines both sides of the sidewalk that starts at
the bottom of the grand stone staircase at the school's main entrance
and expands to a field bedecked with flowerbeds sprouting daffo-
dils, geraniums, and pansies. The one sure sign that the school year
is coming to an end and going home for the summer is on the horizon; you could photograph our anticipation and get bright pictures.

The circuit completed, the march comes to an end at the towering
flagpole in front of the school where stands Father Laval, the school's
new principal, with his hair-plugged nostrils and hirsute hands. Before
him hangs horizontally, at belly-button level, a ten-foot length of
scarlet ribbon three inches wide. Attached to stepladders at opposite
ends, it ripples in the breeze awaiting an event that will snap it in two.
Yet another piece of handiwork accomplished by the nuns, it is the
cherry on the icing of this spectacular production.

For if Brother Menard has been at it again with his handiwork,
then so have they as, indeed, has a virtual army of staff—keepers,
teachers, clergy, janitor, seamstress, nightwatchman, the engineer

Mr. Van Dyke, cooks including Darlene Sawchuk—who have volunteered as scorekeepers, referees, and such. In the past four years have all these people organized a "field day" each spring for two reasons. The first is health, has said Sister Ann; the second, our sense of pride. A sort of Olympic Games for young Native people, it features all the races and tests of skill seen at all such events the whole world over, or so we are told.

The over two hundred students now standing motionless on the gravelled parking lot, the staff standing scattered here and there across the expansive lawn, we launch into a chorus of the national anthem—*a cappella*, of course, for neither of Sister St. Aramaa's piano or organ can be transported from their respective places of concealment, not for this event which is open-air. We come to a finish. At which point Father Laval raises his right hand in which materializes a pair of scissors that glint in the sun. He brings them down, snaps them open, and snips the red ribbon right down the middle. Carried by the breeze of the warm spring morning, the two strands of tissue flutter off and away, and the games are on.

The high jump comes first. Like sheep in a dream, the Small Boys leap over the two-foot-high barrier, a long, thin pole made of red plastic, one after the other after the other, and land in the sawdust which has been installed in a sort of sandbox to receive such impact. Some graze the barrier just enough to bring it down, in which case, it gets reset by a keeper who is there for the job. Some hit it outright, thus causing it again to fall to the ground, in which case it gets reset again; but some clear it neatly. Eight-year-old Alfred Mitaas of South Indian Lake is one of these. Not only that but he jumps highest, so he will surely get a prize, a bright silk ribbon to pin on his chest. Keeper Norman Dubois raises the barrier by a foot and now it is the turn of the Medium Boys. Some make it, others don't. At age twelve, my brother Rene is among the latter; he grazes the barrier with his bone-thin bum, falls in the sawdust, and almost cries, he is that disappointed. But thirteen-year-old Patrick Wachask of Beaver Lake, Saskatchewan, jumps highest of all in this division, for his bones are light and his legs so long he looks like a spider. He will get a ribbon,

I am sure of it, though I grapple with a small surge of jealousy. Next come the Big Boys and, for this stage, keeper Norman Dubois raises the barrier even higher—to four feet, in fact. Big Boys jump and Big Boys fall. When my turn comes, not only do I graze the barrier, so hard do I hit it that I almost break it right down the middle. Someone boos. The tall, gangly, large-boned, and swarthy-complexioned eighteen-year-old George Peter Buckskin of Pelican Narrows, Saskatchewan, however, jumps so high that he almost flies and ends up winning, closely followed by the movie-star handsome Marvin McMillan of South Indian Lake. (The McMillan brothers of South Indian Lake are all movie-star handsome.)

Philbert Nigik, also of Pelican Narrows, who is known for his acting—he once played a woman at a Christmas concert, to great success—and not for his prowess in athletic endeavour, surprises everyone with his adeptness at the shot put. For this sport, the athlete takes, with one hand, a ball of solid and very heavy steel the size of a grapefruit which is called, for some reason, the "shot," and throws it, the person who throws it farthest winning the contest. Unfortunately, in order to give it the momentum it needs to do this, one must swing the projectile around and around. But because the object weighs a good fifteen pounds, at some point in its spin it takes over as "driver," so that the thrower himself ends up being spun like a mouse being twirled by the tail, especially if he has the frame and weight of a string bean as does Philbert Nigik. If the thrower were to forget to let go of the ball, in fact, he would break the sound barrier and disintegrate, thus becoming part and parcel of the ether from whence he came. Fortunately, the thrower does let go when he feels he has gathered said force of momentum, if he knows what he is doing. So that when the time comes for Philbert Nigik to twirl his body around and around with the ball in hand, his twirl amasses such blinding speed that he turns into a blur of the kind Bugs Bunny's nemesis, the Tasmanian Devil, is known for.

Fortunately, Philbert Nigik lets go and, thus, reappears. Flung to the side by the force of the trajectory, he lies in the gravel as spent as Jesus after the nailing. Which doesn't stop a rumour from spreading to the effect that the ball he threw that bright spring morning disappeared in the distance towards Flin Flon. And was never found. Which is how seventeen-year-old Philbert Nigik of Pelican Narrows, Saskatchewan, gets crowned "world champion of the shot put" that day. Me? I don't even rate in the top ten. In fact, of the fifteen throwers, Lady Beksaka and I end up second-last and last, embarrassing me to the point of suicide. I don't want to be here. I am no good at this. Still, I have no choice but to go on with the battle.

The throwing of the javelin is another story. In this sport, the girls, for some reason, excel. Some theories argue that it has to do with the ligaments. For example, the seventeen-year-old Agoo-chigan Kamaa-magoos of Island Falls, Saskatchewan, who has inherited all the sensual allure of her elder sister, Bathsheba Kamaa-magoos, is known and admired for the strength of hers. In fact, it is rumoured that when she jumps, she can hover in the air for three whole seconds, that's how strong are her ligaments. Why she doesn't enter the high jump event that day is due—at least as rumour has it—to a toe she has stubbed on the statue of *Kichitaw Maaree* in the grotto behind the girls' yard while breastfeeding Father Laval. Though Agoo-chigan Kamaa-magoos roundly refutes it to me in the boys' yard that day when I happen by her seat in the bleachers—"*Taapwee chee eegee-noothat* Father Laval?" ("Is it true that you actually breastfed Father Laval?") But then there are theories that extol the virtues of the gluteus maximus. Bertha Mistat of Nelson House, Manitoba, for instance, is known and admired for the elasticity of hers. I should be admired for my gluteus maximus, I think that day as I watch her bend over to re-tie the laces of her running shoes. There are arguments for the thorax, the humerus, the cervix, the cervical clavicle, the *waski-gan*, the *mispitoon*, the *ooskaat*, the *watay*, the *mitatha-gachak*, the *kaski-pichi-gan*, the *oochees-tatay*, even the *weekwi*, and, of course, the various *ootak-seeyaa-peeya* that thread their way through the human corpus from crotch to neck and back again.

Whatever the source of the strength for throwing a javelin, Ann Mitaas has it. And has it a-plenty. For when the completely nondescript sixteen-year-old from South Indian Lake, Manitoba, whom I love with all my heart because she sounds like a woodpecker when she laughs, crosses ten yards of ground on the run to amass momentum for the throwing of the object—a jet taking off, remark observers, is what she looks like—and then, with a grunt, throws back the hand and the arm that hold her spear, which is made of plastic and thus light as paper, and lances it, the distance the object traverses is so unseemly that it takes ten minutes for Onyx Mobster of Nelson House, Manitoba, to retrieve it, thus assuring Ann Mitaas of certain victory. I roundly applaud her; she is my hero, the kind of woman I want to be when I get my sex change. There are, of course, other competitors. Even Lotte Van Dyke, daughter of engineer Mr. Van Dyke and therefore Dutch and not Cree or Dene, takes her turn but, alas, is wanting in lightness of step and strength of tibia. But no one—no one—stands a chance when it comes to competing, in the event known as the javelin, against the mighty Ann Mitaas, my dear friend and colleague. For her, I am proud, for me, not so. Yes, that's what I will do; I will cheer for the others and forget myself; that's how I will survive this hellish ordeal.

With the 100-yard dash for the girls, it is Ella Fitzgerald, a mere slip of a girl at age fifteen, who leaves all and sundry choking in the wake of her *oopas-choosoos* which she leaves so far behind her that it might as well be in Koogoom Oogoot, Saskatchewan. Of medium height, swarthy of tint, roomy of nostril, steak-thick of lip, and with limbs that seem to be made of rubber, they are that pliable, she runs so fast that I can't see her for entire stretches of moments. When she arrives at the finish line, not one pulsation of her chest to denote excessive expenditure of *pagi-tataa-moowin* (breath) is evident, that's how effortless the act of running is for Ella Fitzgerald of Granville Lake, Manitoba. In fact, they say—at least in the legends of Guy Hill School—that the next contestant after her arrives at the finish line two hours later. Then again, I am the one who spreads that rumour.

Keesk'wee Chaanee, a sixteen-year-old Dene from Brochet who is known for the size of his lower regions (they say he is hung like a horse) wins at the broad jump—which surprises, as one would have thought that those regions would have weighed him down. Nameegoos

Kipawm of Brochet and Chally Canoe of Nelson House, Manitoba, tie at the 200-yard dash for boys my age.

Still, when it comes to baseball, no one is more powerful than Ass-Lick ("Angelique" pronounced in Cree) Askeek of Puck, Manitoba. So powerful is Ass-Lick Askeek that I am in awe—in fact, rather scared—of her. For this sport, we are broken up into ten teams or so to play what, in effect, is a day-long tournament peppered here and there through the various other contests. And the games take place in both boys' and girls' yards because, of course, both have baseball diamonds. We play all day, boys against boys, girls against girls. Each team having named itself, the Bobcats play the Chickadees, the Blackbirds the Mink, the Huskies the Panthers—which last team is mine. Game after game is played. In my game, I strike out so many times that someone yells, "Get off the field!" A knife plunged into my back would have been less painful; I walk off the diamond with my cheeks burning.

Finally, the stakes narrow down to the Otters and the Bears, the latter of which have the advantage of Ass-Lick Askeek as their team captain. She plays left field. And when the tall and angular Mildred Kitoo of The Pas hits what looks like a home run towards left field and Mildred starts running, Ass-Lick Askeek catches the flying ball neatly in her glove and throws it to first base where Norma Saagweesoo of South Indian Lake catches it before Mildred Kitoo has come anywhere near said base—that's how good is Ass-Lick Askeek. Which is why I am not surprised when her team, the Bears, wins the tournament. Nor am I surprised when the Panthers, us, end up last.

But all day long, the boys' and girls' yards are a tempest of youth and children leaping and running and screaming and laughing, the dust their feet churn up an atmospheric disturbance unseen in this part of the world to this point in time.

As day's end nears and spectators begin thinning out from sheer exhaustion, the three-legged race appears on the programme. I am paired with William Peeskwa of South Indian Lake and we are to compete with twelve other pairs in the Big Boys' division. At the moment, Gilbert Mitaas of South Indian Lake and Jughead Mistat of

Puck are behind us, Kipoots McDonald of Pelican Narrows and
Martin Wachask of Beaver Lake ahead. With one leg only left free for
movement, the race is a clumsy affair. You don't so much run as limp
and, because it is so easy to trip, you have to hold your left arm entwined around your partner's right. And we limp along and we limp
along, me and William Peeskwa. My left leg, the one that is tied to that
of Mr. Peeskwa's right, starts hurting. I start crying. I want to stop.

"You can do it, you can do it," exhorts William Peeskwa like a
mantra and holds my arm even tighter. I grit my teeth and continue,
if only for the sake of my partner who, at this point, is basically dragging me along like a dishrag. And against all odds, we end up third,
behind Vernon Zipper of The Pas, Manitoba, and Choggy-lat Kipawm
of Brochet, who finish second, and Caayoots Beksaka of Brochet and
Martin Wachask of Beaver Lake, Saskatchewan, who win.

And then, thank God, comes day's end, when this event from hell—
the Guy Hill Olympics, keeper Erik Laporte calls the entire day—is
finally capped off by a ribbon-giving ceremony. For this, three wooden
platforms of three different levels and three different colours have
been constructed by Mr. Babchuk and set up in front of the school
by the flagpole. And there we amass, all two hundred of us students,
male and female, together with the staff, religious and lay, and their
families. Holding a clipboard on which the names of the winners in
all the events are tabulated, Father Laval stands behind what is basically a pedestal, beside him Sister Ann who, in turn, stands behind
a table with trays full of ribbons, silk, in the colours red, white, and
blue. Each one fixed with a mini safety pin so that they can be pinned
on shirts and blouses, they flutter in the breeze of that golden late
afternoon. And as Father Laval reads out the winners in the order
of third, second, and first, they step up to the platforms and mount
them. For the throwing of the javelin in the girls' division, for example, the beautiful Gloria Moostoos of Puck, Manitoba, third in the
contest and flushed with pride, steps up to the lowest of the three
little platforms and is showered with words of praise by Father Laval,
who then pins a white ribbon on her chest. The applause is generous,

for Gloria Moostoos is a popular girl. Called up second, Bertha Mistat of Nelson House steps up to the second platform and has her fulsome chest pinned with the red ribbon. Same words of praise, same applause (though somewhat less), same aspect of pride. And, of course, Ann Mitaas's name is announced for the mounting of the third and highest platform to receive the blue ribbon. Never has applause on Clearwater Lake been louder or longer. And never have you seen a girl as proud as Ann Mitaas. And so it goes for all the other events, of which there are fifty, the final result being fifty-times-three-winners makes for one hundred and fifty very proud young Native people standing on platforms being decorated, applauded, admired, and neck-deep in happiness. That whole school pulsates that day, and for many days thereafter—years, in fact, if truth be told—with pride, a sense of accomplishment, a sense of self-worth.

The last ribbons given out are those for events considered least important, the three-legged race among them. When our names are called, William Peeskwa and I step up to the lowest of the three wooden platforms, receive our white ribbons and take in applause which, when compared to that received by Ann Mitaas and Ass-Lick Askeek, is . . . well . . . quiet. But polite—though Rene's clapping I hear loud and clear for he stands six feet before me beaming with pride. As for William Peeskwa, he foresaw it: that I would win nothing. And so he made sure that I did—which is why he chose me as his partner in the three-legged race. Yes, it was him who chose, not keeper Butch Bouchard of St. Anne, Manitoba, as I had thought. We win the white ribbon only; but, to me, it is blue. Decades later will Mr. Peeskwa turn out to be the kindest and wisest Elder ever to emerge from northern Manitoba.

48

When I first arrived at the Guy Hill Indian Residential School at age three-months-short-of-seven, I knew not one word of English. Nine years later, I know it well enough to be inspired by German-Dutch writer Anne Frank, whose diary has marked me for life. If she could write like that at age thirteen and in such circumstances, I ask myself, then why can't I at age fifteen? When it comes to my final assignment for my English class in June of 1967, I think of Dad's words—*Go out there and save our people. Ergo*, my objective in this essay, my farewell gift to the Guy Hill School. That objective? To prove to the world that, if any one force will save my people, it will be laughter. It will be the joy that anchors Cree. It will be the Trickster-fuelled, spectacular sense of humour that sparks it to life. I have, of course, since touched up the text—inserting Cree, for example, at certain points—but this, at base, is my mother tongue as filtered through an English paid for with blood . . .

"THE LAPWACHIN"
(a.k.a. The "National Dish of the Great Cree Nation")
by Tomson Highway

Controversy swirls from one end of the country to the other as to the nature and identity of the much-loved *lapwachin*. "Is it not a cake?" asks one school of thought. "Is it not a pudding?" asks another. "Is it not both?" asks a third—"that is, a combination of both cake and pudding?" And the three schools of thought have been at logger-heads since 1860, when Father Cheepoogoot first brought the recipe from his native Quebec. In fact, one time—at Ann Kaakaa's wedding to Cheepooti William, when I was four—the debate came near to destroying what little bit of unity that ruled Brochet, though the pro-pudding faction may hold the advantage insofar as the word "*lapwachin*" has its roots in the French word for "pudding," according anyway to Father Cadeau.

Pronounced in his language as "la pudding," with the double "d" pronounced as "dj," the "u" as "oo" as in "cook," and the "g" at the end left silent, it was merely a matter of the Cree tongue adjusting the syllables to accommodate its innate sense of humour, thus transforming in a trice "la poodjin" to "*lapwachin*."

An advantage enjoyed by the first school of thought, the two other schools refuse to concede. "Puddings, strictly speaking, are liquids, are they not?" ripostes the second, "And *lapwachin* is solid, no? If anything, more solid than a cake?" With which pointed question purveyors of this school will cite the example of Ice-keemee Minette and the time she made a *lapwachin* that was so hard it gave her husband, Zebedee Zipper, a case of "blockage of the *kipoochim*" (constipation) that almost killed him.

Myself personally, I am of the third school of thought—*lapwachin*, that succulent dessert that is served at weddings and other events of similar import, is a hybrid, is it not? A cross between a pudding and a cake? In the English-speaking world, is the Christmas pudding not more the idea exemplified by a *lapwachin*? A dessert that is called a pudding when it, in fact, is a cake? Blame it all on the English language and its way too many exceptions to the rule, is what I say.

Exceptions aside, there are women in Brochet who are known for their *lapwachin*s. Isabel Fitzgerald is one; with hers, you can press one slice onto your plate with your fork until it is flatter than a spatula, lift the fork, and—*choing!*—the slice springs back to its former fullness of figure and richness of texture. Filament Mosquito, Caleen-ns Fitzgerald, Poosees Fitzgerald, Louise Cheepay, Tarees Naasi-peeti-meek, even Ann Kaakaa Kipawm, all are admired for the flavour and texture of their *lapwachin*s. But no one—no one—makes a *lapwachin* like Balazee Highway.

Her recipe is simple. Flour, baking powder, lard, sugar, raisins, a teaspoon of salt and, of all things, tea well-steeped, the last for imparting to the *kipoochim*, as it gives Masky Jimmy Perkins immense enjoyment to call it, its warm brown colour. You mix the ingredients and, as you stir, you pour in the first cup of tea thus turning the powder into a soup. You pour a second cup and stir some more, thus transforming the soup into a paste. A third cup, a fourth, etc., the mixture becoming progressively thicker until you can no longer stir it and thus are forced to knead what is now a blob of flesh-like consistency. And you knead and knead until the heel of your hand goes numb from the effort at which point you find yourself with a ball of dough most fearsome in size, pocked with raisins, and as beige as a moose hide that's just been smoked, not too hard, not too soft, just solid yet rubbery enough for you to pick it up and fling it either at the wall or your worst enemy.

To feed two people, the ball of dough might be the size of a grapefruit, thus making for a cute little *lapwachin*. This size of *lapwachin*, however, is rarely made. To feed ten people, the ball of dough would have to be the size of a "bolly ball." To feed one hundred, it would have to be "one mother of a *lapwachin*," as Lawrence Loon, the fiercely admired Cree/Dene/English interpreter, once archly put it. To feed three hundred, you would have to make three entire *lapwachin*s of the size just cited. Still, the best part is to come, the part that gives Rene and me such wanton amusement, and this is the *maskimoot* (the bag).

The *lapwachin* of yore is not the *lapwachin* of today. And the reason for this difference is the *maskimoot*. Much to the sadness of lovers of *lapwachin* on Earth and in heaven, its kind went obsolete in the 1960s. You see, pro-cake school of thought or anti-cake school of thought, *lapwachin* is boiled, not baked. In a *maskimoot*. And not just any *maskimoot*, but the kind that holds the flour we purchase in ten-pound units from Maagisit McMillan at the Companeek store. Made out of cheesecloth with the trademark and data such as weight splashed across its surface in bright red lettering, it is a *maskimoot* that, once emptied and laundered, is valued by Cree women as the perfect receptacle for the boiling of *lapwachin*. The pastry's spherical solidity, that is to say, fits into that *maskimoot* with a snugness that makes cooks squeal with piercing delight.

After you have soaked that *maskimoot* in lukewarm water, you either drop, slide, or stuff into its orifice the ball of dough you have just finished kneading. If it is to be a small *lapwachin*, you drop it in. If it is to be a medium *lapwachin*, you slide it in. But if it is to be a mega-*lapwachin* of the kind that is eaten at weddings, you will have to stuff it into the *maskimoot* with the strength of a moose. At this point in the process, tiny, wiry Balazee Highway in her floral-print granny smock and white cotton apron looks like Goliath, the giant in the Scriptures, twisting to a sinew the boy named David. Such huffing and panting and groaning and cursing has not been heard on Reindeer Lake since the day Oos-eye Naapao, the great Cree shaman, wrestled the *Weetigo* and almost killed him. As Rene and I stand there cheering. And laughing.

Then she ties it shut with a string. One good knot and one good grunt generally suffice, at which point she sinks the bulging monstrosity into a cauldron of water that is boiling and bubbling. And she boils it and boils it and boils it—on an outdoor fire in summer or on her woodstove inside in winter, the source of the fire doesn't matter, she just boils it. She boils it for three hours or she boils it for six. If she has to boil it for nine, then so be it. The size of the *lapwachin* decides. Still, one has to be vigilant for three reasons. The first is that you have to keep turning the bag this way and that so that the heat filters its way into the dough evenly, for the last thing you want is to end up with a product that is raw, pasty, and as sticky as *pawpilly-cum*. The second is that the fire will die unless you feed it on a basis semi-regular (these days, of course, electric stoves make this task unnecessary. And boring). And the third reason is that water kept boiling for that length of time evaporates so that you have to keep replenishing it unless you want your pot to dry up, spring a hole, and destroy your masterpiece, which has happened to more than one less-than-skilled, first-time maker of *lapwachin*. Or unless you want your *lapwachin* to end up as dry as uncooked *oochak-seesa* and as hard as a rock.

Finally, it is time to take the *lapwachin* out of the water and out of the *maskimoot*. With a heave and a ho and considerable grunting, Mom lifts the shining, bulging *maskimoot*—which has expanded due to the cooking of the monster inside it and which takes muscle, for a *lapwachin* suffused with liquid is heavy—and manoeuvres its bulk onto a pan, snips the string, and peels off the *maskimoot* like one would a sweater. *Et voilà*, as Father Cadeau would say, the steaming concoction's former beigeness has deepened in colour. The raisins, moreover, are black where they were brownish before and it is covered with what looks like wax but is actually residue of boiled white flour. And its breast-like roundness wheezes and sizzles and sputters and hisses, as if it has its own mind, its own personality. Then Balazee Highway leaves the concoction in the pan to let it cool off. And while it does, she makes the sauce that will coat each slice—once the *lapwachin* is cut into slices, that is to say—with a gooey viscosity that brings out its intended, planned-from-the-start orgasmic proclivities.

But what, pray tell, is this sauce? asks the pro-cake school of thought on the *lapwachin*'s identity. Is it not icing? As for a cake? The answer given by the third school of thought? It is and it isn't. All one knows is that its ingredients, again, are simple: flour, water, sugar and, this time round, a spoonful or two of vanilla, a product not available at the Companeek store unless one has connections which, of course, Mom has; didn't her eldest son just come from Lynn Lake, where are found such *Moony-ass* temptations?

The sauce now ready and the *lapwachin* cooled, she takes a knife and slices it into these half-inch-thick wedges, wedges she serves on dessert plates, and wedges, moreover, that look like slices of fruit cake of the kind that is served to *Saanchi Giloss* on Christmas Eve, at least in cultures where flourish the *Moony-ass*. The sauce she places on the table in ceramic gravy boats, so that each person served can pour the amount he wants on his slice of cake for, indeed, the proof

of the pudding is as incontestable as Noah counting the animals—
what has started out as pudding, that is to say, has ended up as cake,
thus bestowing the laurel of victory in this thorny debate to the pro-
cake school of thought.

For a recipe so simple, it is remarkable how delicious the result is.
Maagisit McMillan, much to the ire of his fiery wife, Fire McMillan,
can't say enough about its mink-like texture, the way it melts like
caribou marrow on his leathery tongue, makes vibrate his "five hundred tastebuds," and then slides down his cavernous esophagus. Then
again, Balazee Highway, like her husband, has always had the proverbial magic touch in all she does.

As for the *maskimoot*, the cheesecloth bag, at one point in its life,
goes the way of the gramophone, plunging *lapwachin* fanatics across
northern Canada into extended, and pitch-black, bouts of depression.
Sometime in the early sixties, the Companeek store starts selling its
flour in bags made of paper of the kind used for parcels. An outcry
ensues wherein is heard like a rolling of thunder the phrase, "You
can't boil paper!" To a goodly portion of Brochet's population, this
spells Armageddon for a dessert that has marked many a signpost
in life and love. Fortunately, they are wrong (about the Armageddon,
not about boiling paper). No one remembers—it might even be the
old Dene woman, my mother's poker-playing buddy, Old Dice
Chagaazay, of all people—but someone, at one point, comes along
with an idea for a possible replacement for the *maskimoot*: the pillowcase. It isn't quite the same, of course, as a pillowcase is generally
roomier than is a ten-pound sack made for flour. Faster than a fox
can pounce on a mouse, a school of thought that pops from the mind
of the fiery and tempestuous Fire McMillan pooh-poohs the idea. Its
prediction? *Lapwachin* boiled in, of all things, a pillowcase will come
out lacking in symmetry, shape, proportion, and succulence; it will
fall apart. But no, says Balazee Highway by way of rejoinder, if you
tie the pillowcase as tight as the ligament on a caribou tibia, your
lapwachin will be as firm as a buttock, just as spherical and, to boot,
not fall apart. "As for its succulence?" she expostulates, with barely

a glance at her sourpuss arch-rival, Fire McMillan. "*Tanpay-weegit-soo!*" ("It will kill you [with its flavour]!")

So thanks to the wise and crusted Old Dice Chagaazay, the *lap-wachin* lives on to thrill to a cinder yet another generation of lovers of cake. Or pudding, for the second school of thought refuses categorically to lie down and die. One word of warning from, of all people, Masky Jimmy Perkins: "Please make sure your pillowcase is washed before you use it to boil your *kipoochim*"—which *does* rhyme with *lapwachin* but . . . well . . . you'd have to have a word with Masky Jimmy Perkins.

I get an A. Plus.

49

It is the end of June, 1967, and I find myself standing in a line of fifteen boys Big, Medium, and Small. We are in the hallway on the second floor of the Guy Hill School awaiting our turn in kind Mrs. Rasmussen's sewing room across from the Medium Boys' dormitory. Rene stands one place before me, before him Philbert Nigik of Pelican Narrows, behind me Harold Mitaas of South Indian Lake. But why this room? Because it is where we are packing for our annual end-of-school-year journey back to our homes for the summer. Yes, we are going home. To this end, Butch Bouchard of St. Anne, Manitoba, the Big Boys' keeper who has just marked his twentieth birthday, has been busy bringing our suitcases from their winter storage somewhere in the bowels of this great big building. Three Big Boys his gung-ho helpers, he has placed the luggage in rows on great long tables of varnished pine and is presently prepared to receive us. The line advancing, Rene and I are now inside this medium-sized room that seethes with such promise. Philbert Nigik hands Mr. Bouchard a collection of Batman comic books he got somewhere; three in number, they are for his two little brothers—"*niseem-sak kichi*"—who are waiting for him at his home in Pelican Narrows, Saskatchewan, he tells me. The taut-muscled keeper who looks like a gymnast takes the magazine and puts it in a suitcase that belongs to the boy. Thrilled to the bone, jangly Philbert Nigik takes his departure, merrily dancing a fractured jig. Behind me, meanwhile, stands an increasingly impatient Harold Mitaas. Why impatient? Because he has cradled in his hands a life-sized owl he has carved for his parents in Mr. Babchuk's woodworking class. And now for Rene. His face stark-white with excitement, he is holding in his hands a plastic sailboat the length of a hotdog, a prize he won in "token, please" the March just prior. That's for his suitcase. After finding the suitcase among all the others, the kind Mr. Bouchard brings it over, takes the little boat from Rene, and puts it in the box whose handle reads "Rene Highway." While this is happening, I take a fleeting glance at the line of boys with glassy eyes behind me; all hold an object dear to their hearts—bags of marbles won at tournaments, teddy bears received as Christmas presents, a favourite drawing from art class, all gifts for their families whom they've seen neither hide nor hair of since last September. My turn comes. My gift? A sapphire-blue, faux-crystal rosary which I won as first prize in Father Grew's catechism class; my knowledge of the life of Jesus Christ is "exquisite," he had said to the class as he handed it to me. A gift for my mother who prays with verve, she will love it, especially as sapphire blue is among her favourite "of all God's colours." Encased in a box that is tied shut with string, I hand it to Mr. Bouchard; he puts it in my suitcase. And I am ready. After having studied, and studied obsessively, for nine long years, I am leaving the Guy Hill Indian Residential School for the last time in my life. My final average? Ninety-five percent, the highest in the school and among the highest, so it is said, in all Manitoba. Next year? For me? High school in Winnipeg.

Some five days later—on the twenty-fifth of June, 1967—I am sitting on a plane with eleven other students aged six to eighteen both male and female with family names like Kamaa-magoos, Kipawm, Wachask, Beksaka, and others; the Brochet contingent. The single-engine Lamb Airways Otter roars for takeoff from Clearwater Lake. The plane constructed with two rows flanking a single aisle, I am sitting by the window with, by my side, my adored baby brother. Below us sparkle the emerald-green waters of a lake we've come to love and that I'll miss for its beauty, unique in the world, as says keeper Butch Bouchard (with whom I am madly in love). Against that backdrop, I superimpose one after the other after the other the faces of the students I have loved, all these years, and the students who have loved me, all these years, at this institution, some of them already gone off to high school in Winnipeg: Chally Canoe, William Peeskwa, Ass-Lick Askeek, the Mobster sisters Onyx, Opal, and Pearl, Annie Duckbill, Rita Duckbill, Ella Fitzgerald, Machaa-is Bacheese, Wilfred Gunpowder, Elizabeth Gunpowder, Rufus Skylark, Rachel Skylark, Gilbert Mitaas, Ann Mitaas, Michael Mitaas, Sexy Sally, Gregory Crumple, the list goes on *ad infinitum*. In fact, I think it takes me the entire two-hour flight north to Brochet to count them. My young heart weeps for I miss them already. Rene is sleeping; I must not wake him.

Me? Unable to sleep, I fly over lake after lake after river after lake, the forest between them stretching out to infinity until its green turns blue then misty then becomes indistinguishable from the clouds in the distance. Unlike jet planes that fly so high they could well be spaceships—way above the clouds, as keeper Butch Bouchard has kindly informed us—bush planes fly low enough for passengers to see certain details in the landscape they pass over, trees, rocks, even animals. In fact, at one point in the flight, I see a moose urinating in a bog with one hind leg raised (as I will tell Masky Jimmy Perkins when I get home). And my little heart sings to the drone of the engine producing in my bones a certain buzzing, sustained major-second that makes my marrow simmer with an almost painful yearning to see Mom, Dad, Louise, even Doggy, even Seagull's Little Poop, the old Dene woman with the great big bum. Until, finally, Reindeer Lake drifts into view first with one island then another then another. The plane isn't going fast enough, not for me, but there in a minute that seems like an hour sits old Brochet far down below us, a magic little village, a cartoon town. There, Filament Mosquito hanging her laundry, there, Mrs. Permafrost sweeping the front steps of her red-roofed store, there, the one-room school, the church, the rectory, then . . .

"Our house, our house, our house!" I scream to Rene, jabbing at his arm with my right elbow. He snaps to awakeness but is deaf to my voice, grace of the motor that spits and roars. Obliged to read my trembling lips, he leans over me to look out the window, holds my hand, and bursts into tears. And as the aircraft swoops over Moomoos Island to come in for landing, we see people streaming from east, west, and centre as they make their way to Father Cadeau's now rickety dock to meet their children. With no roads or vehicles to speak of, all are walking in pairs and threes, ragtag bunches that thread their way through the network of trails concealed in part by tall waving grasses. And now we are taxiing across the last stretch of water and up to the dock where stands our priest-in-residence with his black cassock billowing and rope at the ready.

In a desperate attempt to see our parents, Rene and I peer through the window as hard as we can at the faces in the crowd. Going from one to the other and back to the other, we search for them and search for them. And we recognize Aroozalee Kipawm, Samba Cheese Choowis, Samba Cheese Weetigo, Jemima Perkins, the wife of Moomoos Perkins (without Moomoos), Meat Toss Yazzie and his towering wife Kinaws-koo Sophie, my wicked but beautiful Aunt Peechoochee with the fourth of her five sons, the impossibly handsome Tyrone Gunpowder, now sixteen (the one who looks like Elvis), the sisters Cheechees McMillan and Oos'chi-gwaan McMillan with her purplish lips, Lucy St. Anne, Filament Mosquito, my pretty-as-a-picture Uncle Horace Zipper (Mom's younger brother), the list goes on. But where are Joe and Balazee Highway?

When we climb down the ladder that connects the body of the plane to its left pontoon, step off the aluminum floating device and onto the dock, we stand there dumbfounded. And we wait on that dock for what seems like hours but is probably something more like five minutes. Until everyone has met their children and has climbed uphill to take them home and the plane has floated away, taxied off, then flown southward from whence it came. The silence it leaves behind is jarring. Add to that element a dock now emptied of people and we feel naked, exposed to the elements. We don't know what to do, we don't know where to go.

Our cheeks sting. I feel them blushing. We have been abandoned, I am sure of it. Now aged twelve, Rene is on the verge of another flood of tears. I, aged fifteen, take hold of his hand. (Now nineteen,

Daniel is gone, wandering the world, God knows where.) Which is when I see Mary Rose Gunpowder, our eldest sister Vi's eldest daughter and thus our eldest niece, even though she is actually five years older than me. The twenty-year-old is lingering shyly on the little stretch of sand between the priest's corrugated, aluminum-walled boathouse and the foot of his dock. And what she says surprises us utterly. She is taking us to Laughing Aunt Margaret's house, she says, where we will wait it out.

"Wait what out?" I ask, puzzled.

"Another plane."

"Another plane?"

Sure enough, there is another. God bless his kindness but Dad has chartered a Cessna 185 to transport Rene and me the extra one hundred and fifty miles from Brochet north to a lake called Clifton Lake, where we will be fishing this summer. So much Mary Rose explains as we walk to our Laughing Aunt Margaret's. Mom's beloved younger sister, God bless her, has apparently pitched in to help with our lodging, for the plane comes not today but tomorrow. Located at the end of the village where juts into the lake this point we call Minee-waati-meek, her house stands between Mrs. Permafrost's little trading post with its jukebox, and the house where lives Filament Mosquito and her husband, Archie. And, lo and behold, early next morning, the little wooden house that is Laughing Aunt Margaret's is buzzed by the plane that is so tiny it makes no sound, or just barely, and looks like a glider. Rene and I jump out of bed, jump into our clothes, grab our suitcases, and run to the dock, Laughing Aunt Margaret Kipawm trailing behind us cackling her signature witch-like laugh which we love hearing.

The point here being: the sons of Joe Highway, and the sons of Joe Highway only, are being given their own private plane to fly them home. And now two princes, the most beautiful man who ever lived, as many will call him in the years to come, and I, his clever elder brother, sit strapped to their seats, me riding shotgun, Rene behind me. And we gaze through the sunshine at the windless lakes and the forests and the rivers and the eskers way down below us. "Permanent Astonishment," I think I will call this godly kingdom . . .

50

At this point in his life, Dad has become Brochet's most successful commercial fisherman. In fact, local legend has it that he owns five fish camps, each one more equipped than the last. One camp each on two different islands on Reindeer Lake, and three on three different lakes in the low sub-Arctic, which includes the one that we are flying to today. At each camp, goes this legend, he has a fish house, an ice house, the three hundred–some nets it takes to operate a successful commercial fishing enterprise, and all the attendant equipment: the buoys, the crates, the canoes, the paddles, the miles of twine, the motors, the drums of gasoline.

His *modus operandi* is to spend one summer fishing on Mariah Lake a hundred miles north of Brochet, the next on Boundary Island in Reindeer Lake fifteen miles west of Brochet, the next on Robinson Lake a hundred and fifty miles northeast of Brochet, the next on Zangeza Bay at the far northwestern corner of Reindeer Lake, and the fifth I don't even remember. And once one cycle is completed, he starts it all over again, the whole point being to let lakes, or sections of lakes, lie "fallow" through the course of a cycle of five years so their fish can replenish their depleted populations. Only Joe Highway. Only he has the vision. Still, if the rumour about his having five fish camps is mere steps from fiction, it is close enough to the truth to arouse his appetite for life and laughter. For here we are, Rene and I, flying up to the southernmost edge of the Northwest Territories to see yet another one of these heart-stopping places.

The plane banks in for landing. We look through the windows. The island Dad has chosen for our residence this summer is a sandbar, in effect, that protrudes in a crescent from an island big enough to accommodate a hundred campers. A half-mile long and ten yards wide at its narrowest, the sandbar thus entails two beaches—the north for Rene, the south for me, I imagine on the spot; we will be able to chase the toothpick-legged, egg-sized sandpipers across that sand as they run from our clutches chirping all along in their high-pitched *you can't catch me, you can't catch me!* Impossible to outrun, they take off in triumph, their winglets fluttering. And our camp of a half-dozen tents stands at the tip, where the sandbar widens out to a grove of spruce—forming, in the process, what in essence is a smaller sub-island; again, as with Boundary Island, a peninsula, an "almost island."

The silver Cessna lands on the water and putt-putts up to the dock made of spruce logs. Dad has built it, so much is evident, for he's built others just like this one over the years. And at its tip he stands with Mom. And Doggy, who wags her tail like a car will do with its windshield wiper—though Mom, too, is just as happy. As is Dad. Now fifty-eight and brown as bark, he still has the body of a man of thirty. Every bit as fit, every bit as muscular, he looks like a tree, a part of the forest. And Mom, too, is solid. Now fifty-five and brown as a *lapwachin*, she still looks capable of bending over, grabbing her dog by her curly tail, twirling its owner above her head, and throwing it to the wild blue yonder. Balazee Highway. Just the thought of her engenders smiling.

Like everyone on Earth, Mom has a ritual before she retires. The first part of three is that she rolls two dozen cigarettes for Dad's day of fishing on the morrow. One of his few simple pleasures in a life filled with labour—and labour and labour and yet more labour—he says he will quit the day he dies. For the task at hand, Mom sits on the floor with its spruce-bough carpet and, legs straight out before her, uses the front of her cotton granny smock as her work table. There on the floor beside her, the pot-sized tin of Player's tobacco. There, the booklet of papers, there, her fingers flashing by the light of a lamp lit by kerosene, there, her tongue on the paper to moisten the gummed edge and, boom, twenty-four cigarettes in a white plastic case ready to confront what storm might come (the twenty-fifth cigarette is for herself, as you'll soon see). Be that as it may, we have always been in awe of her quicksilver fingers.

"All by feel, my sons, all by feel," she assures us. The second part of three on her list of nocturnal rituals? Prayer. And this she does with Dad. Side by side do they kneel on the carpet of spruce boughs beside their bed, home-made, of course, as with all "furniture," such as it is, at fish camps in general. She in her slip, he in his long johns, their elbows on the mattress, their rosaries wrapped around their fingers, they mouth like fish one silent *Nootaawinaan* (Our Father), ten *Kichitaw Maarees*, (Hail Marys), and one *Igwaani keeyaam* (Glory Be). Sharing as we do their tent this summer, Rene and I are already half-asleep in the bed that sits foot-to-foot against theirs. Meaning to say that I, in particular, am privy to the praying—I see it all.

Some forty feet away and into the forest, Suzette and Swanson, too, have retired, with a boy born four months prior and their toddler, Molly—except that Suzette, this summer, has a transistor radio, a gift from Swanson. A music obsessive since age one day, she enjoys, in particular, its gospel programming. So once night has fallen and the airwaves are alive, she plays it softly though not soft enough that we can't hear it, if only faintly, from one tent over.

Our parents' prayers are ardent; they mean what they say; they believe, implicitly, that Jesus Christ, the true Son of God, lives here with us, right on this island on this lake in Canada's sub-Arctic. And as with every other night of their long lives, they are with him on the mountain when he speaks to the masses, his every word alight with hope and *saagee-itoowin* (love). They are with him when he weeps in the garden as he pleads for mercy from his Father the night before his death by fork. (In Cree, crucifixion translates as "to be pierced by a fork.") For they, too, are weeping, literally. Why? Because they are thanking him for taking such good care of their five small children whom they lost to his Kingdom all those years ago and whom they miss, still, to this day. They are with him when he is out on the water walking the waves of the Sea of Galilee . . .

"On the sea (the sea, the sea)," sings the Carter family on Suzette's little radio, "Of Galilee (of Galilee), my Jesus is walking on the sea . . ."

We are battling the waves of the Sea of Galilee, my father and I, looking for that net that we set here yesterday—except that we can't see the buoy. The waves are too high, the white foam swirling. The north wind screaming, it lashes at my face, stings my skin. The spray of water is blinding me, choking me. The deluge starts entering the boat in torrents. We are going to sink, I know it. We are going to drown. Dad screams something. Though I can hear his voice, I can't make out the words it is saying, for the wind conceals them. And because he is sitting on the crossbeam at the prow, he has to face away from me, so I can't see his face either, and he can't turn to me because he has to hang on to that crossbeam or he will be thrown from the boat and drown like his brother, Samba Cheese Highway, did at age sixteen, he, Joe Highway, then just thirteen.

"Please, God," I scream, "please don't take this man from me." The words, for some reason, have sprung from the depths of my puny existence of their very own accord and I don't doubt them. "I don't want to leave him, I don't want to leave him, I don't want to leave him." They pummel me and pummel me and pummel me until I am left a quaking mass.

"But my son," Dad screams through the squall. "You have to go. You have to go to that school. You have to save our people."

"No," I scream, "no, no, no!" All of a sudden, I am a six-year-old boy standing on a dock in Koowap, Saskatchewan, he squatting before me, me embracing his flannel-clad warmth and embracing it and embracing it, unwilling to go. But he hands me to the pilot and, in one instant, I am sitting on that plane, absconded by a system that I as a child have no comprehension of. "No, no, no!" the word screams through me.

I wake to a light that is arcing up and arcing down, almost dance-like in its gentle curves. And arcing up and arcing down. It is my mother smoking a cigarette, the one and only she smokes each day, the third and final part of her tripartite nighttime ritual. My face still covered in tears from my dream, no one will see them for the darkness is total. Except for the tip of that cigarette, its searchlight arcing up and arcing down. And arcing up and arcing down . . .

At four next morning after one long and restless night, we are on the waves of Clifton Lake, Dad and I, searching for that next net, searching for that next net, our pathetic little boat being tossed about like a toothpick—we will surely capsize and drown completely. Still, I keep driving our motor against those waves. And driving and driving, Dad and I both bouncing so hard that my bones rattle. And what is he doing? Still sitting on that crossbeam with one hand clinging to its painted wood for balance, and calm as Jeezoos walking the sea, he is smoking a cigarette. Somehow, amidst all that violence, he has reached under his suit of frog-green rubber, under his coat, into his flannel shirt pocket, extracted his white plastic cigarette case, opened it, pulled a cigarette from its interior, put it in his mouth, and slipped the case back into his shirt pocket under all that other clothing. Somehow, he has taken out a match made of wood, sparked it to life with a thumb, the thumb well-sheltered by a cupped hand, lit his cigarette, and is smoking. Against a wind so strong it could flatten ten tents and an entire forest. All with one hand. Classic Joe Highway, always doing the impossible. As will I. The tempest passes, the wind fades to nothing, we go back to fishing.

"*Nigoosis?*" ("Son?") Dad says to me towards day's end once all is calm, he disentangling a trout from the last net of the day.

"*Eehee?*" ("Yes?") I say, our only radio five Arctic terns hovering ten feet above us. Their killdeer-like cries pleading like children for a morsel of fish to come their way, they circle and circle. All while I sit in the middle of the vessel gutting the five-hundredth fish that day. Through the years, fishing with this man, I will have gutted a million fish.

"*Kimith-weethee-teen awa-simee waathow tantay-schooloowee-in tagwaa-geegi?*"

"*Eehee*"—the islands in the distance floating off into the blue with their beaches sparkling, our only TV.

"*How, neeyaa. N'tay-schooli-wi. Maw weegaach kamee-taateen kwayas eegee-schooloo-wee-in. Keespin kwayas kigeeschool-oowin, maw weegaach oomsi isi kataach keetha ka-isi-atooskaan. Ispeek keesoo-pigi-ini, igoota poogoo kaapin kitay-meechigan asichi.*" He is telling me to go back to school; if I continue, he says, I will never have to undergo extreme suffering like he has—his fingers blue by mid-September from icicles clinging to canvas gloves that are only partly waterproof—my life will be easier. Knowing I am hesitant—and, yes, I am torn; I ache to stay with him at the same time as I want a fantastic education—he pauses. And here he releases his left hand from the net and makes as if holding a book: "*Igwa aaskow oomsi isi poogoo ka-itoo-teen.*" And here he releases his second hand from the net ever so briefly to make the motion of turning the page of the book. "Ho-*ho!*" he yodels with joy unapologetic as he snaps both hands right back to the net. The reason? A twenty-pound trout has come glimmering from the inky depths, its fat white belly the telltale sign. And, at age fifteen—sixteen come December—I am ready in my heart, come September, for high school in Winnipeg, a thousand miles from Joe Lapstan Highway. This, in other words, will be my last full summer with the King of *Keeweet'nook*.

Going home that evening with the sunlight fading, we pass one island after another, I, as always, driving the motor. Dad, mean-while—and as always—is sitting at the prow facing forward, his left hand on the crossbeam to keep himself from falling, and smoking, as always, a Balazee Highway home-crafted cigarette. Suddenly, he points to the left. I swerve accordingly. And now we are heading for an island so small it is actually more shoal than island. Its piles of rock piled helter-skelter by the shifting movement of melting spring ice and its scraggly stands of windblown willow both indicate quite clearly that this is a nesting place for Arctic terns. The five or six who circle high over its half-acre surface while clucking plaintively their Antarctic anthem certainly confirm it. I know in a flash—Dad has a treat for the magic eleventh-born of his twelve children . . .

51

The seagull is a clunky, large-boned bird. In the avian world, it is not a star, not one of its more sophisticated or attractive members. Like the crow and the vulture, it scavenges—though, at least, it stops at carrion. Roadkill, for example, it will not eat, not like crows will. But garbage? Leftover meat, fish, bread, fruit, even cookies? That's another story. People eating meals at island campfires, fishermen fishing on glass-smooth waters, people gutting fish on slats of granite, garbage cans, garbage dumps: any sign of food will attract the attention of *keeyask*, the seagull. Tricksters of a sort, they will hover here, they will loiter there, they will stare, they will glare, they will hop and dance about as if for amusement when what they are doing, in reality, is waiting for the first opportunity to jump to the fore and grab some scraps should the owner of the food lapse into non-vigilance. Even its cry—and who hasn't heard it?—is not very pretty; sharp, raucous, discordant, it grates on the ear. As omnipresent as the English language and therefore as common—what country in the world doesn't have them, and have them in spades?—they are a nuisance. Not a feather on their bodies can be called exotic.

"My son, he don't like seagull," Dad once said to a Ukrainian bush pilot based in Lynn Lake named Fred Chuipka.

The Arctic tern, on the other hand, is an aristocrat. If the seagull is as clunky as a half-ton truck, then the tern is as graceful as a ballet dancer. She is exotic, she is a star. Apart from extreme northern people such as us, and extreme southerners such as those in Argentina's fabled Tierra del Fuego, few people have ever seen her live. Which is what makes her special—it is unique to the corners of the world where Arctic and Antarctic climates flourish. In fact, Reindeer Lake is probably the furthest south they will take up residence when in Canada, if only a residence that is seasonal, and then only at the lake's northern tip. On Clifton Lake, which is one hundred and fifty miles northeast of Reindeer Lake, they are legion.

Similar in look and in colouring to the common northern seagull with whom she shares the same lakes, rivers, and air space, at least when in Canada, the tern is much smaller, perhaps half its size and thus much lighter, finer of bone structure. Like the seagull, she is white for the most part, especially the underside that is visible to us when she is in flight, with shadings of grey on her back as well as on the upper surface of her wings. While her legs are short, red, and spindly, which is misleading for they are actually as strong as steel, her beak is red and pointed, the top of her head as black as ink with a pattern that looks like a beanie if one that is oval. Last—and this her most striking physical feature—her tail is V-shaped in a manner that is elegant, stream-lined for steering.

Fleeter of flight than the seagull, her wings when airborne resemble boomerangs. In fact, that's what she moves like when she flies, a darting, diving movement though one that is subtle, refined, balletic. Like a kite, she glides this way and glides that way high over the water, her killdeer caw, this ringing falsetto somewhere halfway between legato and staccato, piercing the air. As she flies, she looks in that water for the minnows she needs to feed her babies, until she sees one glimmering like tinsel a mere five inches beneath the surface of even choppy water. At which point she swoops like an arrow and, *splash!* Her head, her neck, her entire body, tail included, all cut like a blade into the crystalline blue. If that water is smooth, the commotion of a bird's wings flapping at liquid effects its own visual and aural excitement. And in that turmoil, the bird's beak snaps shut on her victim, this four-inch creature that looks like mercury, only to re-surface in an explosion of light created by water fracturing into a million shards. The minnow wriggling out its last breath on Earth, its tail flaps desperately out one side of the bird's beak, its head out the other, the tern shooting back into the sky with the sureness of bullets. The event never ceases to stop my breath. Assured that her children will eat that day, she soars off ecstatically thus establishing the fact that her vision is as sharp as a *saapoo-nigan* (needle). From a height of as much as fifty feet? With an object as miniscule as a four-inch *kinoo-seesis* ("small fish," i.e. minnow)? Apparently, says Masky Jimmy Perkins to me one day, they can see a hair human, *maskwa* (bear), or *poosees* (cat), lying hidden in the grass from a mile up in the air; "*Taapwee, maw weegaach neetha nigi-thaaskin*" ("It's true, I never lie"), lies Masky Jimmy Perkins to me that one day.

In fact, while the seagull splits its day equally between air, land, and water, the Arctic tern, even though her legs, too, can walk, run, and hop, even though she swims, lives almost exclusively in air, in permanent flight. Which is not surprising as her main claim to fame, the reason she is admired by ornithologist, birdwatcher, and layman alike, is her migration pattern. Twice a year, year in and year out for the twenty-something years of her lifespan, does she traverse, with an endurance that is genuinely astonishing, the entire distance between the Arctic and Antarctic, a flight that takes, apparently, about two months. If the distance between North Pole and South is 12,500 miles, then she travels easily twice that flying south in the fall and north in the spring following not a straight line but a zigzag pattern across both North and South Atlantic thus making for the longest migration route of any animal on Earth. They don't even stop to sleep for—and this is one of the miracles of nature—they have a mechanism inside their bodies, a kind of automatic pilot, that lets them sleep while flying! For a bird so small and so fragile-looking, when compared especially to its large-boned cousin, the seagull, its wings are as powerful—apparently, say ornithologists, who know these things—as the wings of an eagle. Or a jet plane, say, a Boeing 747. Certainly, she can fly further than the latter. And higher than Nepal's Mount Everest, say ornithologists, who know these things.

Another fascinating aspect of their lives is their eggs. Once arrived from Antarctica, they nest in numbers as vast as hairs on an old black *poosees* (to paraphrase Masky Jimmy Perkins) on these small islands, these rocky outcroppings. A thousand to a colony would not be exaggerating their numbers. Away out in the middle of nowhere, such a shoal might be, say, five hundred square feet in area, though irregularly shaped. Bodies of water in northwestern Manitoba and the lower part of the Northwest Territories are known, of course, for their beauty. But not for their depth. The ice of the ice age that gouged out the form that these lakes, rivers, rapids, and waterfalls evidence today was not quite as thorough in its gouging action as it might have been, for it left holes, bumps, and jagged rock formations in unlikely places. Which is why these "bumps" that jut from the water. Which is why the five thousand islands of Reindeer Lake. And which is why these shoals.

The shoals, moreover, are pocked with boulders which, of course, are mere extensions of the shoals themselves and are scattered, moreover, with handfuls of dirt and sand and soil blown in from the mainland and nearby islands from which sprout low-lying scrub, tall waving grasses, and willows and birches in clumps of twos, threes, and fours. And as the nearest island can sometimes be as far as one mile off in either direction, these willows and birches find themselves at the complete mercy of winds that can be as kind as they can be brutal. The north wind, in particular, stunts their growth with callous alacrity so that they end up looking rather scraggly, even pathetic. The birches, in particular, are more sapling than tree, saplings that lean decidedly away from their vaunted arch-rival, this fascistic *thootin* (wind).

At the foot of these willows and stunted birches, around these rocks, and in and among these tall, swaying grasses, in any case, is where the Arctic terns build their nests. Of straw, leaves, and small clumps of earth, they resemble the nests of every other bird that exists on Earth, so far as I know. Larger than those of robins and smaller than those of seagulls, their architecture is as solid and intelligent as that of a church.

They arrive in late May to mid-June when snow on the ground is not quite gone, ice on the lake still floating in sections. By month's end, they have nested, mated, and laid their eggs, and go on nesting for a month. Having driven by any number of these shoals-cum-islands on our daily rounds of harvesting our nets, my father and I have a general idea as to which ones harbour the greatest number of nests—where, that is, the eggs are most abundant. So that, come our one day off of the week, which is Sunday, Mom and Dad like to amuse us by taking us to one of these islands to collect these eggs and boil them for supper. And here's how it's done . . .

Generally the driver when he's off work, Dad stops the motor a quarter of a mile or so offshore from the shoal. Then he and whoever is sitting at the bow, usually Daniel, paddle in silence the remainder of the way. We are not allowed a peep, the reason being that we have to surprise the island's inhabitants, says Mom, so they won't fly away before we get there. Half the fun after all, she says, is watching them fly off from under our noses. As we approach, a few, probably the males, circle some fifty feet overhead surveying their families (so, in any case, I like to imagine), protecting them from possible intruders, their cries intermittent, their flight patterns lazy, directionless. The others, meanwhile, are invisible, at home in their nests. The soaring watchmen, as they seem to be, might be doing their "warning call," for all I know, except that no one is listening.

We land. As noiselessly as possible, we disembark with our equipment: saucepans and pails of plastic or of metal and cardboard boxes. And sticks. In our bulky outfits, and like Sylvester the cat sneaking up on his dinner, Tweety the songbird, we skulk up the slope of grey-black granite towards the island's interior, fanning out all along this way and that so that, by the time the big moment comes, we will have the entire island covered. Until, on a raised hand signal from Dad, we stop. And stand stock-still. Containers hanging empty from our ungloved hands, we don't even breathe. Then, his face beaming, Dad shouts.

"*Igwa!*" ("Go!") Screaming and yelling such as ours has not been heard in any natural disaster on Earth or in heaven. Scurrying like madmen onto the island, we zigzag here and zigzag there. At one point, Rene trips on an exposed tree root and tumbles over. He laughs then rallies. Our faces white as with flour, we wave our pails and saucepans and cardboard boxes this way and that, banging them all along with our stakes of birch, and shouting at the creatures to leave their nests. Even Mom and Dad join in the mayhem, which thrills us because Mom, in particular, looks so funny in her cotton granny smock, her faux-silk head kerchief, her knee-high Wellingtons, and with her pail-sized saucepan just waving away. She even clangs it on rocks and trees for optimum effect.

"*Awas, awas!*" she yells to the birds. ("Get away!" or "Shoo!")

Startled to within an inch of their lives, one thousand Arctic terns take to the air in one huge cloud, so many that we are lucky if we can get even two per cent of their eggs in the short time we have. Their sound is infernal, an all-encompassing ringing and roaring, the cacophony so mesmeric that I start hearing one steel-like note piercing through it, and holding and holding, until the very island itself seems to be singing one note in unison. The sky above us, meanwhile, has turned into one impenetrable surface of white feather, that roof vibrating, throbbing, a human heart in the act of pumping. Which is what I see with my family at least five times each summer. And which is what I am seeing today, at this moment, at age fifteen, with my father standing beside me.

And in that white-out, a dogsled is travelling, travelling, travelling, its eight grey huskies straining at harness. Its limits unknown to the world as we know it, the landscape it crosses is beyond human imagining. And beyond earthly beauty. The question being: Where is the driver of this phantom conveyance? The answer? Enveloped completely in a mountain of goose down, I, Tomson Highway, am lying in blissful and complete comfort inside that sled. And in that comfort, I am dreaming already. And dreaming and dreaming, the one thing I know, the one thing I am sure of being: When I wake up five, ten hours later, or ten, fifty years later, I will be at my destination. For now, however, one mere second before sleep takes me, six words surface, of their own volition, inside my heart. And those words are:

"I think I'll take a nap."

ACKNOWLEDGEMENTS

A great big thanks for helping me in writing this book in one form or other—some as readers of early drafts, some as guides/editors, some as friends—go to Dinah Forbes, Jay Rankin, Suzanne Keeptwo, Schuyler Gilbert, Nancy Lang, Peter Raymont, Evelyn Laliberte, my theatre agent, Kate Mensour, my publishing agent, Jackie Kaiser, my editor Martha Kanya-Forstner, my copy editor Melanie Little, my partner Raymond Lalonde (*kisaagee-itin*), my grandchildren, Milena Faucher and Marek Faucher—*parce qu'ils me font rire, toujours, toujours*—their mother my daughter, Alexie Lalonde-Steedman, and her husband, my son-in-law and my grandchildren's father, Louis-Jean Faucher, my parents, the late Joe and Pelagie Highway (the best parents anyone could ever hope to have), and my late younger brother, Rene Highway, not only the most physically stunning but most humble man who ever lived. All held my hand every step of the way, all loved me. I thank as well the people of Brochet, Manitoba, every one of them my kith and kin—*n'tootee-mak, neet-saanak*. Thanks to the staff of the Guy Hill Indian Residential School. But even more important, even more exciting, even more profound, a great big thanks to the students of the Guy Hill Indian Residential School near The Pas, Manitoba, whom I love to this day with all my heart and will forever; you are more than friends, you are my sisters, you are my brothers, you are family. *Kina-naaskoo-mitin-aawow kaagi-thow eetaas-ee-ik. Igoosi.*